The Early Poetry

VOLUME I:

Mosada and
The Island of Statues

THE CORNELL YEATS

PLAYS

The Death of Cuchulain, edited by Phillip L. Marcus
Purgatory, edited by Sandra F. Siegel

POEMS

The Early Poetry, Vol. I: *"Mosada" and "The Island of Statues,"* edited by George Bornstein

The Early Poetry

Volume I: *Mosada* and *The Island of Statues*

MANUSCRIPT MATERIALS

BY W. B. YEATS

EDITED BY

GEORGE BORNSTEIN

Cornell University Press

ITHACA AND LONDON

THIS PUBLICATION HAS BEEN SUPPORTED BY THE NATIONAL ENDOWMENT FOR THE HUMANITIES, A FEDERAL AGENCY WHICH SUPPORTS THE STUDY OF SUCH FIELDS AS HISTORY, PHILOSOPHY, LITERATURE, AND LANGUAGES.

First published 1987 by Cornell University Press.

LIBRARY OF CONGRESS CATALOGING-IN-PUBLICATION DATA

Yeats. W. B. (William Butler), 1865–1939.
Mosada; and, The island of statues.

(The Early poetry ; v. 1) (The Cornell Yeats)
1. Yeats, W. B. (William Butler), 1865–1939—Manuscripts—Facsimiles. 2. Manuscripts, English—Facsimiles. I. Bornstein, George. II. Yeats, W. B. (William Butler), 1865–1939. Island of statues. 1987. III. Title: Mosada. IV. Title: Island of statues. V. Series: Yeats, W. B. (William Butler), 1865–1939. Poems. Selections; v. 1. VI. Series: Yeats, W. B. (William Butler), 1865–1939. Works. 1982
PR5902.B67 vol. 1 821′.8 s [822′.8] 85-28036
ISBN 0-8014-1855-0 (alk. paper)

Printed in the United States of America

The paper in this book is acid-free and meets the guidelines for permanence and durability of the Committee on Production Guidelines for Book Longevity of the Council on Library Resources.

THE CORNELL YEATS

The volumes in this series will present the manuscripts of W. B. Yeats's poems (all extant versions), plays (complete insofar as possible), and other materials from the rich archives preserved in the collections of the National Library of Ireland and elsewhere. The primary goal of the editors is to achieve the greatest possible fidelity in transcription. Photographic facsimiles will be used extensively to supplement the texts.

The series will include some important unpublished works of high literary quality, and individually and as a whole the volumes will help to illuminate Yeats's creative process. They will be essential reference works for scholars who wish to establish definitive texts of the published works. They will contain many passages of biographical interest as well as passages that will be helpful in interpreting other works by Yeats. The emphasis throughout, however, will be on the documents themselves, and critical analysis will be limited to discussion of their significance in relation to the published texts; the editors assume that publication of the documents will stimulate critical studies as a matter of course.

THE YEATS EDITORIAL BOARD

To the memory of C. A. Patrides and F. S. L. Lyons

"Truth flourishes where the student's lamp has shone"

Contents

Preface

The manuscripts transcribed for this volume represent over half of all known surviving manuscripts of the poetry of W. B. Yeats through 1895. The other manuscripts will be presented in *The Early Poetry,* Volume II, which will include the remaining material for work in *The Wanderings of Oisin and Other Poems* (1889), *The Countess Kathleen and Various Legends and Lyrics* (1892), uncollected poems, and several poems that Yeats finished or brought to an advanced state but apparently never published. The two works here, *Mosada* and *The Island of Statues,* belong together on account of not only their bulk and genre but also (and more important) their chronology and theme. Yeats conceived and brought both of them near completion during his productive year 1884 and published *Island* in 1885 and *Mosada* (which was begun first) in 1886. He usually referred to them as poems rather than dramas, as the subtitle to the 1889 collection implies, but on occasion could label them plays as well. Scholars have followed his practice (the labels "poems," "plays," "dramatic poems," and "poetic dramas" have all been used), and the works appear both in the *Variorum Edition of the Poems* and in the *Variorum Edition of the Plays.* The present volume follows such mixed usage according to the sense of the context.

Faced with the impracticality of including facsimiles for each page of transcription, I have chosen a group likely to be of most value to scholars. Because the entire manuscript record of *Mosada* totals only forty-nine pages, that has been included in full. So, too, has the first draft of *Island of Statues,* whose distance from the final version gives it particular interest. The exclusion of both the *Mosada* manuscripts and the first draft of *Island* from the filming for the Yeats archive at Stony Brook makes their inclusion here doubly valuable. The remaining facsimiles offer four pages from each of the three intermediate drafts of *Island of Statues* and five from the more complex printer's copy, chosen to illustrate particularly difficult or interesting cases. The use of the facsimiles was made possible by the Hugh Walpole Collection, King's School, Canterbury; The Board of Trinity College Dublin; and the Department of Special Collections, State University of New York at Stony Brook.

My greatest debts in working on this volume have been to Richard J. Finneran and to the late F. S. L. Lyons for scholarly help, and to Senator Michael B. Yeats, Mrs. Gráinne Yeats, and Miss Anne Yeats for permission to examine and reproduce the unpublished materials from Senator Yeats's collection (now in the National Library of Ireland) and for going out of their way to make it possible for me to see those materials. For generous assistance of various kinds I also thank Heather Bryant, Mary FitzGerald, George Mills Harper, Carolyn Holdsworth, Marjorie Howes, John Kelly, Greg Kucich, Jennifer Lyons, Phillip L. Marcus, William M. Murphy, Maurice R. O'Connell, Edward O'Shea, Thomas Parkinson, Stephen

Parrish, Ann Saddlemyer, Ronald Schuchard, Jon Stallworthy, and Mary Helen Thuente. My wife has displayed a glad kindness throughout this project.

The staffs of many libraries have been remarkably helpful. I particularly acknowledge those of the following institutions: Harvard University, King's School, Canterbury (Hugh Walpole Collection, especially David S. Goodes), University of Michigan (especially Don Callard), National Library of Ireland, New York Public Library (Henry W. and Albert A. Berg Collection, especially Lola Szladits), State University of New York at Stony Brook (Department of Special Collections, especially Narayan Hegde), Princeton University (especially Richard Ludwig), Reading University, University of Texas (Humanities Research Center, especially Cathy Henderson), Trinity College Dublin, and Yale University (Beinecke Rare Book and Manuscript Library).

Financial support for this project was provided by the National Endowment for the Humanities, the American Council of Learned Societies, the American Philosophical Association, and the Horace Rackham Graduate School and College of Literature, Science, and Arts at the University of Michigan.

GEORGE BORNSTEIN

Ann Arbor, Michigan

Mosada and *The Island of Statues*

Introduction

"It's certain there is no fine thing / Since Adam's fall but needs much labouring," wrote W. B. Yeats in "Adam's Curse," first published in 1902.[1] Thanks to the pioneering work of Curtis Bradford, Jon Stallworthy, and others, scholars have long known that Yeats practiced what he preached by subjecting his major verse from *The Wind Among the Reeds* onwards to laborious revision both before and after publication. The present volume shows that Yeats had done so from the very beginning of his poetic career. Publication first of two of its lyrics and then of the entire *Island of Statues* in the *Dublin University Review* from March through July of 1885 constituted his first published work, while the separate reprinting of *Mosada* from the *Review* the following year became his first publication in book form. These early successes did not come easily. Manuscripts survive of all or part of three major versions of *Mosada* and five of *Island;* most of these versions, furthermore, constitute at least two stages of the text, in that they contain either heavy emendations or else successive versions of the same passage. That would yield a count of six stages of one work and ten of the other, not including presumably lost revisions in between the major versions of the surviving record. If the seams still show occasionally in these early works, it is not for lack of stitching and unstitching.

The order of publication of the manuscripts reverses that of their composition. In 1888 Yeats recalled for his friend the poet Katharine Tynan the period around 1884 when he was "living a quite harmonious poetic life": "'Mosada' was then written and a poem called 'Time and Vivien' which you have not seen. . . . The 'Island' was the last."[2] The evidence of the manuscripts themselves in this instance supports Yeats's sometimes wayward memory. An undated early notebook at Trinity College Dublin (TCD 3502/2) contains the three poems in the following order: a draft of *Time and the Witch Vivien,* the first versions of scene 3 of *Mosada,* and the first draft of *Island.* That notebook, which must precede one containing the third draft of *Island* and dated August 1884, probably dates from earlier in the same year. The manuscripts thus suggest that Yeats worked on both poems at overlapping times but started *Mosada* first, while the letter indicates that in the main he must have finished it first as well.

The two works have much in common. Both present tragically unsuccessful love relationships, one between Mosada and Ebremar and the other between Naschina and Almintor.

[1]*The Variorum Edition of the Poems of W. B. Yeats,* ed. Peter Allt and Russell K. Alspach (New York: Macmillan, corrected 3d printing, 1966), p. 205. Hereafter cited as VP followed by page number.

[2]*The Letters of W. B. Yeats,* ed. Allan Wade (London: Rupert Hart-Davis, 1954), p. 88. Hereafter cited as L followed by page number.

In each case the very power which might enable the lover to succeed causes his or her failure instead; the force of the Inquisition embodied in Ebremar drives Mosada to suicide before he can recognize her, and Naschina's vanquishing of the Enchantress to save Almintor ironically turns her into an immortal figure who will survive her earthly lover. Both heroines turn to magic as a means of regaining their lovers, only to find that such wizardry proves their undoing. The verse and situations recall the same models, particularly Shelley and Spenser, and the remote settings of Arcadia and medieval Spain would shortly yield to Irish ones in Yeats's work.

When in exploring the ideas and images of his own model, Shelley, Yeats observed that "I do not think men change much in their deepest thought,"[3] he might have been thinking of himself. *Mosada* and *The Island of Statues* contained much that would exfoliate into his own mature art. Perhaps most central was the Yeatsian notion of antinomies, the opposites into which all experience falls in human consciousness. *Mosada* deploys the secular against the spiritual, heterodox magic against orthodox doctrine, love against hatred, self against mask, and heart against mind. *Island* stresses peace against happiness, nature against art, youth against age, and time against eternity. The list could be extended, but the point is not just that these terms form antinomies, but that they constitute many of the same antinomies to which Yeats devoted his later art. So, too, does much of the imagery of the two poetic dramas. The island, for example, turns up ubiquitously in Yeats's early period, whether in tropical seas or the waters of Lough Gill. For Yeats as for Keats, statues dramatize both ideals and costs of human devotion, whether in the form of a bronze head or of Greek sculpture with its plummet-measured faces. Similarly, the boat and star passage from *Mosada* ("We'll fly from this before the morning star," VP 702) echoes from the early verse through *The Shadowy Waters* to Byzantium.

The boat and star passage, like much else in the early Yeats, derives from works of Shelley like *Alastor,* as the island does from Spenser's *The Faerie Queen.* The manuscripts enable us to trace his creative transformations of Shelley and Spenser, among others, throughout their evolutionary stages rather than merely in the final version that he published. In so doing, we better understand the working of his own creative imagination, in which timeless works of art derived from the human heart on the one hand and from other works of art on the other. Additionally, the manuscripts suggest at least two wholly unexpected new sources for *The Island of Statues* and offer unique insight into the early stages of Yeats's making as a poet. It is time to turn to them individually.

Mosada

The appearance of *Mosada: A Dramatic Poem* in book (or at least booklet) form in 1886 raised little fanfare except in the Yeats family. John Butler Yeats had arranged for its reprinting from the *Dublin University Review* by the same firm of Sealy, Bryers, and Walker that also handled the review. The elder Yeats both executed a portrait of his son for the

[3]*Essays and Introductions* (New York: Macmillan, 1961), p. 69. Hereafter cited as E&I followed by page number.

frontispiece and collected subscribers to make separate publication possible. In the latter task he had the assistance of Edward Dowden, who persuaded his brother, the bishop of Edinburgh, to take a dozen copies.[4] JBY fondly pressed copies on anyone he thought would be helpful, including a young lecturer at the Catholic University College named Gerard Manley Hopkins. Commending WBY for having "written in a Trinity College publication some striking verses," Hopkins told Coventry Patmore:

> I called on his, young Yeats's, father by desire lately; he is a painter; and with some emphasis of manner he presented me with *Mosada: a Dramatic Poem* by W. B. Yeats, with a portrait of the author by J. B. Yeats, himself; the young man having finely cut intellectual features and his father being a fine draughtsman. For a young man's pamphlet this was something too much; but you will understand a father's feeling. Now this *Mosada* I cannot think highly of, but I was happily not required then to praise what presumably I had not then read. . . .[5]

Hopkins's reaction may have been shared outside Yeats's own circle, for the volume attracted only a single review. Even so, brother Jack kept up the family loyalty by urging "Willy" to send "a copy of the *Mosada* or any other thing that has been published" to their uncle George Pollexfen.[6]

So few letters or other biographical material survive from the years 1884–1885 that Yeats's own comments on *Mosada* all date from after the composition and initial publication of the work. They are also far fewer than those on *Island of Statues,* which assumed a more prominent place in his account of his own career. On March 11, 1887, he wrote to an unnamed correspondent, offering to send a copy of "my poem *Mosada*" and mentioning T. W. Lyster. Yeats made sure that Katharine Tynan, who had written the only known review of *Mosada,*[7] received an advance copy of *The Wanderings of Oisin and Other Poems* (1889) as well. Shortly thereafter, he wrote to ask, "Does 'Mosada' or 'Oisin' please you most?" His longest and most revealing comment had come in a well-known letter to her almost a year earlier, when he had been revising *Mosada* for inclusion in that volume:

> I have much improved 'Mosada' by polishing the verse here and there. I have noticed some things about my poetry I did not know before, in this process of correction; for instance, that it is almost all a flight into fairyland from the real world, and a summons to that flight. The Chorus to the 'Stolen Child' sums it up—that it is not the poetry of insight and knowledge, but of longing and complaint—the cry of the heart against necessity.[8]

[4]Joseph Hone, *W. B. Yeats, 1865–1939* (London: Macmillan, 2d ed., 1962), pp. 49–50.

[5]*Further Letters of Gerard Manley Hopkins,* ed. Claude Colleer Abbott (London: Oxford University Press, 2d ed., 1956), pp. 373–374.

[6]*Letters to W. B. Yeats,* ed. Richard J. Finneran, George Mills Harper, and William M. Murphy (New York: Columbia University Press, 1977, 2 vols.), 1: 3.

[7]"Three Young Poets," *Irish Monthly,* 15: 165 (March 1887): 166–168, partially reprinted in *W. B. Yeats: The Critical Heritage,* ed. A. Norman Jeffares (London: Routlege and Kegan Paul, 1977), pp. 66–67.

[8]L 32, 101, and 63, respectively.

Evidently, polishing the verse of *Mosada* precipitated Yeats's discontent with its theme, of which "the cry of the heart against necessity" remains a fair summary. Yeats never wholly left that theme, even while he strove to place the heart's cry more firmly in the real world and to alter its tone. He would deploy the antinomies already embryonic in the early work to suggest insight and knowledge rather than longing and complaint. The self-transformations that marked his entire career had begun.

Mosada itself represents a process of evolution from the earliest surviving draft (TCD 3502/2, a notebook containing two versions of scene 3) through an intermediate one (TCD 3502/1, a notebook containing a version of the entire play) to the nearly final stage (TCD 3502/3, loose foolscap containing scene 1 and most of scene 2).[9] At first Yeats aimed primarily at setting down a rough version of the action of the drama, together with some of the dialogue. The earliest version of scene 3, much shorter than the final one, centered on Ebremar's call for Mosada to wake, her speech about the darkness of the night, and her death. The immediately following revision of the scene in the same notebook preserves that emphasis. Only with the next stage did Yeats begin to polish dialogue and to introduce such complexities as the final version would contain.

Initially, Ebremar appeared a more sympathetic character, almost wholly defined by his role as lover rather than as Inquisitor. In the early version, for example, his opening speech to Mosada lacks the harshness of these two and a half lines preceding his recognition of her in the final version: "Young Moorish girl, thy final hour is here; / Cast off thy heresies, and save thy soul / From the undying worm" (VP 701). Similarly, the two early versions of scene 3 end at Ebremar's resolution to importune the remaining prisoners to penitence rather than with his more aloof direction of the monk to change his hood for one better suited to their appearance before the crowd. Yet in presenting Ebremar as a more lyric lover, the scene lacks the dramatic tension which his later characterization provides. In the next draft Yeats swung toward presenting a much harsher Ebremar before finding a middle ground in the final one (for example, by balancing his denunciations of the heathen with the hesitation of his "and yet—" in line 49 of scene 2).

A deleted passage from the earliest notebook contains a seed from which would germinate many of the antinomies not only of the play but also of Yeats's future career. Immediately after Mosada's death, Yeats first had Ebremar exclaim "Hence forth I'm but the actor of a part" and then immediately revised that to "She['s] dead's and I alone have left a ma[s]k / To play a part" (TCD 3502/2, 12). That passage implies that Ebremar found his true self in his secret identity as Mosada's lover and only a false one in his public role as Inquisitor. It engenders the alignment of self with heart, love, spirit, and magic and, correspondingly, of mask with mind, hatred, institution, and dogma which the finished play displays. A more subtle and sustained manipulation of the dialectics of masking would inform much of Yeats's great mature work, both in poetry and in prose. In *A Vision,* for example, the image of the wandering lover forms a true mask for the man of phase seventeen (to which Yeats assigned himself) to enable him to achieve simplification through intensity, while the false mask of

[9]Hereafter cited as manuscript number followed by a comma and the page number. For the purposes of the introduction, I have followed Yeats's last wording on a given draft unless otherwise indicated, have supplied occasional missing letters or punctuation within square brackets, and have introduced small emendations to improve comprehension; readers will find a full and exact transcription below in the appropriate section of the transcriptions themselves.

abstraction leads to hatred and dispersal. Such a contrast already lay latent in the characterization of the divided Ebremar forty years before. So, too, does the "hollow face" of Dante (another man of phase seventeen) in one of Yeats's greatest mask poems, "Ego Dominus Tuus," match that of Ebremar "hollow-cheeked / From fasting" in 1886.

If Ebremar became harsher as the poem evolved, the boy Cola grew more sympathetic. The first draft in which he appears (TCD 3502/1) de-emphasizes his deformity and unpopularity. For example, it lacks his early declaration, "They say I am all ugliness; lame-footed / I am; one shoulder turned awry" (VP 692). Even more important, here he seems motivated by hatred and resentment of Mosada rather than by the evident devotion of the final draft. He disrupts her conjuring and denounces her as a heretic:

> burn, burn, thou moorish witch[.] I scatter thus
> These thing[s] of crime that you may hide them not
> Burn, Burn, thou heretic[.] (TCD 3502/1, 10)

This draft lacks, too, the suggestion that the Inquisitors misled Cola about their intentions. Whereas in the final version they tell him that they intend only to "fright her from her sin" (VP 695), here they lead him to betray her out of concern only with his own fate.

By making Cola more sympathetic, Yeats set him up as a foil to Ebremar. His gentleness contrasts with Ebremar's harshness, and his human love with Ebremar's abstract devotion to a cause. His devotion to Mosada recalls Ebremar's own previous feeling. Both the powerless boy and the omnipotent but not omniscient Inquisitor end up destroying the woman they love. Just as Cola uses his one moment of power to betray Mosada and then mourns the result, so, too, does Ebremar drive her to suicide and then repent. Indeed, after recognizing Mosada, Ebremar can conceive of no alternative but fleeing his own authority and reverting to a Cola-like condition of love outside the social order. Even at this early stage of Yeats's development, humans do not put on knowledge with their power.

The changes in Ebremar and Cola cause Mosada herself to grow in stature. Just as her refusal to condemn the boy after his betrayal moves her to a higher moral order than the Inquisitors of the first scene, so does her steadfast devotion to her lover contrast with his abandonment of her and tardy repentance. Condemned for heresy, she had practiced her arcane art only to conjure up a glimpse of her absent lover. Her devotion to magic aligns her with other enchantresses in Yeats's early work, such as Naschina and the Enchantress in the nearly contemporaneous *Island of Statues*. Indeed, the phantom she beckons to her aid recalls the Enchantress herself:

> She was a great enchantress once of yore,
> Whose dwelling was a tree-wrapt island, lulled
> Far out upon the water world and ringed
> With wonderful white sands, where never yet
> Were furled the wings of ships. There in a dell,
> A lily-blanchèd place, she sat and sang,
> And in her singing wove around her head
> White lilies, and her song flew forth afar
> Along the sea; and many a man grew hushed

In his own house or 'mong the merchants grey,
Hearing the far-off singing guile, and groaned,
And manned an argosy and sailing died. (VP 693)

For "singing guile" Yeats originally wrote "tuneful guile," a phrase that surfaced in the title of the second draft of *Island* ("The lady of tuneful guile") before finding a final incarnation as the "melodious guile" of the shell in "Song of the Happy Shepherd," first published as a separate "epilogue" to that play and *The Seeker*. Apart from minor details like the ocean instead of lake or the song being sung by the enchantress herself rather than a Voice, the description from *Mosada* clearly parallels that of *Island*. In both cases, as so often in Yeats, a magical female figure beckons a male to a perilous quest dramatizing the dialectic between the supernatural and natural worlds, itself a paradigm of the other antinomies.

Just as Yeats's revisions complicated and deepened the original sketchy architectonic structure, so did they enrich the diction of individual speeches. The boat and star passage of scene 3 offers a ready example. Both early versions of the scene lack the speech altogether as they pass through drastically condensed versions of the exchange between Ebremar and the dying Mosada. The next draft contains the essence of this part of Ebremar's speech:

We'll fly, from here There is a secret way
From near by tunneled to the river's marge
Where lies a boat among the shadowy reeds
That sigh to one another all year long—
Awake awake and we will sail afar
Afar along the fleet white rivers face
We two alone upon the river wan
Alone among the murmurs of the dawn—
Far 'mid thy people none will know that I
Was Ebremar whose thoughts were fixed on god
Whom I now lose, awake Mosada 'wake
Thy Vallance is by thee[.] (TCD 3502/1, 22–23)

The published version introduces crucial changes at the beginning and end of the passage:

We'll fly from this before the morning star.
Dear heart, there is a secret way that leads
Its paven length towards the river's marge
Where lies a shallop in the yellow reeds.
Awake, awake, and we will sail afar,
Afar along the fleet white river's face—
Alone with our own whispers and replies—
Alone among the murmurs of the dawn.
Once in thy nation none shall know that I
Was Ebremar, whose thoughts were fixed on God,
And heaven, and holiness. (VP 702)

The opening revisions deliberately bring the passage closer to Shelley.[10] They include his frequent image of the morning star and the substitution of "shallop" (a word he and Keats both favored) for "boat." In his perceptive essay "The Philosophy of Shelley's Poetry" Yeats would argue that "the most important, the most precise of all Shelley's symbols, the one he uses with the fullest knowledge of its meaning, is the Morning and Evening Star" and would identify his great predecessor's most characteristic vision as "a boat drifting down a broad river between high hills . . . following the light of one Star" (E&I 88, 95). The late changes bring a Shelleyan counterpoint into a context recalling one of Yeats's favorite Shelleyan enchantresses, Cythna in *The Revolt of Islam,* and establish the relevance of perhaps Yeats's favorite Shelleyan poem, *Alastor,* to his own early quest. Like Ebremar, the Alastor-poet fails through devotion to an unearthly ideal resulting in a lack of human sympathy. The revisions at the end of the passage reinforce that parallel by substituting the objects of Ebremar's devotion ("God, / And heaven, and holiness") for the effect of his loss ("god / Whom I now lose"). Yet *Mosada* as a whole already displays the embryonic antinomies by which Yeats would eventually move away from his early, Shelleyan model.

The Island of Statues

The Island of Statues occupies a crucial place in Yeats's development, both in actual chronology and in the mythic self-constructions that periodically delighted him. To begin with, *Island* was his first major published work, appearing in the *Dublin University Review* from April through July of 1885. Indeed, except for two of its lyrics ("Song of the Faeries" and "Voices," which appeared in the March issue of the same journal) *Island* was the first of his works to be published at all. As such, it claims a special place in his development, the point of origin for all the later work. Yeats slyly preserved that status when he arranged his 1933 *Collected Poems,* where he for the first time chose to open his canon with "The Song of the Happy Shepherd," itself first published as "An Epilogue to 'The Island of Statues' and 'The Seeker' " in the *Dublin University Review* for October 1885.[11] *Island* thus served the aged Yeats as the suppressed origin of his poetry, even as it had served him in youth as the first public announcement of his powers.

Yet the poem itself stood for culmination as much as for commencement. It marks the final work in the series of mostly unpublished productions which Yeats recalled in 1914 when preparing *Reveries over Childhood and Youth:* "I had begun to write poetry in imitation of Shelley and of Edmund Spenser, play after play—for my father exalted dramatic poetry above all other kinds—and I invented fantastic and incoherent plots."[12] Except for *Mosada* and the brief "Time and the Witch Vivien" (salvaged in 1889 from a much lengthier two-act

[10] I have discussed Yeats's profound relation to Shelley more fully in *Yeats and Shelley* (Chicago: University of Chicago Press, 1970) and *Transformations of Romanticism in Yeats, Eliot, and Stevens* (Chicago: University of Chicago Press, 1976), as has Harold Bloom in *Yeats* (Oxford University Press, 1970). See also Adele M. Dalsimer, "My Chief of Men: Yeats's Juvenilia and Shelley's *Alastor,*" *Eire-Ireland,* 8 (1973): 71–90.

[11] In between, it appeared as "Song of the Last Arcadian" in *The Wanderings of Oisin and Other Poems* (1889). The present title first appeared in *Poems* (1895).

[12] *Autobiographies* (London: Macmillan, 1966), pp. 66–67. Hereafter cited within parentheses as A followed by page number.

version entitled *Vivien and Time*), the numerous plays that Yeats wrote between the autumn of 1882 and his appearance in the *Dublin University Review* have remained unpublished. Besides *Vivien and Time,* they include *Love and Death* and the variously titled play known as *The Blindness.*[13] Perhaps the best work of its period, *The Island of Statues* presented a plot certainly fantastic but not necessarily incoherent. It closed Yeats's obscure apprenticeship and inaugurated his long and productive public career.

So important was the acceptance of this first work to Yeats that he left us not one but two accounts of the moment, once as recollected in middle age and the other the year before he died. Happily, they do not contradict each other in essentials. Here is the better-known version recorded in his autobiography:

> I had been invited to read out a poem called *The Island of Statues,* an Arcadian play in imitation of Edmund Spenser, to a gathering of critics who were to decide whether it was worthy of publication in the College magazine. The magazine had already published a lyric of mine [in fact, two], the first ever printed, and people began to know my name. We met in the rooms of Mr. C. H. Oldham, now Professor of Political Economy at our new University; and though Professor Bury, then a very young man, was to be the deciding voice, Mr. Oldham had asked quite a large audience. When the reading was over and the poem had been approved I was left alone, why I cannot remember, with a young man who was, I had been told, a schoolmaster. I was silent, gathering my courage, and he also was silent; and presently I said without anything to lead up to it, 'I know you will defend the ordinary system of education by saying that it strengthens the will, but I am convinced that it only seems to do so because it weakens the impulses'. (A 92–93)

One can appreciate the joyful release of the young Willie, fresh from approval by the literary organ of the College which his father had wanted him to attend but for which he doubted his own ability to pass the entrance examination. The moment vindicated his own, more eccentric education. He returned to it in his second-to-last publication in his lifetime, the radio talk "I Became an Author," which was never broadcast by the BBC series for which it was intended but which appeared in *The Listener* on August 4, 1938. Yeats devoted almost a third of that reminiscence to *The Island of Statues,* retelling the account of its acceptance, placing it between the unpublished early work and the later *Wanderings of Oisin,* and adding Keats, Shelley, and Ben Jonson to the list of influences.[14] Clearly, the work and its publication held a pivotal and enduring importance for him.

[13]David R. Clark and Rosalind E. Clark will present a reading text (not a diplomatic transcription) of *Vivien and Time* in their book *Visible Array,* forthcoming from Dolmen Press and Barnes and Noble. For an account of much of the work of this period see Richard Ellmann, *Yeats: The Man and the Masks* (New York: Dutton, 1948), chaps. 3 and 4. The August 1884 date that Ellmann gives for completion of *The Island of Statues* in fact marks only the completion of the third draft transcribed in the present volume.

[14]The essay is reprinted in *Uncollected Prose by W. B. Yeats,* vol. 2, ed. John P. Frayne and Colton Johnson (New York: Columbia University Press, 1976), pp. 506–509, hereafter cited within parentheses as Uncoll2 followed by page number. In contrast to his usual favorable opinion, Yeats there recorded his most negative if slightly hedged one: "I have not looked at it for many years, but nothing I did at that time had merit." He also accounted for the continuing presence at the start of *Collected Poems* of lyrics associated with the play by his standard evasion of pleasing old friends, a ploy that he used elsewhere with other early lyrics and which seems intended more to disarm criticism than to provide an accurate record.

That importance did not have to wait for Yeats's middle or old age to manifest itself but was already clear to him in his youth. It surfaces repeatedly in his correspondence immediately before and after publication of his first full-sized volume of poetry, *The Wanderings of Oisin and Other Poems* (1889). The book provided the first of a series of occasions throughout his career when Yeats would review his work to date, discard some poems, revise others, and end up with a canon which was also an imaginative construction of his career. The opening and closing poems often assume particular stress in such arrangements, as the alpha and omega of the volume. For his first collection Yeats placed the title poem at the beginning and took care to include "The Island of Statues: A Fragment" at the end. "I have added to the book the last scene of 'The Island of Statues' with a short argument to make all plain," he told Katharine Tynan in the fall of 1888. "I am sure the 'Island' is good of its kind" (L 87). The "fragment" thus comprised scene 3 of act 2, together with a prose summary of the plot to that point. Yeats had wanted to include the entire poem, but limitations of space prevented him. Writing to George Russell (AE) shortly after publication, he confessed: "I am sorry that the whole of 'The Island of Statues' is not in my book. It would have increased the book in size too much. It will be printed later on in some future volume" (L 112).

Yeats was not the only one at the time who wished that he had been able to include the whole *Island of Statues* in his 1889 volume and hoped that he would reprint it soon. Edward Dowden of Trinity College, who wavered between the roles of mentor and antagonist to Yeats, responded warmly to the poem in a letter of January 28, 1889, in which he concentrated on the beginning and end of the collection. "I decidedly think the 'Wanderings of Oisin' the best thing in the volume, but I wish you had made the book a little larger so as to include the whole of the 'Island of Statues,' " he wrote to its author. "Fragments are very provoking & somewhat illegitimate things."[15] T. W. Rolleston, one of O'Leary's disciples who assumed editorship of the *Dublin University Review* from August 1885, shared Dowden's desire for more of *Island,* which he preferred to *Oisin.* Four days before Dowden's letter Yeats told Katharine Tynan that Rolleston had sent a note to say "that he could have spared some of 'Oisin' for the sake of 'Island of Statues' " (L 102). Two months later he noted with delight W. E. Henley's article "A New Irish Poet," which praised both *Oisin* and *Island* while, in Yeats's words, labeling "Song of the Last Arcadian" as "more subtle than any other poem in book" (L 116). A decade later, friends like George Russell still hoped for a reprinting of the entire poem. Russell even offered to arrange for a pirated edition by the American publisher Thomas Bird Mosher of Maine, for which he volunteered to write a preface stating that the work "was too good to lose in the opinion of friends."[16]

One friend whose opinion particularly interested Yeats was Maud Gonne. At the start Maud had reminded Yeats of perhaps his first love, his flirtatious cousin Laura Armstrong. The correlation mattered, because Yeats had designed the part of the Enchantress in *The Island of Statues* and a similar one in *Time and the Witch Vivien* for Laura Armstrong to act (L 118), as he would later design roles for Maud herself. Maud's response to the poem at her first meeting with Yeats was striking, to say the least. As Yeats recounted it to Katharine Tynan, "Miss Gonne (you have heard of her, no doubt) was here yesterday with introduction

[15]*Letters to W. B. Yeats,* 1: 4. Dowden had been more ambivalent in 1885. See the account of his exchange with Todhunter on Yeats's early work in William M. Murphy, *Prodigal Father: The Life of John Butler Yeats (1839–1922)* (Ithaca: Cornell University Press, 1978), p. 144.

[16]*Letters to W. B. Yeats,* 1: 65.

from the O'Learys; she says she cried over 'Island of Statues' fragment, but altogether favoured the Enchantress and hated Na[s]china'' (L 106). One might have expected Maud to sympathize more with Naschina, for whom two hopeless lovers die and a third undertakes a perilous quest from which only she can rescue him. But Maud's sympathies lay more with the Enchantress, who rules the Island whose magical flowers turn men to stone until she is undone by her own love for Naschina and by Naschina's for Almintor. Yeats had developed the relationships among those three characters through at least five major manuscript versions. An examination of the drafts themselves illuminates the sources of the play, its progressively more subtle manipulation of antinomies and character, and the surprisingly late stage at which Yeats by a bold stroke found the true resolution of this important early work.

The names of the characters in *The Island of Statues* suggest some of the antecedents which Yeats transformed into his own art. While those in the published versions support his publicly acknowledged influences, particularly the Spenserian ones, those in the drafts open additional possibilities. Most strikingly, throughout the first draft Yeats called the heroine who later failed to win Maud Gonne's sympathy not Naschina but rather Evadne. The name suggests at least two other works, both of them poetic dramas with obvious if superficial links to Yeats's own play. The first is *The Maid's Tragedy,* first published in 1619 and often regarded as the best of the dramas by Beaumont and Fletcher. That play turns on the forced marriage of Evadne to the gentleman Amintor, whose name clearly suggests the Almintor of Yeats's Evadne. Although Beaumont and Fletcher's lovers fail in the quest for their union, too, the series of dark Jacobean convolutions leading up to their double suicide seems far removed from Yeats's admittedly troubled Arcadia; he apparently absorbed little from *The Maid's Tragedy* except the names of the thwarted pair.

Closer to Yeats's own time lay the work of Richard Lalor Sheil (1791–1851), an Irish dramatist and politician who fought for Catholic emancipation in Ireland and for repeal of the Act of Union. A play of his first performed in 1819 bears special relevance to Yeats's work both in title and subtitle—*Evadne; or, The Statue.* There the cynical and corrupt Evadne plans to marry the virtuous Vincentio as a cloak for her adulterous relation with the king but eventually repents and brings the king to repentance as well. The drama features not one statue but rather a whole gallery of them, images of Evadne's virtuous ancestors whom she invokes at the climax to reform the king. Besides Evadne's name and the group of statues recalled to figurative if not literal life, however, Sheil's work seems to have contributed little more to Yeats's own than did that of Beaumont and Fletcher.

Yeats rightly identified Spenser and Shelley as the two chief influences on *The Island of Statues,* and the drafts reinforce the presence of both from the beginning. To Spenser's *Faerie Queene* he partly owed the magic boat that ferries first Almintor and then Naschina across the lake, the enchanted island, the Enchantress herself, and the generalized Arcadian setting. Even the faeries were not wholly Irish, but derived from Spenser's Faery Land as well. The names of the singing shepherds Colin and Thernot (or Thenot, as Yeats sometimes wrote in the drafts) recall the Colin and Thenot who appear throughout *The Shepherd's Calendar* (so does another shepherd called Willy) and stage a singing match in the November eclogue. For all these similarities, Yeats still detaches his vision from Spenser's in an important way. Despite the overt Christian reference to Eve's sin in the Voice's song, Yeats seizes the mythic and romantic components of Spenser even while rejecting the Christian context which they serve in his great precursor. Twenty years later, he would formalize such division in the introduction to his own selection of Spenser's poems.[17]

Shelley himself had admired Spenser, and Yeats found confirmation in the romantic poet for some of his own redactions, particularly those connected with the quest motif. The magic boat, for example, derives as much from the shallop of *Alastor* and magic vessel of *The Witch of Atlas* as from the craft which takes Spenser's Cymocles over the idle lake to the wandering island in *The Faerie Queene;* Yeats himself later scribbled a comparison to Shelley's boats in the margin of his own copy of Spenser.[18] Many of the images he ascribed to Shelley in "The Philosophy of Shelley's Poetry" had already appeared in his own work from *Island of Statues* onward, particularly those of boat, water, stars, and fountain. The drafts reinforce the presence of Shelley from the very beginning. For example, the Voice's song at the end of act 1, scene 2 of *Island,* with its "And follow, and follow!" clearly recalls the "O follow, follow!" song of the Echoes at the end of act 2, scene 1 of Yeats's beloved *Prometheus Unbound.*[19] Yeats began from that point of closest resemblance. In the first draft, indeed, he has not yet composed the song itself but simply indicates: "the voice sings / a song who's chorus is / follow follow follow" (TCD 3502/2, 20^{v}). When the song does finally appear in the next draft, it already refers to the myth of the Fall instead of to the world of potentiality hymned by Shelley's spirits. Yeats had begun by then the evolution of his work from its initial happy resolution to the more troubled Arcadia that it finally portrays.

In his first draft Yeats had sketched the action and provided a rough version of some of the dialogue. Both the main plot involving Almintor, Naschina (Evadne at this time), and the Enchantress and the subplot featuring Thernot and Colin were in his mind from the start. Even the byplay of Naschina disguised as a shepherd and mocking herself appears fleetingly. The Enchantress claims a much smaller role, however; Yeats's development of her love for Naschina and the pathos of her condition belong to later stages of revision, in which the play as a whole grows darker and more problematic. Two key examples illustrate the difference. The first concerns the bumpkin lovers Colin and Thernot. In the later versions both die, one in their swordfight and the other in trying to swim to the island; in the first version, however, neither dies, and their comic chivalry forms an agreeable contrast to the main plot. The action involving Almintor and Naschina shows a similar evolution. Ending with Naschina grown shadowless because immortal, the published version portrays the frustration of the lovers' quest for fulfilled love in the real world. But the first draft closes with Almintor exclaiming, "My Evadne the world and thee / once more" (TCD 3502/2, 30^{v}). The transition from a sunny to a clouded Arcadia underlies most of Yeats's thematic revisions. He

[17]The issues raised in this paragraph and the next are discussed more fully in my *Yeats and Shelley, passim,* and "The Making of Yeats's Spenser," in *Yeats: An Annual of Critical and Textual Studies,* vol. 2, ed. Richard J. Finneran (Ithaca: Cornell University Press, 1984), pp. 21–29. See also A. G. Stock, "Yeats on Spenser," and Edward Engleberg, "'He Too Was In Arcadia': Yeats and the Paradox of the Fortunate Fall," both in *In Excited Reverie: A Centenary Tribute to William Butler Yeats 1865–1939,* ed. A. Norman Jeffares and K. G. W. Cross (London: Macmillan, 1965); Dalsimer, "My Chief of Men," cited above; and Michael North, "The Paradox of the Mausoleum: Public Monuments in the Early Aesthetics of W. B. Yeats," *Centennial Review,* 26 (1982): 221–238.

[18]"The Making of Yeats's Spenser," p. 25.

[19]*Shelley's Poetry and Prose,* ed. Donald H. Reiman and Sharon B. Powers (New York: Norton, 1977), pp. 165–166. In "The Philosophy of Shelley's Poetry" Yeats referred to *Prometheus Unbound* as "a sacred book" (E&I 65).

moved from reconciling the antinomies of peace and happiness, art and nature, and eternity and time to showing them in continued opposition.

No part of the play troubled Yeats more than scene 3 of act 2. Besides the four surviving manuscripts of the entire play, two additional ones record his struggles to shape his material to a satisfactory conclusion. The first version lacked almost the entire long dialogue between the Enchantress and Naschina which occupies the first two-thirds of the published version, and it provided only a rudimentary sketch of the briefer final third, with only two Sleepers. The scene continued in the roughest condition of any straight through the revisions and required two separate reworkings just before Yeats prepared the printer's copy. Even in those he had trouble with the character of the Sleepers (in the second he experimented with a Trojan speaker carrying a locket of his beloved's hair) and the exact resolution of the dialectics between the real and ideal worlds with their associated antinomies. As we shall see, his final solution must have come only in now-lost proofs for the *Dublin University Review*.

Two general conclusions emerge at the level not of plot and theme but of diction and versecraft. The first is that the lyrics contained within the play (such as the Voice's song about "follow follow") appeared relatively late. Yeats apparently composed them specifically for the occasion, particularly those tied most closely to the action, but he may have inserted others that he had worked on independently. For example, the song of the Voices at the start of the final scene does not appear until the two separate reworkings of that scene just prior to the printer's copy; the advanced state of the song there, furthermore, suggests that it may have started out as a separate poem (it was in fact one of the two lyrics that he did publish in the magazine just before the play). The second is that Yeats generally, though not invariably, revised diction to add detail and concreteness. The dialogue between Antonio and Almintor at the start of act 1, scene 2 (VP 652–653) offers two good examples. On SB 23.2.230^{r} Yeats first wrote "deep bosomed in the leaves the birds are sad." He then cancelled all but the last two words and wrote above them "the birds that hover in leaves," immediately replacing "hover" with "nestle." The notion of "bosomed" engendered the addition a few lines later of "Yon lake that fills with song the whole / Of this wide vale embossomed in the air." More briefly, the "trees" on SB 23.2.232^{r} eventually became "poplars." This style of revision matches that of another of Yeats's alleged models, Keats, as evidenced, for example, by the revisions to *The Eve of St. Agnes*.[20]

When Yeats came to prepare the final version of *The Island of Statues* for use as a printer's copy, he wisely sought the help of someone who knew more about spelling and punctuation than he did himself. Those were shaky areas for him throughout his career, but never more so than at the start. Spellings like "lafter," "wrapsedy," "falkan," and "vains" dot the transcriptions that follow. For aid Yeats turned to T. W. Lyster, later director of the National Library of Ireland and best known to posterity as the Quaker librarian of Joyce's *Ulysses*. Ten years Yeats's elder, Lyster helped the young poet emend not just his punctuation and orthography but also his diction and rhythms. In his speech at the unveiling of the Lyster

[20] See Walter Jackson Bate, *John Keats* (Cambridge: Harvard University Press, 1963), pp. 448–451, for a short discussion of Keats's revisions to that poem and, for a longer one, M. R. Ridley, *Keats' Craftsmanship* (London: Oxford University Press, 1933), pp. 112–190.

memorial in 1926, the year after Lyster's death, Yeats aptly and generously recalled their sessions together:

> My first published work owed much to his correction. I wrote a long pastoral play, which was accepted by the short-lived 'Dublin University Review.' When a young man writes his first poems, there will often be a good line followed by a bad line, and he should always go to a scholar to be advised; and Mr. Lyster did that for me. I used to go to his house, and he would go over the manuscript of my play with me, and help me to correct the bad lines. (Uncoll2 471)

These corrections still exist on the manuscript at King's School Canterbury, together with Yeats's directions that proof be sent to himself and to Lyster (whose name he characteristically misspelled there). An ambiguous note written in pencil on KS 7 suggests that the sometime possessor of the manuscript, Dr. W. Frazer of 20 Harcourt Street, might also have had a hand in the revisions, but for reasons described in the headnote to the transcriptions of the King's School version that seems unlikely.[21]

One change not present even in the manuscript that Yeats and Lyster polished is the important final stage direction, which must have been added at the proof stage. It reads: "*The rising moon casts the shadows of* Almintor *and the Sleepers far across the grass. Close by* Almintor's *side,* Naschina *is standing, shadowless*" (VP 679). That direction alters the meaning of the entire play by undermining the union of Almintor and Naschina. Until this point in the evolution of the manuscripts, the lovers' final success symbolized the resolution of the antinomies like nature and art, time and eternity, and real and ideal which the play presents. But the new philosophy calls all in doubt. Naschina's lack of a shadow suggests that she has joined the realm of the immortals, that her reunion with Almintor can persist but briefly, and that the antinomies remain at war with each other. Such a conclusion better fits the ambivalent Arcadia of Yeats's drama than did its optimistic predecessor. The stage direction ironically contradicts the positive exclamations of Naschina, Almintor, and the Sleepers, implicitly anticipating the poet's later contention that man can embody truth but he cannot know it.

Yeats did know the crucial significance of that change not just to *The Island of Statues* but to his entire early career. He acknowledged as much in his autumn 1888 letter to Katharine Tynan (quoted earlier in regard to the chronology of *Island, Mosada,* and *Time and Vivien*). Here is the full passage, which identifies the final stage direction of *Island* as the start of a phase of Yeats's art that persisted at least through *Oisin:*

[21]Dr. William Frazer lectured on Materia Medica at Carmichael School, Dublin, and published *Treatment of Disease of the Skin* in 1864. Yeats wrote him a letter on June 23, 1888, which suggests no intimacy. Given Yeats's account of Lyster's role, the likelihood that the corrections made during their sessions could have been suggested and recorded by either (though always with Yeats's approval), and the fact that the emendations were accomplished over a period of time allowing for different black inks and instruments, there seemed little point in attempting infrared or ultraviolet photography here. The only scholar to have recorded such an attempt with Yeats, William H. O'Donnell when working on *The Speckled Bird* manuscripts, concluded that "infrared and ultraviolet photography can achieve spectacular results only in sharply limited and, for the most part, unpredictable instances." See his "Infrared and Ultraviolet Photography of Manuscripts," *Publications of the Bibliographic Society of America,* 69 (1975): 574–583.

> I was then living a quite harmonious poetic life. Never thinking out of my depth. Always harmonious, narrow, calm. Taking small interest in people but most ardently moved by the more minute kinds of natural beauty. 'Mosada' was then written and a poem called 'Time and Vivien' which you have not seen. It is second in my book. Everything done then was quite passionless. The 'Island' was the last. Since I have left the 'Island,' I have been going about on shoreless seas. Nothing anywhere has clear outline. Everything is cloud and foam. 'Oisin' and the 'Seeker' are the only readable result. In the second part of 'Oisin' under disguise of symbolism I have said several things to which I only have the key. The romance is for my readers. They must not even know there is a symbol anywhere. They will not find out. If they did, it would spoil the art. Yet the whole poem is full of symbols—if it be full of aught but clouds. The early poems I know to be quite coherent, and at no time are there clouds in my details, for I hate the soft modern manner. The clouds began about four years ago. I was finishing the 'Island.' They came and robbed Naschina of her shadow. As you will see, the rest is cloudless, narrow and calm. (L 88)

Completion of *The Island of Statues* thus marked for Yeats a major change in his early career. The clarity born of his love for natural beauty and avoidance of real human passion (though not of derivative literary ones) yielded to a cloudiness of unresolved antinomies and large ambitions which would be relieved only by the integrated symbolism he came to in the nineties by way of *Oisin*. That resolution would in turn yield to new doubts and syntheses as his career unfolded itself, with the development of the work a perpetual mask to the development of the man. It was always Yeats's self that he remade. The transcriptions that follow provide a record of the earliest stage of that process.

Transcription Principles and Procedures

As the earlier volumes of the Cornell Yeats indicated, Yeats's manuscripts are impossible to transcribe with absolute fidelity. His hand was often difficult to read, especially when he was writing for his eye alone and with a carelessness reflecting the excitement of literary creation. He left the endings of many words unfinished or represented by an unclear line, formed letters carelessly and inconsistently, was a poor and erratic speller, and punctuated unsystematically and often incorrectly when he did so at all.

The selection of photo-facsimiles in this volume will enable the interested reader to *see* what Yeats actually wrote. The task of the editor is to present a transcription in which the often highly obscure documents are *read,* and this inevitably requires a certain amount of interpretive "translation." Because this volume contains facsimiles for less than one-third of the transcriptions, I have followed a conservative policy of transcription. The principles by which that process has been carried out and the conventions used in presenting the resultant text are listed below.

1. In rendering Yeats's words, I have followed his actual spelling when it is clear, even if it is incorrect or if he finished only part of a word. In cases where Yeats's actual spelling is difficult or impossible to determine, the standard spelling is given. Thus in line 15 of SB 23.2.230^{r} Yeats unquestionably wrote "wrapsedy" for "rhapsody" and his spelling is given; similarly, he clearly omitted the final "e" from an intended "shone" in line 1 on TCD 3502/2, 5, and the transcription accordingly reads "shon." But in line 29 of TCD 3502/3, 2^{v} the exact letters at the end of "sailing" are impossible to distinguish, so the standard spelling is given.

   In *Mosada* and *Island of Statues* the speakers' names are a particular source of difficulty. Where Yeats's spelling of, for instance, "Almintor" or "Naschina" is clear, I have followed it, whether such spelling is correct or incorrect. Likewise, I have transcribed only the letters he actually wrote in cases where he obviously did not finish the name. In the remaining cases—where the exact spelling is unclear or where it is impossible to determine if Yeats wrote the entire name—I have given the standard spelling used elsewhere in the manuscript.
2. A similar policy has been used for Yeats's sometimes unclear, sometimes erratic capitalization, a problem that arises often though not always at the beginning of verse lines. Where the first letter of a word is clearly either capitalized or lower-

cased, I have transcribed accordingly; where the letter is ambiguous, I have standardized according to normal practice.

3. Yeats frequently broke words at unusual points, or broke words not normally divided. Such words are joined in the transcriptions unless either the resultant division makes possible sense as two separate words or the width of the break approximates the spacing Yeats normally left between words, indicating that he considered or heard the word in question to be actually two words or one needing hyphenation (though he himself rarely inserted hyphens). Thus on TCD 3502/2, 5, "tune ful" in line 8 has been joined but "in to" in line 7 has not; similarly, because of the width of spacing, "nighting gale's" in line 16 on TCD 3502/2, 16^{r} has been left as two words.
4. Symbols for illegible words and editorial conjectures:

[?]	a totally illegible word, with the space between brackets corresponding approximately to the length of the word
stran[?]	a partially illegible word
[? ? ?]	several totally illegible words, with the number of question marks corresponding to the apparent number of words
[~~—?—~~]	a cancelled and totally illegible word
[?sing]	a conjectural reading (used only when the editor feels more than ordinary uncertainty)
[?sing/?say]	equally possible conjectural readings

5. Overwritings are indicated thus: ha{s/ve = "have" converted to "has." In some cases a letter has not been changed but merely overwritten to make it clearer; such reinforced letters have not been noted.
6. There are throughout the drafts certain obscure marks or blots, which may have been made accidentally. In cases where their significance has not been determined, they are silently omitted.
7. Cancellation of single lines or of words within a line is indicated by a single horizontal cancellation line. (This line is straight and single even where Yeats's was wavy or multiple.) Parallel lines are used to indicate cancellation first of a word or phrase and then of the entire line or a greater portion of it. Where Yeats intended to cancel an entire word but only struck through part of it, the cancellation line in the transcription extends through the entire word. However, even when it seems likely that Yeats meant to cancel an entire phrase or line, no word that he did not at least partially cancel (or extend a cancellation mark over or under) is cancelled in the transcriptions.
8. Except when Yeats used a separate horizontal cancellation mark for each line, the cancellation of entire passages is indicated by vertical brackets in the left margin. Arrows indicating relocation of words and passages only approximate the originals. Where typographical limitations make it impossible to print a marginal revision in its actual position, it is given immediately below the transcription of the page on which it occurs. Arrows leading from such passages are not reproduced.
9. Yeats's "stet" marks, underscorings to indicate italics, and other copyediting

marks are preserved. Caret symbols just below or above the line are raised or lowered to line level when their exact placement is clear; however, carets under a cancelled word meant to indicate substitution of a new word written above it have been left in place.

10. A special problem of Yeats's lifelong erratic punctuation that appears in the present manuscripts is his frequent use of a mark resembling a dash but placed at the level of the bottom of the line, often where one would expect a period. The placement of such marks is sometimes precisely or virtually on the notebook line in a way that seems to preclude mere carelessness, as though Yeats—always shaky in punctuation—was using the symbol as a nonce mark indicating a pause or possible future place for conventional punctuation. I have transcribed the mark as a line-level dash, except in cases where it is far enough above the line reasonably to be construed as a conventional dash or short enough reasonably to be construed as a period.
11. Problems in the transcription of words and passages are discussed in footnotes keyed to line numbers in the margin of the transcriptions. Because some of these problems pertain to stage directions, speaker tags, or widely separated half lines, I have assigned an individual number to each line of text, including each of the above categories. Instances where Yeats could not fit all of a line of verse onto a notebook line but had to write part of it immediately below have not received separate numbers, and such turnovers have been aligned at the right margin.
12. Although spacing of words and lines generally approximates the originals, a degree of typographical regularization has been employed for such elements as indentation, half lines, the placement of above-the-line revisions, turnovers, stage directions, and speaker tags. Yeats often omitted apostrophes in possessive constructions. Such omissions are clear in the case of proper nouns and have been indicated by a thin space before the final "s," as, for example, "Almintor s." Cases involving ordinary nouns admit of so many uncertainties that the convention has not been followed for them.
13. Although the manuscripts are written almost entirely in one instrument (usually black ink), two type styles have been used throughout this edition to facilitate distinction of revisions made in a different instrument. The conventions are as follows:

roman	ink
italic	pencil
heavy ~~cancellation line~~	deletion, ink
thin ~~cancellation line~~	deletion, pencil

In cases where the use of pencil amounts only to a punctuation mark or individual letter, a note to the line calls the reader's attention to the fact; in cases where there is enough revision to make the use of italic apparent, such a note is not given. Yeats used both lead and blue pencil in no apparent pattern on the drafts, and such variation is not noted.

A special problem of the printer's copy of *Island of Statues* is the presence of a hand other than Yeats's. For that manuscript only, an additional type style,

boldface italic, has been used; cancellations to permit revisions have been indicated with the thin line used elsewhere for revisions in pencil and should be understood to be by this same other hand unless a note indicates otherwise.

14. In general, each of Yeats's manuscript pages is recorded on a separate page of transcription. However, in cases where Yeats wrote relatively little on a page—usually a line count or short insertion on an otherwise blank notebook page facing a much fuller page of manuscript—I have recorded the information in the notes at the bottom of the fuller page.
15. The quotations in the notes and apparatus often involve Yeats's punctuation as well as diction. To avoid confusion of that punctuation with the editor's own syntax, quotations there follow the British convention of placing editorial punctuation outside the quotation marks.

Mosada

MANUSCRIPTS, WITH TRANSCRIPTIONS AND PHOTOGRAPHIC REPRODUCTIONS

With the exception of one leaf from the collection of Michael B. Yeats, now in the National Library of Ireland (NLI 30,430), all known surviving manuscripts of *Mosada* are in the library of Trinity College Dublin, to which they were presented by Mrs. W. B. Yeats on the occasion of the W. B. Yeats Exhibition, 1956. The three main manuscripts represent all or parts of three distinct drafts of the play. They are transcribed in chronological order, as follows:

MS TCD 3502/2, a notebook of which foliated pages 5–8 and 9–13 represent successive early versions of part of scene 3

MS TCD 3502/1, a notebook containing "Mosada a Tragedy in three scenes"

MS TCD 3502/3, sheets of loose foolscap containing a later version of scene 1 and most of scene 2, together with a one-page fragment of scene 3; the leaf in the National Library of Ireland continues scene 2 almost to the end

In addition, Appendix One lists changes recorded on galley proof, on copies of *The Wanderings of Oisin and Other Poems* at Princeton University and the University of Reading, and on a transcript prepared later by Mrs. Yeats.

The first two manuscripts are in maroon notebooks stamped inside the front cover with an oval device giving the name and address of "W. CARSON BOOKSELLER & STATIONER." The pages are lined and measure 19.8 cm by 15.7 cm. Yeats used similar notebooks for the drafts of *The Island of Statues*. The large, unlined sheets of loose foolscap in 3502/3 include both separate leaves measuring 33 cm by 20.3 cm and larger leaves folded in half vertically to make individual pages of that size; they are countermarked SUPERFINE FOOLSCAP. The additional leaf containing the fragment of scene 3 is on a worn fragment of a different, light green, unlined paper folded to make four sides that measure 21.7 cm by 15.5 cm. The leaf in the National Library of Ireland is on unlined white paper measuring 20.3 cm by 16.8 cm.

To facilitate identification, I have included in the top left brackets on each page of transcription the number of the manuscript in Trinity College followed by the foliated page number written on each leaf by the staff of the library. Thus, [TCD 3502/2, 5] refers to the foliated page 5 in the notebook labelled 3502/2 in the Trinity College Dublin library. For the convenience of North American readers I cite the manuscripts from the Michael B. Yeats collection, now in the National Library of Ireland, by their reference numbers in the Yeats Archive at the State University of New York, Stony Brook. Thus [SB 22.7.14] refers to page 14 of volume 7 of the hard copy derived from reel 22 in the Stony Brook archive. For the convenience of readers in Ireland and the United Kingdom a conversion table showing the designation of the original manuscripts in the National Library of Ireland is provided as Appendix Two. The second set of brackets at the top of each page indicates the scene and line numbers to which the page corresponds in *The Variorum Edition of the Poems of W. B. Yeats,* ed. Peter Allt and Russell K. Alspach (New York: Macmillan, corrected 3d printing, 1966). Thus [VP 3:50–55] indicates lines 50–55 of scene 3 of *Mosada.* Readers using *The Poems of W. B. Yeats: A New Edition,* ed. Richard J. Finneran (New York: Macmillan, 1983; London: Macmillan, 1984), will find the numbering identical through line 40 of scene 3; thereafter, the reader should add 1 to the Finneran numbering, which follows a copy text on which Yeats deleted line 41. In the case of the roughest drafts, the correspondence is sometimes only approximate.

One name in the transcriptions requires explanation. In both the *Dublin University Review* text (June 1886) and its reprinting by Sealy, Bryers, and Walker (Dublin, 1886), the former name of Ebremar is ''Vallence'' rather than ''Gomez.'' In the manuscripts, the exact spelling varies but is most often ''Vallance.''

First Version: Two Early Drafts of Scene 3

The earliest surviving drafts of *Mosada* consist of two versions of part of scene 3 in maroon notebook TCD 3502/2, which contains in order: a draft of *Time and the Witch Vivien,* with the last page possibly belonging to a different work; the *Mosada* material; and the first draft of *Island of Statues*. Because a later draft of *Island of Statues* appears in a notebook dated August 1884 by Yeats, and because the next version of *Mosada* appears in a different notebook dated June 7th, 188[?], by him, it seems reasonable to assign that version of *Mosada* to June 7, 1884, and hence to date the present drafts as prior to that time.

Both drafts of scene 3 in the 3502/2 notebook are far from the finished version, so much so as sometimes to make correlation problematic. The first version appears to begin at line 50 of the VP numbering and proceeds until the end of the play. On the next page, Yeats began again with the same material, but this time commencing with the "Awake Mosada wake" line from the top of the second page of the first version, and again continued until the end in somewhat more finished form. Nowhere in these two drafts did Yeats number the scenes as "3", nor did he give any indication of an earlier part of the play. Hence, although it is possible that Yeats wrote earlier drafts of scenes 1 and 2 to precede 3502/2, it is also possible that these versions of scene 3 represent the germ of the entire play. Of course, these versions of scene 3 themselves may represent an advance on an earlier, now lost draft.

Both versions are written in black ink. With the exceptions of the first page (TCD 3502/2, 5), which is a recto facing a verso that contains either a continuation of the *Time and the Witch Vivien* draft or a fragment of something else, and of the last page, for which Yeats turned the notebook upside down and began again at the back, all the other pages are written on rectos facing otherwise blank versos of the preceding page.

T'is thus they shone the night
When my lost love passed down among the hills
O Vallance Vallance we shall meet at last
St The stars of thy nativity and mine
Burn side by side two ministering light
Throbing within the circle of ~~the~~ green dawn
Souls, dawn, pour down your beam in to my heart
~~And~~ it will answer lonely with old memories tune of joy
To Cate To Cate for I am near to death

I raise to thee no praying voice
In the old times ancient fashion
~~For~~ the great seers under position

Tis thus they shon the night
When my lost love passed dowm among the hill
O Vallance Vallance we shall meet at last
~~St~~ The stars of thy nativity and mine
Burn side by side, two ministering lights
                                                    {c   green
Throbing within the cir{lle of ~~the~~ dawn
                                                                   { a
Souls dawn, pour down your be{[?]ms in to my hea
        t'will
~~And it~~ ~~will~~ answer with old [?manners] tuneful joy
To late To late for I am neer to death

I ~~raise to the no praying~~ voice
~~In the old times ancint~~ fashion
                                                          {a
~~For the great sees endless~~ pash{tn

The draft begins at the present line 50 of VP, immediately after Mosada has drunk the poison (which is not mentioned in this draft).

5 The last two letters of "ministering" are formed particularly poorly.

7 "Souls" may be intended for either a singular or a plural possessive; "hea" is presumably intended to be "heart".

10–12 These lines may belong to the draft of another work on the verso page of the notebook facing TCD 3502/2,5. Both the original and emended spelling of the last word of l. 12 are difficult to decipher and at one stage may contain an "i".

She

Awake Mosada wake
Thy Valence is by thee
Mosada
Go not this eve for it ~~very late~~ down ~~~~ below the hill
The way is very long and it is late
Ebremar
O
Lift up thine eyes tis Valence kneels by thee
Who leaves thee nevermore
Mosa
Mosada I do not go
O stay one moon de
Tis dark I never new so dark a night
Ebreme
~~Upon the brest of ~~valence~~ Valence lies thy head~~
O still the trouble of thy wandering ~~~~ mind
Upon the brest of Valence lies thy head

1 She
2 Awake Mosada wake
{V
3 Thy {valance is by thee
4 Mosada
down ~~amo~~ below the hills
5 Go not this eve for ~~it very dark~~
6 The way is very long and it is late
7 Ebremar
8 ~~I~~ {kn
9 Lift up thine eyes tis Valance {neels by thee
10 Who leaves thee nevermore
11 ~~Mosad~~
12 Mosade ~~I do not go~~
{I
13 {[?O] stay one more da
14 Tis dark I never new so dark a night
15 Ebreme
~~Valance~~
16 ~~Upon the brest of [?] lies thy head~~
17 O still the troubles of thy wandering ~~mid~~ mind
18 Upon [?the/?thy] berst of Valence lies thy head

Mosada 7

~~Let us sit here a little for ye~~ go
~~And put my~~ Cloak ~~about for us for~~ the cold
I ~~never knew a night so bitter~~ cold

The way is very long and it is ~~very~~ late
She go now like the cold dew on my face
Ebremar
~~Mosada~~
Oh look one look.
Mosada
~~On the smooth mossy ro~~
By this wide mossy root
Let us sit here a little for ye go
And put ~~us~~ my cloak ~~[illegible]~~ about us
for tis cold
I never knew a night so bitter cold
(dies)
Ebremar
Mosada Mosada

1 Mosada
2 ~~Let us sit here a litle fore you~~ go
3 ~~And put my cloak about far ti for~~ tis cold
4 I ~~never new a night so bitter~~ cold
5 The way is very long and it is ~~very~~ late
how
6 She yo lies the cold dew on my face
7 Ebremar
8 ~~Mosada~~
9 On look one looke
10 Mosada
11 ~~O this smoot mossy roc~~
[?See] this wide moosy [?root/?rook]
12 Let us sit here a litle for yo go
13 And put ~~a~~ my cloak [~~—?—~~] about me
for ti's cold
14 I never new a night so bitter cold
15 (dies)
16 Errib
17 Mosada Mosada

6 "She" is presumably an error for "See".
16 There may be another letter after the "b" of "Errib".

Enter Monks

1 Monk

My Lord you called

[illegible]ren

Not

Not I! Not I — this morish maid is dead

1 Monk

a Suicide you cannot trust the moor

Your pale my lord

Ebrena

I am not very well

'twill pass — I'll see ~~speak~~ ~~with~~ the other prisoners

now

and Importune them that they may repent

again

and save their soul. My crusofix

(A Monk hands it him)

2 Monk

often said

I ~~always~~ ~~knew~~ you could not trust these moo

Enter Monks
1 Monk
My lord you called
Ebrem
~~Not~~
{N
Not I! {not I—thiis morish maid is ded
1 Monk
{ y
A suiside {[?]ou cannot trust the moor
Your pale my lord
Ebrema
I am not very well
see
T'will pas —I'll ~~speak~~ ~~with~~ the other prisnors
now
And Importune them that they may repent
dying
And save their souls My crusafix
(a Monk hads it him)
1 Monk
often said
I ~~alway~~ ~~new~~ you could not trust these moors

---

8 "moor" may have an "s" at the end.

15–16 In both these lines Yeats apparently changed his mind about the letter or numeral preceeding "Monk"; l. 15 may have a capital "A" overwritten with a small "a", and l. 16 appears to have a "1" written over "a".

awake Mosada wake
Thy Vallance is by thee
Mosada
talk
Let ~~talk~~ and grieve
For thats the sweetest music for sad souls
Day's dead all flame bewildered and the hills
In listening silence gaze upon our grief
Ebremar
Her thoughts hold commune with old times
awake
Grieve not thy Valance kneels by thee
Mosada
Vallance
Tis late, wait one more day, below the hills
The shadowey way is long and it grows dark
It is the darkest eve I ever knew
Ebremar
I kneel by thee I leave thee never more —
with
She smiles in happy ~~in~~ her wondering griefs

awake mosada wake
Thy Vallance is by thee
Mosada
talk
Lets ~~talk~~ and grive
For thats the swetest music for sad souls
Day's dead all flame bewildered and the hills
In listning silence gaze apon our grief
Ebremar
Her thoughts hold comune with old time
—awake
Grieve not thy Valance kneels by thee
Mosada
Vallance
Tis late, wait one more day, below the hills
The shadowey way is long and it grows dark
It is the darkest eve I ever knew
Ebremar
I kneel by thee I leave the never more—
with
She smiles is happy ~~in~~ her wandering griefs

With this page Yeats begins a new version of the immediately preceding draft. TCD 3502/2, 9–13 are a revision of TCD 3502/2, 5–8.

7 Yeats may have written "gries" for "grief".

10

Mosada

Ah must you go, kiss me before you go
Oh would the busy minutes might fold up
There thieving wings that we might never part
I never knew so still and sweet a night

Ebremar

All parting now is past I go no more
Upon the brest of Valana lies thy head
unhappy one

Mosada

Go not – go not . go not
For fast night comes look down on me my Love
And see how thick the dew lies on my face

Ebremar

O still the wandring sorrow of thy mind
One look one look who such you asked so
Why fall you back so heavy in my arms
As thou sleepst sleep was siting by one look
O will you die when we have meet one look
~~Cast on~~ giv to thy Vallance ~~[illegible]~~

Mosada
~~A~~
Ah must you go, kiss me before you go
Oh would the busy minutes might fold up
There theiving wings that we might never part
I never knew so still and sweet a nighit
Ebremar
All parting now is past I go no more
Upon the brest of Valance lies thy h{e / iad}
Unhappy one
Mosada
Go not — go not — go not
look down
For fast night comes ^ one me my love
And see how thick the dew lies on my face
Ebremar
O still the wandering sorrow of thy mind
One look one look why sink your eylids so
Why fall you back so heavy in my arms
As thou sleep sleep was siting by one look
O will you die when we have meet one look
Give to
~~Cast on~~ thy Vallance ~~sad~~

15–16 These two lines are squeezed into one line of the notebook. Yeats may have added l. 15 later, but he may also simply have wanted to conserve space to enable Ebremar's speech to end at the bottom of the page.

Vallence he has gon

From sights along the shadowy path that ~~go~~ wind
along ~~sort,~~ close by the river ~~wong~~ ~~the~~ wanders, ligne
I'll see him longer if I stand out here
upon the mountain brow
(She tries to stand and with
Ezremiel supports her stands she
points as if down into ~~an~~
~~imaginary~~ ~~too~~ a visionary valley)

Mosad.

~~along the path~~
yonder he ~~goes~~ treds
The path over muffled with the leave
– dead leaves
Like happy thoughts grown sad in evil days
He fades among the mist how fast it come
and poors upon the world ah welladay
Poor love and sorrow with their arms thrown round
each others necks and whispering as they go

1 Vallance he has gon
wind
2 From sighs along the shadowy path that ~~go~~
Its [—?—] way
3 ~~Along~~ close by the river ~~mong~~ ~~the~~ wandering light
{ll
4 I'{d see him longer if I stand out here
5 Upon the mountain brow
6 (She tries to stand and totters
7 Ebrenar suports her [?stands/?starts] she
8 points as if down Into ~~an~~
9 ~~imaginary [?wa/?va~~] a visionary valley)
10 Mosada
11 ~~Along the path~~
yonder he ~~goes~~ treds
12 The path oer muffled with the leave
—dead leav
13 Like happy thoughts grown sad in evil days
mist
14 He fades among the ^ how fast it come
15 And poors upon the world ah welanday
round
16 Poor love and sorrow with there arms thrown
17 each others necks and whispering as they go

---

1 Yeats has forgotten to include a speaker tag assigning ll. 1–5 to Mosada.
3 There may be an "s" at the end of "light".
6 One of the letters is missing from the end of "totters".

Still wonders thro the world — he's go he'll go
I'm wearied out and it is very cold
I'll draw my cloak about me it is cold
I never knew a night so bitter cold

(dies)

~~Ebremar~~

~~Mosada Mosada~~

Ebremar

~~Henceforth I'm but the actor of a part~~

She deceivs and I alone have left a mask
To play a part

Calls

Peter and Gomez come

Enter monks

My Lord

Peter this moorish maid is dead

" .. 1 ~~monk~~ ~~Peter~~ 1 monk

A suicide you cannot trust this moor
You pale my Lord

[TCD 3502/2, 12] ~~[VP 3:121–127]~~

Still wande through the world—he's go he's gone
I'm wearied out and it is very cold
I'll draw my cloak about me its cold
I never new a night so bitte cold
(dies)
~~Ebrenar~~
~~Mosada Mosada~~
Ebrenar
~~Hence forth Im but the acter of a part~~
s'
She dead's and I alone have left a mak
To play a part
calls
Peter and Jerome come
enter monk
my lord
Peter this moorish maid is dead
~~1 monk Peter~~ 1 monk
A suiside you cannot trust thes moors
You pale my lord

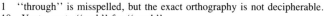

1 ''through'' is misspelled, but the exact orthography is not decipherable.
10 Yeats wrote ''mak'' for ''mask''.

13

Ebremar

~~Fasts pass~~

I am not very well

*Fasts pass

I 'll see the other prisoner now

and I importune them that they may repent

and deny save the ~~sons~~

my crucifix

(a most such is as when

it had fallen ere in the sea

and handit him)

| most

I often said you could not trust thy moor

1 Ebrena
2 ~~T'will pass~~
3 I am not very well
4 'Twill pass
I'll see the other prisners now
5 and IImportune them that they may repent
6 and dying save thr souls
7 my crusafix
8 (a monk picks it up wher
9 it had fallen ear in the [?scene]
10 and hand it him)
11 1 Monk
12 I often said you could not trust these moor

---

9 ''ear'' is presumably intended to be ''earlier''.

Love and sow

9·

~~Pale Love and sorrow pass~~

Pale Love and sorrow pass nor do I greatly grieve
about the ending of their famous wonderings
I see how round each other's necks their arms
they wreath
I see how they do whisper mong their pongerings

[TCD 3502/2, 31^{v}] [VP 3:119–121]

1 Love and sow

2 ~~Pale love and sorrow pass~~

Pale love and sorrow pass nor do I greatly grieve

3 About the ending of their famous wonderings
4 I see how round each other's necks their arms
they wreath
5 I see how they do whisper mong their pongerings

At some point, presumably later than the rest of the draft, Yeats turned the notebook upside down and backwards to write this on the former last page. Although the TCD foliation numbers stop with 30 and are followed by nine blank leaves, this leaf is numbered 31 according to the facing notation on the inside back cover ''Foliated Nov. '65 31 folios''. The lines do not appear in the first version but do pertain to those in the second, TCD 3502/2, 11–12.

1–2 There is an illegible mark between these two lines that may be a cancelled ''I''.

3 ''wonderings'' may be an error for ''wanderings''.

4 There may be an errant apostrophe between the ''k'' and ''s'' of ''necks''.

5 ''pongerings'' is presumably an error for ''ponderings''.

Second Version: ''Mosada a Tragedy in Three Scenes''

This notebook contains the earliest surviving draft of the entire play. It is later than the two early drafts of scene 3 (TCD 3502/2) but precedes the version on loose foolscap. Faded black ink on the cover of the notebook reads ''MOSADA/a Dramatic Poem/June the 7th 188[?]''. Because a draft of *The Island of Statues* which is later than the one that appears in the 3502/2 notebook with the early versions of scene 3 is dated August 1884, it is likely that the present notebook should be assigned to June 7, 1884, though June 7, 1885, is possible. *Mosada* finally appeared in the June 1886 issue of the *Dublin University Review.*

The 3502/1 version of *Mosada* is reasonably finished, though some sections remain far from the eventual version and a few are wholly different (for example, the dialogue between Mosada and Cola near the end of scene 1 on foliated pages 9 and 10). It seems likely that after 3502/2, Yeats worked on the play in a now lost notebook or manuscript. 3502/1 often reads like a fair copy on which Yeats then made minor revisions as he went along. Most of the words made illegible by cancellation appear to be misspellings of the word replacing them, and most of the corrections are entered first in pencil and then reinforced in ink. In several instances a correction was made first in pencil, then erased, and finally entered in ink; such erased pencil corrections have not been noted in the transcriptions, but the notes indicate the most legible examples of the practice.

The notebook is written in black ink, with occasional pencil corrections. Inside the front cover Yeats wrote in pencil: ''W B Yeats / 10 Ashfield Terrace / Rathgar / Dublin''. After the end of the play come ten blank leaves, followed by an eleventh which has a scrap of the unpublished early play ''The Blind'' written upside down on the verso. Inside the back cover appears the notation ''Foliated Nov. '65 / 11 + 28 folios''. As with 3502/2, the manuscript is written on rectos; the versos are blank.

3502/1 1

Mosada
a Tragedy in three scenes
By W B Yeats—

"and my Lord Cardinal hath had strange days in his youth" Extract from a Memoir of the fifteenth century

— Characters —

Mosada	A moorish lady
Ebremar	a monk
Colu	a boy

Monks, & Inquisitors—

Scene ~~xxx~~ in and about Granada

Friday — 3. to 6. —

[TCD 3502/1, 1] [VP 1]

Mosada
A Tragedy in three scenes
By W B Yeats—
"and my lord Cardinal hath had strange days
in his youth" Extract from a Memoir of
the fisthenth century
—Characters—

Mosada	A moorish lady
Ebremar	a monk
Cola	a boy

Monks, & Inquisitors—
Scene ~~nea~~ in and about Granada
Friday— 3 to 6.—

2

Scene 1

a moorish room in the Village
of Azabra. In the room's center stand a chafing dish
upon a tripod

Mosada (alone)

Thrice has the winter come and gone again
~~As Autumn~~
And thrice the roses have grown less and less
~~As Autumn climbed the steps of summer's throne~~
~~When~~ slowly ~~youthful~~
as ~~[illegible]~~ Autumn climbed the golden throne
When sat ~~at~~ old summer fading ~~[illegible]~~ into song
And thrice the ~~[illegible]~~ peaches flushed upon the walls
And thrice the corn around the sickles flamed—
Since to my peoples tents among the hills
He came a messenger. In aprils prime
When swallows flashed their white breasts high above
Or perched upon the tents, ~~slow~~ when weak they seemed
From their long flight yet over ~~[illegible]~~ garrulous,
Along the winding vale I watched him come

1 Scene 1
2 a moorish room in the Village
3 of Azabia — In the room's center stand a chafing dish
4 upon a tripod
5 Mosada (alone)
6 Thrice has the wintėr come and gone again
7 ~~As Autumn~~
8 And thrice the roses have grown less and less
9 ~~As Autumn climbed the steps of summer's throne~~
10 ~~Where~~
slowly
~~youthful~~
11 As ~~tuneless~~ Autumn climbed the golden throne
into
12 Where sat ~~al~~ old summer fading ~~in his~~ song
peaches
13 And thrice the ~~p[?]~~ flushed upon the walls
{kles
14 And thrice the corn around the sic{les flamed—
15 Since to my peoples' tents among the hills
16 He came a messenger. In april s prime
17 When swallows flashed their white breasts high above
when
18 Or perched upon the tents, ~~still~~ weak they seemed
garrulous
19 From their long flight yet ever ~~g[?]s~~,
20 Along the winding vale I watched him come

3 Yeats's "a" and "u" are often difficult to distinguish, but here he seems to have written "Azabia" rather than the "Azubia" of the published version.
4 This line is squeezed into the same lined space of the notebook as l. 5.
11 "slowly", Yeats's third choice of modifier, appears on the same level as l. 10.
14 "sickles" is corrected in pencil, overwritten in ink.
19 The illegible word is a misspelling of "garrulous".

3

'Twas autumn when far down the mountains side
The heavy clusters of the grapes were full
I saw him go — He sighed and turned away
I and my people seemed to him accurst
He passed away and down among the grass
I hid my face and cried long bitterly
'Twas evening and I heard the grasshoppers
Sing close around my head among the grass
~~And all around the lemon leaves fell down.~~
And naught I knew ~~[illegible]~~ until a dying ~~leave~~ leaf
Came circling down and softly touched my lips
With dew, as though 'twould seal them up for death—
Yet some where in the world we two must meet
Again before we die for Azolar
The star taught moor said thus it was decreed
By those wan stars that sit in company
Above the Apagarras on their thrones
And gaze upon the silence of the world
That when the stars of our nativity
Draw near as on the evening that he passed

'Twas autumn when far down the mountains side
The heavy clusters of the grapes were full
I saw him go—He sighed and turned away
I and my people seemed to him accurst
He passed away and down among the grass
I hid my face and cried long bitterly
T'was evening and I heard the grasshoppers
Sing close around my head among the grass
~~And all around the lemon leaves fell down~~
until
And naught I knew [~~—?—~~] a dying ~~leave~~ leaf
Came circling down and softly touched my lips
With dew, as though 'twould seal them up for death—
Yet some where in the world we two must meet
Again before we die for Azolar
The star taught moor said thus it was decreed
By those wan stars that sit in company
l
Above the A^pajarras on their thrones
And gaze upon the silence of the world
That when the stars of our nativity
Draw near as on the evening that he passed

12 The apostrophe before "twould" is in pencil.

4

Vallies
Down those long ~~[illegible]~~ from my peoples tents
Then ~~in~~ the world some where we two must meet
(She opens ~~the~~ casement – the mingled
Sound of the laughter and voices
of the apple gatherers float in)
Mosada
How merry all these are among the fruit
each heart a kingdom for winged laughter sway
But yonders Cola sitting by himself – apart
Twere sad if my unlawful spells ~~[illegible]~~ weighed down
His boyant heart
aye how the slanting sun
Sinks down at last with yonder minaret
Of the Alhambra black ~~a[illegible]~~ athwart his disk
#. That is the sign and Cola comes this way
(She throws herbs upon the chafing
dish)
So do I burn these ~~[illegible]~~s fragrant herbs whose smoke
Pours up and floats along the roof
In coil on coil of green
(Enter Cola)

vallies
Down those long ~~valley~~ from my peoples tents
{n
Then i{[?] the world some where we two must meet
{the
(she opens {a casement—the mingled
sound of the laughter and voices
of the apple gatheres floats in)
Mosada
How merry all these are among the fruit
each heart a kingdom for winged laughter sway
But yonders Cola sitting by himself apart
weighed
T'were sad if my unlawful spells [~~?~~] down
His boyant heart
aye how the slanting sun
Sinks down at last with yonder minaret
{*A* athwart
Of the {alhambra black [~~?atwart~~] his disk
[~~?~~] That is the sign and Cola comes this way
{t
(she throws herbs upon {ahe chafing
dish)
{a {a {se
So do I burn this ~~herbs~~ fr{egr{ent herbs who{'se smoke
Pours up and floats along the roof
In coil on coil of green
(Enter Cola)

8 This line is squeezed into the same lined space of the notebook as l. 9.
13 The capital "A" of "Alhambra" is in pencil.
17 The full words "fragrant" and "whose" were first written above the line in pencil and then erased, with more limited corrections entered in ink.

5

Mosada
All is prepared
Cola
Mosada it is then so much the worse
~~I will not look and share thy sin against~~
I will not aid thy spells and share thy sin
'gainst the far reaching power of the church
Mosada
Why these new fears?
Cola
The dark still man ~~has~~ come
The great ecclesiastic ~~[illegible]~~ and his ~~boast~~ / ~~[illegible]~~ boast
Is of the countless heathen he has burnt
Moscada
Fear not the sin is mine and think you I
would sin if he might know — what sin to see,
Within the charméd ~~[illegible]~~ depth of whirling smoke,
What one who left me long ago does now —
Some say to wish is half the sin itself
Well then it has been ~~[illegible]~~ sinned full many times

1 Mosada
2 All is prepared
3 Cola
4 Mosada it is then so much the worse
5 ~~I will not look and share thy sin against~~
I will not aid thy spells and share thy sin
6 'Gainst the far reaching power of the church
7 Mosada
8 Why these new fears?
9 Cola
{ h
10 The dark still man { [?]as come
ecclesiastic boast
11 The great ~~E~~ [?~~ecleastic~~] and his ~~boas~~ / ~~bost~~

12 Is of the countless heathen he has burnt
13 Moscada
14 Fear not the sin is mine and think you I
15 would sin if he might know—what sin to see,
16 Within the charméd ~~deapth~~ depth of whirling smoke,
17 What one who left me long ago does now—
18 Some say to wish is half the sin itself
sinned
19 Well then it has been s[—?—] full many times

10 There is a mark before "as" in "has" that may be either a misplaced apostrophe or the start of another letter.
11 The slash mark after "boas" may be an uncrossed "t".

6

This is a harmless art my father old
Who dreamed unto a wonderous age ~~[illegible]~~ taught me
He was a man most learned and most mild
Why he would spend the live long day to train
And tend the roses round about his door
For many years his days had come and faded thus
Among the plants — The flowery silence fell
Upon his soul like rain upon ~~the~~ a soil
Worn by the ~~[illegible]~~ solstice ^ weary and made it pure —
And when 'twas dark his faded eyes would gaze
On those ~~[illegible]~~ wan mariners who sail and sail
Upon thei~~r~~ ^r ever foamless sea, the stars —
Would he teach ~~its~~ any its

Cola

I will not look

Mosada

O child you cannot tell how yearnings for
A sight of far off ones can fill sick hearts
I'll show you things to tell of when ~~[illegible]~~ you're old
Beneath a lemon tree before thy door

This is a harmless art my father old
taught
Who dreamed unto a wonderous age [~~—?—~~] me
He was a man most learned and most mild
Why he would spend the live long day to trail
And tend the roses round about his door
For many years his days had come and faded thus
Among the plants—The flowery silence fell
a
Upon his soul like rain upon ~~the~~ soil
solstice fearce
Worn by the [~~?Solystice~~] ^and made it pure—
And when 'twas dark his faded eyes would gaze
wan
On those [~~?want~~] mariners who sail and sail
Upon their ever foamless sea, the stars——
Would he teach ~~ill~~ any ill
Cola
I will not look
Mosada
O child you cannot tell how yearnings for
A sight of far off ones can fill sick hearts
you're
Ill show you things to tell of when ~~your~~ old
Beneath a lemon tree before thy door

---

2 The cancelled word appears to be a misspelling of "taught".
9 Yeats may have written "pare" for "pure".
11 The apparent "t" of "~~?want~~" may be a "d".
12 Yeats may have first written "there" for "their". At the end of the line, he first made a short dash on the level of the printed line in the notebook and then extended it diagonally into a very long dash.

7

and all the elders sitting in the sun
Will wondering listen and thy tale will ease
For long the burden of their talking griefs

Cola

I will not look for you, look for your self

Mosada

no no none but the innocent can see
are you afraid — you'll see no fearful sight
I'll call ~~up~~ unto thine aid a spirit fair
and calm, robed all in raiment moony white—
She was a great enchantress once of yore
who lived upon a tree wrapt Island called
Far out upon the ocean world and ringed
With wonderful white sand where never yet
~~[illegible]~~ were furled the wings of ships— There in a dell
a lily blanched place she sat and sang
and as she sang she'd ~~bu~~ bind about her head
White lilies and her song would ~~pass~~ fly afar
From where the ~~[illegible]~~ lilies of the wan lips grew,
~~across the~~ sea

and all the elders sitting in the sun
Will wondering listen and thy tale will ease
For long the burden of their talking griefs
{ C
{ [?]ola
I will not look for‸ you; look for your self
Mosada
No no none but the innocent can see
Are you afraid—you'll see no fearful sight
I'll call ~~up~~ into thine aid a spirit fair
And calm, robed all in raiment moony white—
She was a great enchantress once of yore
Who lived upon a tree wrapt Island lulled
{u
Far out {apon the ocean world and ringed
With wonderful white sand where never yet
were
[—?—] furled the wings of ships—There in a dell
A lily blanchèd place she sat and sang
And as she sang she'd ~~ba~~ bind about her head
{ie fly
White lil {y s and her song would ~~pass~~ afar
lilies
From where the ~~lilys~~ of the wan lips grew.
~~Acros the sea~~

7 Yeats eventually moved this line to 59 in the VP numbering.

8

Along the sea, and many a man would hear
At his own house or 'mong the merchants grey
And at the sound of that far tuneful guile
Would groan as one who knows no hope and then
He'd man a ~~[illegible]~~ vessle and would sailing die—
At last ~~[illegible]~~ she sang herself to sleep. Her soul
I'll conjure hither and by her will show
His form in smoke

Cola

I will not look

Mosada

Look child
And I will teach thee how to sing the song
The shepherd boys on the Apajurras' side
The many clefted sing their ~~[illegible]~~ browsing sheep

Cola

You said none but the innocent can see
The figures on the smoke how do you know
~~[illegible]~~

Mosada that I'm innocent

Along the sea, and many a man would hear
At his own house or 'mong the merchents grey
And at the sound of that far tuneful guile
Would groan as one who knows no hope and then
vessle
He'd man a ~~vessal~~ and would sailing die—
At last [~~?sher~~] she sang herself to sleep. Her soul
I'll conjure hither and by her will show
His form in smoke
Cola
I will not look
Mosada
look child
And I will teach thee how to sing the song
{A
The shepherd boys on the {apajairas' side
The many clefted sing their ~~brr~~ browsing sheep
Cola
You said none but the innocent can see
The figures on the smoke how do you know
~~That~~
Mosada that I'm innocent

9

Mosada

O yes

For why should not the young be innocent

Cola (Start and listens)

Now I will do what e'er you wish

Mosada

Thanks! Thanks!

Stand thou aside and I will chant the spell
For thee — 'Twas by a famous poet made
In an unremembered tongue — He loved
~~The princess~~ of
It was a touching and unhappy tale,
The princess of a town who's very name
None know and where it was none now can tell

(there is a faint sound without)

Why do you grow so pale and sit apart
Like to a startled ~~[illegible]~~ hare — fear not we're far
From all the world among the climbing coils
Of this green smoke — when I have sung the spell
To call the song-soul of that ancient isle

Mosada
O yes
For why should not the young be innocent
Cola (starts and listengs)
{N
{Iow I will do what e'er you wish
Mosada
Thanks! Thanks!
Stand thou aside and I will chant the spell
For thee—'Twas by a famous poet made
In an unremembered tongue. He loved
~~The princess~~ of
It was a touching and unhappy tale,
The princess of a town who's very name
None know and where it was none now can tell
(there is a faint sound without)
Why do you grow so pale and sit apart
Like to a startled ~~hair~~ hare—fear not we're far
From all the world among the climbing coils
Of this green smoke—When I have sung the spell
To call the song-soul of that ancient isle

Pages 3502/1, 9–10 differ so much in both length and content from VP ll. 92–103 that they are best seen as a rejected extended alternative to the eventual version. The lineation in the righthand brackets at the top of this and the next page indicates placement rather than correspondence.

20 The hyphen is either cancelled or reinforced in pencil.

10

a burning spark shall glimmer in the smoke
That wraps us and —
Cole (darts forward and throws
down the chafing dish the glowing
charcoal and the herbs are scattered)
Ecola
burn burn, thou moorish ~~witt~~ witch
I scatter thus
These thing ~~thing~~ of crime that you may hide them not
Burn, Burn, thou heretic
Mosada
(trying to gather ~~[illegible]~~ together the herbs)
I cannot ~~not~~ now
know where he is — These herbs alone I had
~~kept long for one spell ample and no more~~
And child I know not where to gather new
(the doors are burst open and the
Officers of the inquisition enter)

a burning spark shall glimmer in the smoke
That wraps us and—
Cola (darts forward and throws
down the chafing dish the glowing
charcoal and the herbs are scattered)
Cola
burn, burn, thou moorish ~~with~~ witch
I scatter thus
These thing ~~things~~ of crime that you may hide them not
Burn, Burn, thou heretic
Mosada
together
(trying to gather [~~?togather~~] the herbs)
I cannot ~~not~~ now
know where he is—These herbs alone I had
~~Kept long for one spell ample and no more~~
And child I know not where to gather new
(the doors are burst open and the
Offices of the inquisition enter)

---

6 The "C" of "Cola" is written over the start of an "M".
14 One cancellation mark runs through "Kept . . . ample" and another through "spell . . . more".

I Inquisitor
I here arrest thee in the churches name
Mooren ~~[illegible]~~ surrounded by the impliments
Of thy accursed art
Mosada
'Tis Allah's will
Touch not this boy he is most innocent
Cola
Forgive me lady I have ~~[illegible]~~ told them all
The spells you planned and this the chosen day —
They ~~[illegible]~~ threatened me and said I'd burn in hell
Unless I told them all, and ~~went~~ came to you —
without a word, They wished to come as now
And find you mong the vapour and the herbs —
(She turns away he
clings to her dress)
Cola
O will you not forgive
Mosada
'Twas Allah's will

1 inquisitor
re
I he {ar arrest thee in the churches name
surrounded
Mooress [—?—] by the impliments
Of thy accursed art
Mosada
'Tis Allah's will
Touch not this boy he is most innocent
Cola
Forgive me lady I have ~~tolld~~ told them all
The spells you planned and this the chosen day—
threatened me
They [—?—] and said I'd burn in hell
came
Unless I told them all, and ~~went~~ to you—
Without a word,—They wished to come as now
And find you mong the vapour and the herbs.
(she turns away he
clings to her dress)
Cola
O will you not forgive
Mosada
'Twas Allah's will

---

3 The cancelled word appears to be a misspelling of "surrounded".

12

Colin
Forgive or I will die
Mosada
'Twas Allah's will
(Exeunt)

[TCD 3502/1, 12] [VP 1:118]

Cola
Forgive or I will die
Mosada
'Twas Allah's will
(exeunt)

13

Scene 2

a room in the building of the
inquesition at Greneda, a stained
Window behind representing St James
of Spain –

Monks and Inquisitors talking

1 inquesetor

So she must burn you say

2 inquesitor

She must in truth

1 inquesitor

Will he not spare her life –

1 Monk

The most just man
Will stamp this race of Vipers from the earth

2 inquisitor

In truth these moors are a most evil race
Unto the cross our lives we hold in trust
And we must stamp them out – Why strive for her
~~Tis to~~ She's but a ~~[illegible]~~ little moorish girl

Scene 2
A room in the building of the
{G
inquisition at {greneda, a stained
window behind representing St James
of Spain—
Monks and Inquisitors talking
1 inquisitor
So she must burn you say
2 inquisitor
She must in truth
1 inquisitor
Will he not spare her life—
1 monk
The most just man
Will stamp this race of Vipers from the earth
2 inquisitors
In truth these moors are a most evil race
Unto the cross our lives we hold in trust
And we must stamp them out—Why strive for her
~~'Tis~~ [~~?for~~] She's but a ~~l~~ little moorish girl

14

~~Small~~

1 monk

Small worth

1 inquisitor

I had a sister like her once – My friend

(touches the 2nd monk on his shoulder)

Where is ~~your~~ our brother Peter. when ~~[illegible]~~ you're ~~nigh~~ near

He is not far – I'd have him speak for her

I've seen his jovial mood bring once a smile

To ~~[illegible]~~ sainted Ebremars sad eyes – I think

He loves our brother Peter in his heart

If he would ask he'd grant her life mayhap

2 monk

He digs his cabbages – He brings to mind

A song I've made about a Russian tale

Of holy Peter of the burning gate

A saint of Russia in a vision saw

(sings)

A ~~[illegible]~~ stranger new arisen wait

'Fore the door of Peter's gate

1 ~~Smal~~
2 1 monk
3 Small worth
4 1 inquisitor
5 I had a sister like her once__My friend
6 (touches the 2nd monk on his shoulder)
our you're
7 Where is ~~your~~ brother Peter. When [—?—] ~~nigh~~ near
8 He is not far—I'd have him speak for her
9 I've seen his jovial mood bring once a smile
sainted
10 To [—?—] Ebremar s sad eyes—I think
11 He loves our brother Peter in his heart
12 If he would ask he'd grant her life mayhap
13 2 monk
14 He digs his cabbages—He brings to mind
15 A song I've made about a Russian tale
16 Of holy Peter of the burning gate
17 A saint of Russia in a vision saw
18 (sings)
stranger
19 A [—?—] new arisen wait
20 'Fore the door of Peter's gate

---

19 The cancelled word appears to be a misspelling of "stranger".
20 To correct "For" the word "'fore" was first written above the line in pencil and then erased.

15

And he shouted open wide
The sacred door but Peter cried
No thy home is deepest hell
Deeper than the deepest well —
But the stranger softly crew
Cock-a-doodle-doodle-do —
Answered Peter enter in,
But friend it were a deadly sin
Ever more to speak a word
Of any unblessed earthly bird

1 Monk

Hist I hear the step of Ebremar

(Enter Ebremar the great
Eccleastic they all bow low to him)

1 Inquisitor

Highness my suit to you

Ebremar

I will not hear
I will destroy this nation of the moors
and burn the utter roots of heresy

And he shouted open wide
The sacred door but Peter cried
No thy home is deepest hell
Deeper than the deepest well—
But the stranger softly crew
{le {le
Cock-a-dood {ly-dood {ly-do—
Answered Peter enter in,
But friend it were a deadly sin
Ever more to speak a word
l
Of any unb∧essed earthly bird
1 Monk
Hist I hear the step of Ebremar
(Enter Ebremar the great
Eccleastic they all bow low to him)
1 inquisitor
{u
Highness my s{ait to you
Ebremar
I will not hear
{n
I will destroy this natio{ns of the moors
and burn the utter roots of heresy

16 The "hn" of "Highness" may be written over other letters.

16

Sow salt where they have dwelt – I plant the cross
They die

1 inquisitor

My lord would you yourself descend
Into the ~~dungeon~~ dungeon mong the prisonors
and importune with ~~[illegible]~~ weighty words this maid
That being repentent of her heresy
And bowing to the cross – her life be saved

Ebremar

I see none but the servant of the cross
and dying men – This moorish maid hath ~~[illegible]~~ sinned
and therefore must she die – I will not hear

(he sats down at a table and begins to write)

1 Enquisitor

But mercy is the manna of the world

Ebremar

Stipendium ~~peccati~~ peccati mors est

2 inquisitor

Lets hence

Sow salt where they have dwelt—I plant the cross
They die
1 inquisitors
{s
My lord would you yourself de{ cend
dungeon {o
Into the [?~~duingeon~~] mong the pris{enors
weighty
And importune with [—?—] words this maid
That being repentent of her heresy
And bowing to the cross__her life be saved
Ebremar
{a
I see none but the serv{ents of the cross
sinned
And dying men—This moorish maid hath ~~sinned~~
And therefore must she die. I will not hear
(he sats down at a table and begins
to write)
1 Enquisitor
{s
But mercy i{n the manna of the world
Ebremar
{i
St{ependium peccati mors est
2 inquisitor
Let's hence

On this page the corrections "descend" in l.4, "prisonors" in l.5, "servant" in l.10, and "peccati" in l.18 were first entered above the line in pencil and then erased.

4 The "s" of "descend" was added later.

6 The cancelled word appears to be a misspelling of "weighty".

18 The "pec" of "peccati" is smeared, presumably at the time that Yeats added the second "c" in ink after erasing it in pencil; Yeats may have written an "e" instead of an "i" at the end of the word here and on l. 6 of the next page.

17

It is no use

1 inquisitor

We'll go it is no use

(They bow to Ebremar and go out)

Ebremar (alone

Stipendium peccati mors est, mors est

The wages of a sin is death, tis writ—

High god I have established far and near

Thy fear, and shall destroy this alien church

8

It is no use
1 inquisitor
We'll go it is no use
(They bow to Ebremar and go out)
Ebremar (alone
Stipendium peccati mors est, mors est
The wages of a sin is death, tis writ—
High god I have established far and near
Thy fear, and shall destory this alien church
~~E~~

---

6 As on the previous page Yeats added the second "c" to "peccati" in ink after erasing the penciled correction.
7 Yeats eventually moved this line to 42 in the VP numbering.

18

Scene 3

The dungeon of the inquisition
The morning of the ~~autoda~~ ~~[illegible]~~ auto da Fé-
dawns dimly through a ~~[illegible]~~ barred window -
A few faint stars are still burning
the swallows are circling in the darkness
Mosada (looking at her ring)
My ring where I have stored a poison drop
Twas once but for an ~~[illegible]~~ idle fancy's sake
A fashion with us dreaming moorish maids
But ring I love thee this fair morn - for ring
Thou only in the world obeyst my wish
I will not die just yet my serpent ring
that art so ~~[illegible]~~ fair in thy small coils of gold -
I'll stand a little in the window here
(she gazes out of the window)
O swallows, swallows, swallows will ye fly
This eve, to morrow or to morrow night
Above the farm house by the little lake,
Soon now my brothers will be passing through
The narrow corn field where the poppies grow,
To their farm work - How silent all will be

Scene 3
The dungeon of the inquisition
auto da Fé—
The morning of the ~~autoda~~ ~~[?]y~~
barred
dawns dimly through a ~~b[?]~~ window—
A few faint stars are still burning
the swallows are circling in the dimness
Mosada (looking at her ring)
{o
My ring where I have stored a pois{en drop
{y's
T'was once but for an ~~Idle~~ idle fanc{ies sake
A fashion with us dreaming moorish maids
But ring I love thee this fair morn—for ring
Thou only in the world obey‸'st my wish
I will not die just yet my serpent ring
fair
that art so [~~?fare~~] in thy small coils of gold—
I'll stand a little in the window here
(she gazes out of the window)
O swallows, swallows, swallows will ye fly
This eve, to morrow or to morrow night
Above the farm house by the little lake,
Soon now my brothers will be passing through
The narrow corn field where the poppies grow,—
To their farm work. How silent all will be

The corrections to ll. 8, 9, and 12 were first entered above the line in pencil and then erased.
3 The cancelled and illegible phrase appears to be a misspelling of "auto da Fé".
6 This line was written in pencil and squeezed into the same division of the lined notebook as l. 7.
12 The faint caret is in pencil; the apostrophe and "t" of "obey'st" were added later.
16 This line is squeezed into the same space of the lined notebook as l. 17.
21 The final punctuation mark is a comma with a dash through it at the level of the printed line.

19

But no in this warm weather mong the hills
Will be the faint far thunder sound as though
The world was dreaming in its summer sleep
That will be latter as yet dawn's not come
And Cecco will be with them he was small
a weak thin child, when last I saw him there
He will be taller now – 'Twas long ago
O swallows, swallows, swallows, all I think
Is not right here
(touching her forhead)
I do not weep, and yet
O look ye swallows it is sad to join
All those ~~[illegible]~~ unhapy ones who died in youth
(a pause)
The men are busy in the glimmering square
I hear the ~~[illegible]~~ murmur as they raise the beams
To build the wooden circle of the seats
Where shall the churchmen sit above the crowd
O cowled race – I am too dazed to curse

But no in this warm weather 'mong the hills
Will be the faint far thunder sound as though
The world was dreaming in its summer sleep
That will be latter as yet dawn's not come
And Cecco will be with them he was small
A weak thin child, when last I saw him there
He will be taller now—'Twas long ago
O swallows, swallows, swallows, all I think
Is not right here
(touching her forhead)
I do not weep, and yet
O look ye swallows it is sad to join
All those ~~unhappy~~ unhapy ones who died in
youth
(a pause)
The men are busy in the glimmering square
murmur
I hear the [~~—?—~~] as they raise the beams
To build the wooden circle of the seats
Where shall the churchmen sit above the crowd
O cowled race—I am too dazed to curse

1 The apostrophe before "mong" is in pencil.

I'm not of that pale company who's feet
E're long shall falter through the glimmering
square
And not come thence
(she poisons herself from the ring)
Mosada
This precious poison drop
Will soon thieve from me with it's sleepy mood
My thoughts and yonder brightning patch of
sky
With three bars crossed, and these four walls
my world
~~How soon so small a drop makes one grow~~ weak
~~And yon few stars that~~ grow dim like old mens eyes
And ~~yon~~ few stars so dim like old men's eyes
How soon so small a drop makes one grow weak
Where shall I lay me down that question is
a very weighty question being the last
If here, or yonder alcove shadowed deep
Where I've immagined ghostly feet to pass

1 I'm not of that pale company who's feet
2 E're long shall falter through the glimmering
square
3 And not come thence
4 (she poisons herself from the ring)
5 Mosada
6 [?N/?M] This precious poison drop
7 Will soon thieve from me with it's sleepy mood
8 My thoughts and yonder brightning patch of
sky
9 With three bars crossed, and these four walls
my world
10 ~~How soon so small a drop makes one grow weak~~
~~grown~~
11 ~~And yon few stars that dim like old mens~~ eyes
12 ~~And yon~~ few stars so dim like old men's eyes
{o
13 How so{nn so small a drop makes one grow weak
14 Where shall I lay me down that question is
weighty
15 A very [—~~?~~—] question being the last
16 If here, on yonder alcove shadowed deep
17 Where I've immagined ghostly feet to pass

---

4 Yeats first cancelled "poisans" in pencil and wrote the word correctly above; then he erased both the cancellation line and the new word, and changed "a" to "o" in ink.

11 There is either a caret or a letter cancelled between "that" and "grown".

13 Yeats first cancelled "weak" in pencil and wrote "weaker" above it; then he erased both the cancellation line and the new word.

15 The cancelled word appears to be a misspelling of "weighty". The legible "weighty" was first written above in pencil and then traced over in ink.

On lonely nights – my fading eyes must look
If here – on the long rows of square cut stone
upon the wall, I must look last, their sight
Were very wearisome to dying eyes
Nay here I'll lay me down for I can see
The burghers of the night fade one by one
Five, Five . nay six (she lies down)
(a pause)
'Tis thus they shone the night
When my lost love passed down among the hills
O Vallance, Vallance we shall meet at last
The stars of thy nativity and mine
Burn side by side two ministering lights
Throbbing within the circle of green dawn –
Too late, Too late, for I am near to death
I try to lift mine arm and it falls back
grown very heavy in a little time
a painless death creeps over me like sleep
What do ye mean o stars – when death has come
Shall in his being all my being fade,

On lonely nights—my fading eyes must look
If here—on the long rows of square cut stone
upon the wall, I must look last, their sight
Were very wearisome to dying eyes
Nay here I'll lay me down for I can see
        burghers
The ~~burgers~~ of the night fade one by one
Five, Five. nay six *(she lies down)*
            (A pause)
                        'Tis thus they shone the night
When my lost love passed down among the hills
O Vallance, Vallance we shall meet at last
The stars of thy nativity and mine
                                      {i
Burn side by side two min{estering lights
Throbbing
T[—?—]g within the circle of green dawn—
Too late, Too late, for I am near to death
I try to lift mine arm and it falls back
grown very heavy in a little time
A painless death creeps over me like sleep
What do ye mean o stars—when death has come
Shall in his being all my being fade,

6 "burghers" is written in pencil traced over with ink.
7 The first "Five" may be intended as "Four".
13 Yeats first wrote "minestering", cancelled it in pencil and wrote the correct spelling above; then he erased both the cancellation line and new word, and corrected "e" to "i" in ink.
15 The second "o" of both "too"s probably was added later.
20 The comma is in pencil.

I think all's finished now and all is sealed
(a long pause then enter Ebremar)
Ebremar
Prisoner the final day has come for thee
Repent thy heresies and save thy soul
From endless pain
(he starts & rushes forward)
Mosada O Mosada
Turn round, a word, a look, lie not so still
I thought thou wert on the Apajarra's side
Far, far away from this most ill starred town
O god she lies as still as on a tomb
A sculptured lady in the marble white
Look look
(throws back his cowl)
I am thy Vallance; rise
Magnificent in thy black hair that pours
A shining wonder in its heavy folds—
And then ere fading with the morning star
We'll fly, far from here There is a secret way

I think all's finished now and all is sealed
(a long pause then enter Ebremar)
Ebremar
{o {e
Pris{en{or the final day has come for thee
Repent thy heresies and save thy soul
From endless pain
&
(he starts ∧ rushes forward)
Mosada O Mosada
Turn round, a word, a look, lie not so still
l
I thought thou weret on the A∧pajarra's side
Far, far away from this most ill starred town
O god she lies as still as on a tomb
A sculptured lady in the marble white
look look
(throws back his cowl)
I am thy Vallance; rise
Magnificent in thy black hair that pours
A shining wonder in its heavy folds—
And thither fading with the morning star
~~far~~ from here
We'll fly,∧There is a secret way

The verso of TCD 3502/1, 21, which faces TCD 3502/1, 22, has a pencil sketch of a male figure from the waist up. Opposite l. 19 is the cancelled pencil query, "What does this line mean".

10 The caret and "l" in "Alpajarra's" are in pencil.

16 The semicolon is in pencil.

20 The comma is in pencil.

23

From near by tunneled to the river's marge
Where lies a boat among the shadowy reeds
That sigh to one another all year long—
Awake awake and we will sail afar
Afar along the fleet white river's face
We two alone upon the river wan
Alone among the murmurs of the dawn—
Far 'mid thy people none will know that I
Was Ebremar whose thoughts were fixed on god
Whom now I lose, awake Mosada 'wake
Thy Vallence is by thee

Mosada

Let's talk and grieve
For that's the sweetest music for sad souls
Day's dead all flame-bewildered and the hills
In list'ning silence gaze upon our grief

Ebremar

Her thoughts hold ~~[illegible]~~ commune with old time—
—Awake—
Grieve not—thy Vallance kneels by thee

From near by tunneled to the river's marge
Where lies a boat among the shadowy reeds
That sigh to one another all year long—
Awake awake and we will sail afar
Afar along the fleet white rivers face
We two alone upon the river wan
{urs
Alone among the murm{ [?] of the dawn—
Far 'mid thy people none will know that I
Was Ebremar whos*e* thoughts were fixed on god
Whom now I lose, awake Mosada 'wake
Thy Vallance is by thee
Mosada
Let's talk and grieve
For that's the sweetest music for sad souls
Day's dead all flame-bewildered and the hills
In list'ning silence gaze upon our grief
Ebremar
commune
Her thoughts hold [~~—?—~~] with old time—
—Awake—
Grieve not__thy Vallance kneels by thee

---

1 The apostrophe is in pencil.
3 The dash at the end of the line is in pencil here and in l. 7.
8 The "k" and "w" of "know" appear to have been added later.
9 The "e" of "whose" is in pencil.
14 The "'s" of "that's" appears to have been added later.
15 The hyphen is in pencil.
19 The first "e" of "Grieve" appears to have been added later.

Mosada
Vallance
'Tis late waits one more day, below the hills
The shadowy way is long, and it grows dark
It is the darkest eve I ever knew
Ebremar
I kneel by thee I leave thee nevermore—
She smiles, is happy with her wandering
Griefs—
Mosada
ah must you go, kiss me before you go
Oh would the busy minutes might fold up
Those theiving wings that we might never part—
I never knew so still and sweet a night
Ebremar
all parting now is past, I go no more.
Upon the breast of Vallance lies thy head
Unhappy one
Mosada
Go not, go not, go not—

Mosada
Vallance
'Tis late waite one more day, below the hills
The shadowy way is long, and it grows dark
It is the darkest eve I ever knew
Ebremar
I kneel by thee I leave thee nevermore—
She smiles, is happy with her wandering
Griefs.
Mosada
Ah must you go, kiss me before you go
Oh would the busy minutes might fold up
There theiving wings that we might never part—
a night so honey
I never knew so still and sweet a night
Ebremar
All parting now is past, I go no more.
Upon the breast of Vallance lies thy head
Unhappy one
Mosada
Go not, go not, go not—

---

8 The comma is in pencil.

13 The "k" of "knew" appears to have been added or overwritten later.

15 The period is in pencil.

For fast night comes — look down on me
my Love, ~~see~~
and see how thick the dew lies on my face
Ebremar
O still the wandering sorrow of thy mind
look on me once — why sink your eyelids so
Why fall you back so heavy in my arms
As though Sleep's sleep were sitting by
— One look
O will you die when we have met — one look
give to thy Vallance
Mosada
Vallance he has gone
From sight along the shadowy path that winds
It's way close by the rivers wandering light
I'll see him longer if I stand out here
upon the mountains brow
(she tries to stand and totters Ebremar
supports her standing she points
down as if into a visionary valley

1 For fast night comes—look down on me
my love, ~~see~~
2 And see how thick the dew lies on my face
3 *I never knew a night so de bedrowned*
4 Ebremar
5 O still the wandering sorrow of thy mind
6 look on me once. Why sink your eylids so
7 Why fall you back so heavy in my arms
8 As though sleep's sleep were sitting by
—one look
9 O will you die when we have met—one look
10 give to thy Vallance
11 Mosada
12 Vallance he has gone
13 From sight along the shadowy path that winds
14 It's way close by the rivers wandering light
15 I'll see him longer if I stand out here
16 Upon the mountains brow
17 (she tries to stand and totters Ebremar
18 supports her standing she points
19 down as if into a Visionary Valley

3 Added in pencil, this line is squeezed into the same lined space of the notebook as l. 4; "de" is presumably an unfinished form of "dew"

Mosada

Yonder he ~~[illegible]~~ treads
The path over muffled with the leaves
— dead leaves
Like happy thoughts grown sad in evil
days—
He fades among the mist—how fast ^it comes
And pours upon the world—ah welladay
Poor love and sorrow with there arms thrown
round
Each others necks and whispering as they go
Still wander through the world—he's gone
he's gone
I'm wearied out and it is very cold
I'll draw my cloak about me it is cold
I never knew a night so bitter cold
(dies)

Ebremar
~~Mosada~~
~~dead~~ Mosada Mosada

1 Mosada
treads
2 Yonder he [~~—?—~~]
3 The path oer muffled with the leaves
—dead leaves
4 Like happy thoughts grown sad in evil
days—
it
5 He fades among the mist. how fast ^ comes
6 And pours upon the world. Ah welladay
7 Poor love and sorrow with there arms thrown
round
8 each others necks and whispering as they go
9 Still wander through the world. hes gone
[*?ah*] *me* he's gone
10 I'm wearied out and it is very cold
11 I'll draw my cloak about me it is cold
12 I never knew a night so bitter cold
13 (dies)
14 Ebremar
15 ~~Mosada~~
16 ~~dead~~ Mosada Mosada

---

5 The period is in pencil.
7–9 These lines are cancelled by a large wavy line in pencil.
9 "[?ah] me" is written in pencil and does not appear to be part of the previous line.
12 The "k" of "knew" appears to have been added or overwritten later.

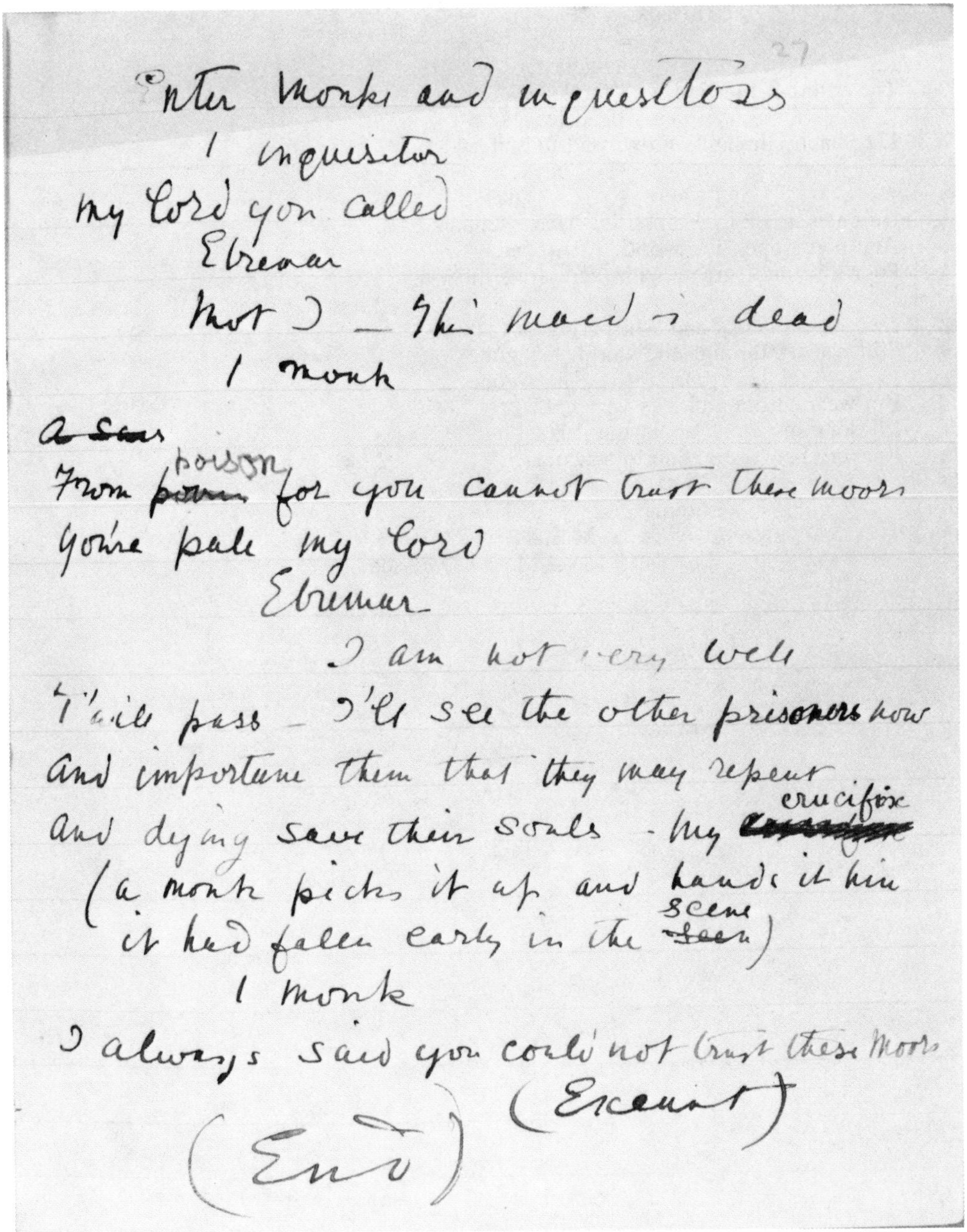
27

Enter monks and inquesitors

1 inquisitor

My Lord you called

Ebremar

Not I — This moor is dead

1 monk

~~a Sans~~

From ~~pain~~ poison for you cannot trust these moors

You're pale my Lord

Ebremar

I am not very well

T'will pass — I'll see the other prisoners now

And importune them that they may repent

And dying save their souls — My ~~crossing~~ crucifix

(a monk picks it up and hands it him

it had fallen early in the ~~seen~~ scene)

1 monk

I always said you could not trust these moors

(Exeunt)

(End)

Enter monks and inquisitors
1 inquisitor
My lord you called
Ebremar
Not I_This maid is dead
1 monk
~~A [?suis]~~
poison
From [?~~poisen~~] for you cannot trust these moors
You're pale my lord
Ebremar
I am not very well
{o
T'will pass—I'll see the other pris{eners now
And importune them that they may repent
crucifix
And dying save their souls—my [?~~crusafix~~]
(a monk picks it up and hands it him
scene
it had fallen early in the ~~seen~~)
1 monk
I always said you could not trust these Moors
(Exeunt)
(End)

7 "suis" is presumably intended to be "suiside", a misspelling used elsewhere.
12 The full correct word "prisoners" was first written in pencil above the line and then erased.

Third Version: Advanced Draft of Scenes 1 and 2

The pages of loose foolscap and additional leaf which comprise TCD 3502/3, together with a separate leaf from the collection of Michael B. Yeats, NLI 30,430, represent the most advanced known draft of the first two scenes of *Mosada.* The exact date of composition is unclear, but it is later than the June 7, 1884 (or possibly 1885), date of the 3502/1 notebook and, obviously, earlier than the date of publication of the June 1886 number of the *Dublin University Review.*

The relation among the materials in this group of manuscripts is more complicated than the simple notebook ordering of the earlier drafts. Unlike his practice of using only one side of the page for the notebook versions, Yeats used both sides of the separate sheets in 3502/3. Accordingly, in following the Trinity College foliation numbers, I have indicated recto and verso as well. The first four pages are written on a single sheet of foolscap folded in half vertically to make four surfaces; they are foliated as 1 and 2. The next sheet, which continues scene 1 to the end, was misfoliated by Trinity College, so that its verso continues from page 2^v and its recto then completes the scene. The third sheet presents scene 2 from the opening as far as line 42 of the VP numbering. A leaf on different paper from Michael Yeats's collection, now in the National Library of Ireland, continues this scene without a break to its conclusion; that leaf is also written on both sides, with its verso containing "A Song of Sunset" written perpendicularly to the lines from *Mosada.* ("A Song of Sunset" is not transcribed here but will be included with the transcriptions in volume two of the early poetic manuscripts.) The leaf (NLI 30,430) is a scrap, roughly 20 cm by 17 cm, torn from paper watermarked with a figure of Britannia seated within a double-crowned oval.

Finally, the remaining leaf at Trinity College presents a special puzzle. It is written on torn, partly charred, light green paper folded in half to make four pages, of which only the first, foliated as 5, and the last have been written on (I have designated the last as 6^v). The page foliated as 5 appears to be the most advanced known draft of the lines that became 84–88 of scene 3 in the VP ordering, principally as the only manuscript to contain the eventual line 88. Yet the lines on 6^v are so rough as to elude certain identification; they may be an early version of Ebremar's immediately preceding speech. It is unclear why one set of lines should be so finished and the other so rough. Perhaps the rough ones belong to another work altogether or the finished ones belong to an early draft that included the eventual line 88, which Yeats then deleted for 3502/1 and 3502/2 but later restored. In view of such uncertainty, I have thought it best to transcribe the leaf in the group with which it is presently found.

The large sheets at Trinity College are written in faded black ink as far as the middle of page 4^v, where Yeats shifted to pencil in mid-line. The sheet at the National Library of

Ireland which continues this page is also in pencil, as is the remaining, fragmentary sheet at Trinity College. It is likely that after finishing the manuscripts in 3502/3, Yeats prepared at least one additional version as a printer's copy.

Mosada

and my Lord Cardinal has had strange days in his youth — Extract from a memoir of the ~~fifteenth~~ ~~fif~~sixteenth Century

Characters

Mosada — a moorish lady
Ebremar — a monk
Cola — a lame boy.

Monks and Inquisitor Etc.

~~Scene~~ ~~Granada~~ —

Scene 1 —
A little moorish room in the village of Azubia In the center of the room is a chafing dish

Mosada (alone)

Three times the roses have grown less and less
As slowly Autumn climbed the golden throne
Where sat old summer fading into song
And thrice the peaches flushed upon the walls
And thrice the corn ~~[illegible]~~ around the sickles flamed
Since ~~to my~~ 'mong my peoples ~~tents~~ tented on the ~~[illegible]~~ hills
He stood a messenger — In april's flush
(Swallows ~~were~~ flew sped flashing their white breasts above
~~Or perched upon the tents~~ a
Or ~~perched~~ ~~perching~~ on the tall tents a weary still
waste seas aw[illegible]
~~From their long flight~~ yet ever garrulous)
Along the velvet vale I saw him come —
In autumn when far down the mountain slopes
The heavy clusters of the grapes were full
I saw him sigh and turn and pass away
For I and all my people were accurst
Of his sad ~~faith~~ God, and down among the grass
Hiding my face I cried long bitterly

1 Mosada
2 and my lord Cardinal has had strange days in
3 his youth—Etract from a memoir of the ~~[?fifteenth] C~~
4 fiftiteenth Century
5 Characters
6 Mosada — a moorish lady
7 Ebremar — a monk
8 Cola — a lame boy.
9 Monks and Inquisitors Etc.
10 ~~Scene~~ ~~Grenada~~—
11 Scene 1—
12 A little Moorish room in the village of
13 Azubia In the center of the room is a chafing dish
14 Mosada (alone)
15 Three times the roses have grown less and less
16 [~~?~~] As slowly Autumn climbed the golden throne
17 Where sat old summer fading into song
18 And thrice the peaches flushed upon the walls
19 And thrice the corn ~~arund~~ around the sicles flamed
tented
20 Since ~~to my~~ 'mong my peoples ~~tents~~ on the ~~dear~~ hills
21 He stood a messenger—In April's flush
~~flew~~ were
22 (Swallows ~~were~~ flashing their white breasts above
23 ~~Or pearched upon the tents a~~
pearching
Or ~~pearched~~ on the ~~tall~~ tents a weary still
waste seas crost
24 From ~~their long flight~~ yet ever garrulous)
25 Along the velvet vale I saw him come —
26 In autumn when far down the mountain slopes
27 The heavy clusters of the grapes were full
28 I saw him sigh and turn and pass away
29 For I and all my people were accurst
God
30 Of his sad ~~faith~~, and down among the grass
31 Hiding my face I cried long bitterly

The black ink of the manuscript has faded to a nearly brownish color except for ll. 26–31 and for the word "tented" and last two cancellation marks in l. 20. These do not seem to represent different stages of composition.

'Twas evening and the cricket nation sang
And danced around, my head among the grass
And all was dimmer till a dying leaf
Came circling down and softly touched my lips
With dew as though twere sealing them for death
Yet ~~some~~where in the ~~world~~ footsore world we meet
We two before we die for Azola
The star taught moor said thus it was decreed
By those seven stars that sit in company
Above the Alpujarras on their thrones
A gazer on the silence of the world
That when the stars of our nativity
~~Shone~~ star to star is on that eve he passed
Down the long valley from my [illegible]
We meet we two (she opens the casement
The mingled sound of the laughter of the laughter)
How merry all there are
Among the fruit — But yonder long Cola crouches
Away from all the others
A shimmy on the little oranges of silver [illegible] at last [illegible] now the sun
Sinks down with yonder minaret
Of the Alhambra black athwart his disk
And Cola seeing knows the sign and comes
Thus do I burn these precious herbs whose smoke
Born up and floats in fragrance or my head
In coil on coil of ~~blue~~ azure
Enter Cola
Cola is ready

Cola
It is Mosada then so much the worse
I will not share your sin.

’Twas evening and the cricket nation sang
(And danced) around my head among the grass
And all was dimness till a dying leaf
Came circling down and softly touched my lips
With dew as though twere sealing them for death
Yet some where in the ~~world~~ footsore world we meet
We two before we die for Azolar
The star taugh Moor said thus it was decreed
By those wan stars that sit in company
Above the Alpajarras on their thrones
agazing on the silence of the world
That when the stars of our nativity
draw
[?~~Shine~~] star to star as on that eve he passed
down the long valley from my beples [?tents]
we meet we two (she opens the casement
The mingled sound of the laughter of the laughter)
How mery all these are
{ut lame{C
Among the fruit—B{y yon~~der~~ {cola Crouches
Away from all the others
Now the sun
A shining on the little crusafix
of silver hung round lame Cola neck
at last
Sinks down with yonder minneret
Of the Alhambra black athwart his disk
And Cola seeing knows the sign and comes
Thus do I burn these precious herbs whose smoke
{P
{Bours up and floats in fragrence or my head
In coil on coil of ~~blu~~ azure
Enter Cola
all is ready
Cola
It is Mosada then so much the worse
I will not share your sin

5 Yeats may have written “seeling” for “sealing”.
8 The “us” of “thus” may be written over something else.
10 Yeats may have written “in” or “an” for “on”.
12 This line was probably added later.

Mosada

O 'tis no sin 2

that you shall see in yonder glowing cloud
Pictured, where wander the ~~be~~ beloved feet
whose foot fall I have longed for, thru sad ~~years~~ summers
Why these new fears

Cola

The dark still man has come
The servant of the Lord and says 'tis sin

Mosada

They say the wish is half the sin its self
Then has this one been sinned a myriad times
yet tis no sin — my father taught it me.
He was a man most learned and most mild
who dreaming to a wondrous age lived on
Tending the roses round his lattice door
For many years his days had dawned and faded thus
among the plants — The flowery silence fell
Down on his soul like rain upon a soil
Worn by the solstice fierce and made it pure
would he teach any sin

Cola

Gaze in the ~~smoke~~ cloud
your self

Mosada

None but the innocent can see

Cola

Lame footed
They say I am all ugliness
I am ~~one~~ shoulder tener ~~any~~ awry Why then
Should I be good But you are beautiful

Mosada

I cannot see your young

Cola

the Bulls and bats
and spiders are my friends I'm thinks they are
not good But you are like the butterflies

Mosada
It is no sin
That you shall see in yonder glowing cloud
Pictured, where wander the [?] beloved feet
Whose foot fall I have longed for three sad ~~years~~ summers
~~C~~
Why these new fears
Cola
The dark still man has come
The servent of the lord and says 'tis sin
Mosada
They say the wish is half the sin its self
Then has this one been sinned a mirriad times
Yet tis no sin—my father taught it me
He was a man most learned and most mild
Who dreaming to a wondrous age lived on
Tending the roses round his lattice door {us
For many years his days had dawned and fadded th{is
Among the plants_The flowery silenc fell
Down on his soul like rain upon a soil
Worn by the solstice fearce and made it pure
{y
Would he teach an{d sin
Cola
Gaze in the ~~smoke~~ cloud
Your self
Mosada
None but the inocent can see
Cola
They say I am all ugliness lame footed
I am one shoulder turned ~~ary~~ arwry why then
Should I be good But you are beautiful
Mosada
I cannot see ~~your~~ ~~yong~~
the
Cola the Beelles and bats
And spiders are my friends Im theres they are
Not good But you are like the butterflies

13 The middle of "mirriad" is written over something else, but the exact relation of the letters is difficult to decipher.

Mosada

I cannot see, I cannot see. But you
Shall see a thing to talk on when your old
Beneath under a lemon tree beside thy door
And all the elders sitting in the sun
Will wondering listen and thy tale shall ease
All day for long the burden of their talking grief

Cola

Down on my knees I pray you let it sleep
The vision —

Mosada

Your pale and weeping, child
Be not afraid you'l see no fearful sight thing
Thus Thus I beckon from her viewless field
Thus beckon to one and a phantom fair
And calm robe robed all in raiment moony white
She was a great great enchantress once of yore
Whose dwelling was a tree wrapt island lulled
Far out upon the water world and ringed
With wonderful white sand where never yet
Ever far led the wings of ships There in a dell
A lily blanched place she sat and sung
And as her song wove around her head
White lilies and her songs, flew afar
From where the lilies of its warm life grew—
Over the sea and many a young man heard grew
In wander his own house or mong the merchants grey
Hearing the far off lureful quire and gleaned
And maned an argosy and surely died
In the far Isle she sang herself asleep
At last But now I anon her to my side

Cola

They stray or I will hold your white arms down
Ah me I cannot reach them — here and there
darling you wave them clutching at the vapour
Heard you your lute upon upon the wall has sounded
Oh horrible I feel a finger drawn across my cheek

Mosada
I cannot see, I cannot see. But you
Shall see a thing to talk on when your old
Under
~~Beneath~~ a lemon tree beside thy door
And all the elders sitting in the sun
tale
Will wondering lilsten and thy shall ease
for long
~~All day~~ the burden of their talking griefs
Cola
Down on my knees I pray you let it sleep
The vision—
Mosada
Your pale and weeping [~~?~~] child
Be not afraid youl see no fearful ~~sight~~ thing
Thus Thus I beckon from her viewless field
Thus beckon to our aid a phantom fair
And calm ~~rube~~ robed all in raiment moony white
She was a ~~great~~ great enchantress once of yore
Whose dwelling was a tree wrapt Island lulled
Far out upon the water world and ringed
with wonderful white sand where never yet
were furled the wings of ships There in a dell
{ly
A li{lly blanchéd place she sat and sang
and in her sing wove around her head
{ies song [?forth/?borne]
White lil{ly and her ~~singing~~ flew afar
From where the lilies of [?its] wan life grew—
Over the sea and many a ~~young~~ man ~~heard~~ grew
~~which~~
In his own house or mong the merchents grey
Hearing the far off tuneful guile and groned
and maned an argosy and sailing died
In the far Isle she sang herself a sleep
{to
At last But now I wave her {[?] my side
Cola
Stay stay or I will hold your white arms down
Ah me I cannot reach them < here and there
darting you wave them [?darting] in the vapour
Heard you your lute upon upon the wall has sounded
O horrible I feel a finger drawn across my cheek

23 Yeats may have written "on" and then overwritten the "o" with "i" to make "in".

ha ha ha
The phantoms come [illegible] they come they come
I wave them hither my ~~heart~~ brain leaps with joy
Ah now I'm eastern hearted once again
And while they gather round my [illegible] arms
I'll sing the songs the [illegible] lovers sing
Wandering in ~~m~~ sultry palaces of Ind
A lotus in their hands —

The door is burst open

Enter the officers of the inquisition

Young moorish girl
Taken in magic in the churches name
I here arrest thee

Mosada
Touch not this boy ~~It is~~ alone [illegible]
for he is innocent

Cola
Forgive me I have told them every thing
They said I'd burn in hell unless I told
Then all and let them [illegible] away the [illegible]

She turns away he clings to her dress

Cola
Forgive me

Mosada [illegible]
[illegible]

1 Inquisitor
now [illegible]

Mosada
No need to bind my hands Where are ye sirs
~~The [illegible] hidden ye~~
[illegible] are [illegible] with [illegible]

2 Inquisitor
round the stake
The [illegible] is much thicker

Cola
gird the stake
Ye said that ye would ~~not~~ fright her from her seat
No more take me with you [illegible] of her great [illegible]
She was my only friend [illegible]
One shoulder [illegible] and the children [illegible]
[illegible] after me

ha ha ~~ha~~
The phantoms ~~come~~ ~~with~~ they come they come
breast heaves
I wave them hither my ~~heart~~ leeps with joy
Ah now Im eastern hearted once again
And while they gather round my becking arms
Ill sing thee songs the dusky lovers sing
Wandering in ~~in~~ sultry palaces of Ind
A lotus in their hands—
The door is burst open—
enter the oficers of the inquisition
Young moorish girl
Taken in magic in the churches Name
I here arest thee
Mosada
{It is
{Tis Allah s will
Touch not this boy for he is inocent
Cola
Forgive me I have told them every thing
They said Id burn in hell unless I told
you
Them all and let them find [?~~thee~~] mong the vapour
{ s
She turns away he cling to her dre{ [?]s
Cola
Forgive me
Mosada ~~it~~
It was Allah s will
{1
{2 Inquisitor
Now chords
Mosada
No need to bind my hands Where are ye sirs
~~This mist has hidden ye~~
for ye are hid with with vapour
2 Inquisitor
round the stake
The vapour is much thicker
Cola god the stake
{id that ye
Ye sa{y ~~ye~~ would ~~but~~ fright her from her sin
No more ^take me ~~with~~ ~~you~~ instead of her great sirs
She was my only fried you see Im lame
One shoulder twisted and the children cry
~~out~~ names
~~Names~~ after me

This page was incorrectly foliated by Trinity College; 3^{v} precedes 3^{r} in proper sequence.
1 The "t" of "with" may be written over another letter.
7 Yeats's pen may have slipped after "A", or he may have accidentally written "s" or "n" after it.
9 Yeats may have dropped the "s" of "oficers".
30 Yeats failed to leave a space between the first two words.

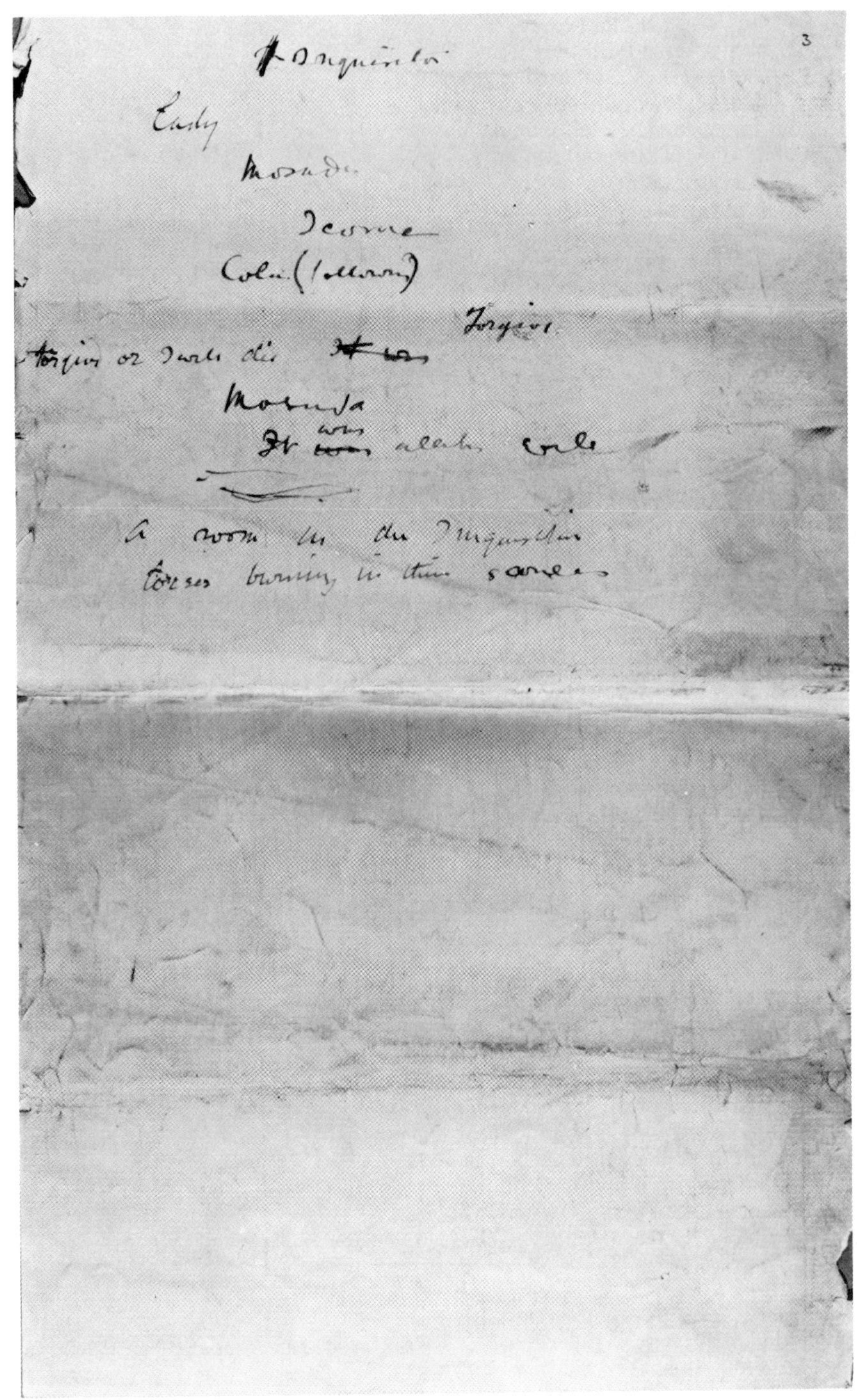

[TCD 3502/3, 3^{r}] [VP 1:117–118]

{1
{2 Inquisitor
Lady
Mosada
I come
Cola (following)
Forgive
Forgive or I will die ~~It was~~
Mosada
was
It ~~was~~ allah s will

A room in the Inquisition
[?torcses] burning in their [?sconeas]

12 The doubtful words are presumably intended to be ''torches'' and ''sconces'', respectively.

4

3rd Scene

A room in the building of the Inquisition of Grenada
stained window behind representing St. [illegible] of Spain

1 monk

Will you not hear my last new song

1 Inquisitor Hush Hush

So she must burn you say

2 Inquisitor

1 Inquisitor She must in truth

Would he not spare her life [illegible] us
for would one matter
When there are many

2 Inquisitor
Ebremar will stamp
This heathen hoard away you need not hope
And [illegible] you not she kissed that proud child
with withered lips and he is pining since

1 monk

Your full of words will you not hear my song

2 monk

In truth an evil race why strive for her
A little moorish girl

2 Inquisitor
Small worth

1 monk
My song

1 Inquisitor

I had a sister like her once
(touches the second monk of the shoulder)
My friend
Where is our brother Peter when your nigh
He is not here — I'd have him speak for her
I saw his jovial mood bring once a smile
To sainted Ebremar's sad eyes I think
He loves our brother peter in his heart
and if he Peter ask her life why then who knows?

[TCD 3502/3, 4^r] [VP2:1–17]

2nd Scene
A room in the building of the Inquisition of Grenida
stained window behind representing St James of Spain
1 monk
Will you not hear my last new song
1 inquistior Hush Hush
So she must burn you say
2 Inquistior
She must in truth
1 nquisitor
Will he not spare her life ~~she~~ is
how would one matter
When their are many
2 Inquisitor
Ebremar will stamp
{ is
Th{ [?] heathen hoard away you ned not hope
know
And ~~heard~~ you not she kissed that pious child
~~vampire~~
With withces lips and he is pining since
1 Monk
wordyness come
Your full of ~~words will~~ ~~you not~~ hear my song
2 Monk
In truth an Evil race Why strive for her
A little moorish girl
{2
{1 Inquisitor
Small worth
1 Monk
My song
1 Inquistor
I had a sister like her once
(touches the second monk of the shoulder)
My friend
{P
Where is our brother {peter when your nigh
He is not far—I'd have him speak for her
I saw his jovial mood bring once a smile
To sainted Ebremar s sad eyes I think
He loves our brother peter in his heart
Peterd
[~~?and~~] ife ~~he~~'d ask her life why then who knows?

21 Yeats's pen continued upward at the end of "an", making it resemble "and".
22 Yeats may have written "litle" for "little".

? monk

He deigns this stranger He brings to mind ~~that~~ song

That song I've made is of a Russian tale

Of holy Peter of the burning gate

A saint of Russia & a Russian saint

(Sings)

A stranger new arisen wait
By the door of Peters gate.
And he shouted open wide
The sacred door but Peter cried
No thy home is deepest Hell
Deeper than the deepest well
Then the stranger softly crew
Cock a doodle dooly doo
answered peter enter in
Friend but twere a deadly sin
ever more to speak a word
Of any unblessed earthly bird

1 Inquisitor

be still [illegible] the step of Ebremar [illegible] eyed
Yonder [illegible] the red light slanting down
from the great painted window wraps his brow
as with an aureole

(Ebremar enter they all bow to him)

My suit to thee

I will not hear ~~for all the~~ I will will slay the Moor

The moorish girl must die

I will burn heresy from this land earth

And 1 Inquisitor

Mercy is the mane of the world

Ebremar

The corpse of a sin is death

1 monk [illegible]

2 monk

{ h
He digs { [?]is cabbages He bring to mind ~~that song~~
That song Ive made is of a russian tale
Of holly Peter of the burning gate
[?A] saint of Russia in a vision saw
(sings
A stranger new arisen wait
By the door of Peter s gate
And he shouted open wide
The sacred door but Peter cried
No thy home is deepest Hell
{er {n
Deep{ [?] tha{ t the deepest well
Then the stranger softly crew
Cock adodle [?dodling/?dooley] doo
Answered peter Enter in
Friend but twere a deadly *sin*
ever more to speak a word
Of any unblessed earthly bird
1 Inquisitor
be still I hear the step of Ebremar
gaunt with long fast bright eyed
Yonder he comes —the red light slanting down
and hollow cheeked
From the great painted window wraps his brow
As with an [?aruroele]
(Ebremar enters they all bow to him)
My suit to thee
{l
I wil{ t not hear ~~for all the I will will slay the~~ moor
The moorish girl must die
I will burn heresy from this mad earth
and 1 Inquisitor
Mercy is the mana of the world
Ebremar
The wages of a sin is death
1 monk No use

Yeats changed from ink to pencil after "deadly" in l. 16 and continued in pencil for the remainder of the scene.
24 "Ebremar" may be written over "the" or "they"; "enters" may lack the final "s".

[—?—]
1 Ebremar
{e
My lord if it must b{ [?] I prey descend
Yourself down to the dungeon neath our feet
moor
And Importune with weight words this ~~maid~~
{her
that she foresweare { [?this] heresy and save
Her soul from seas of endless flame
Ebremar
I see alone the servents of the cross
{no
And dying men—And yet [?I] but { now farewell
1 Monk
No use
~~1 Inquistor~~ Ebremar
~~lets hence~~
Away (they go out
Ebremar
{O
Hear me { o thou Enduring god
Who giveth to the golden crested [?ren]
Her hanging ~~nest~~ mansion give to me I prey
~~and fill~~
the burden of thy truth reach town ~~thy hands~~
thy hand
and fill
~~And fill~~ me with thy rage that I may bruse
The heathen yea and shake the sullen king
~~And the great warriors whose [?names] have~~ sung

This leaf from the collection of Michael B. Yeats, now in the National Library of Ireland (NLI 30,430), continues scene 2 to its conclusion.

10 The possible "I" appears to be two confusing marks, one above the other and with less than usual space on either side.

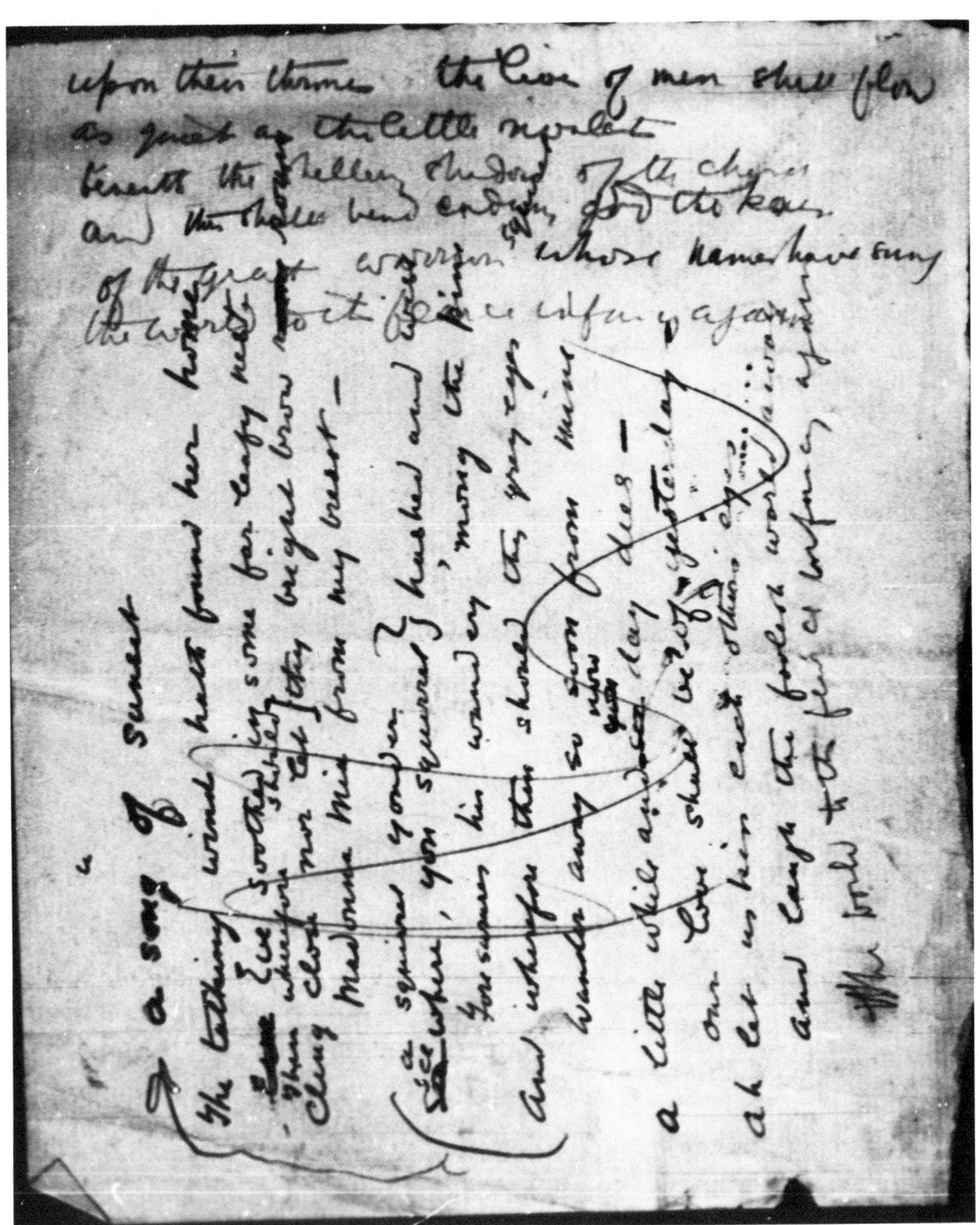

Upon their thrones the lives of men shall flow
As quiet as the little rivulets
beneath the sheltering shadow of thy church
And [?this/?thou] shallt bend enduring god the k{n / eees}
Of the great warriors whose names have sung
the world to its fearce infancy again

These lines appear in pencil at the top of the verso of the previous page. At either an earlier or a later time, Yeats turned the page sideways and wrote "A Song of Sunset" on it; some of the lines of that poem intersect the lines from *Mosada* perpendicularly. The three stanzas of "A Song of Sunset" were published as the central portion of "Life" in the *Dublin University Review* of February 1886. They are not presented here but will be included in the second volume of transcriptions of Yeats's early poetic manuscripts.

6 This line appears again in pencil immediately after "A Song of Sunset."

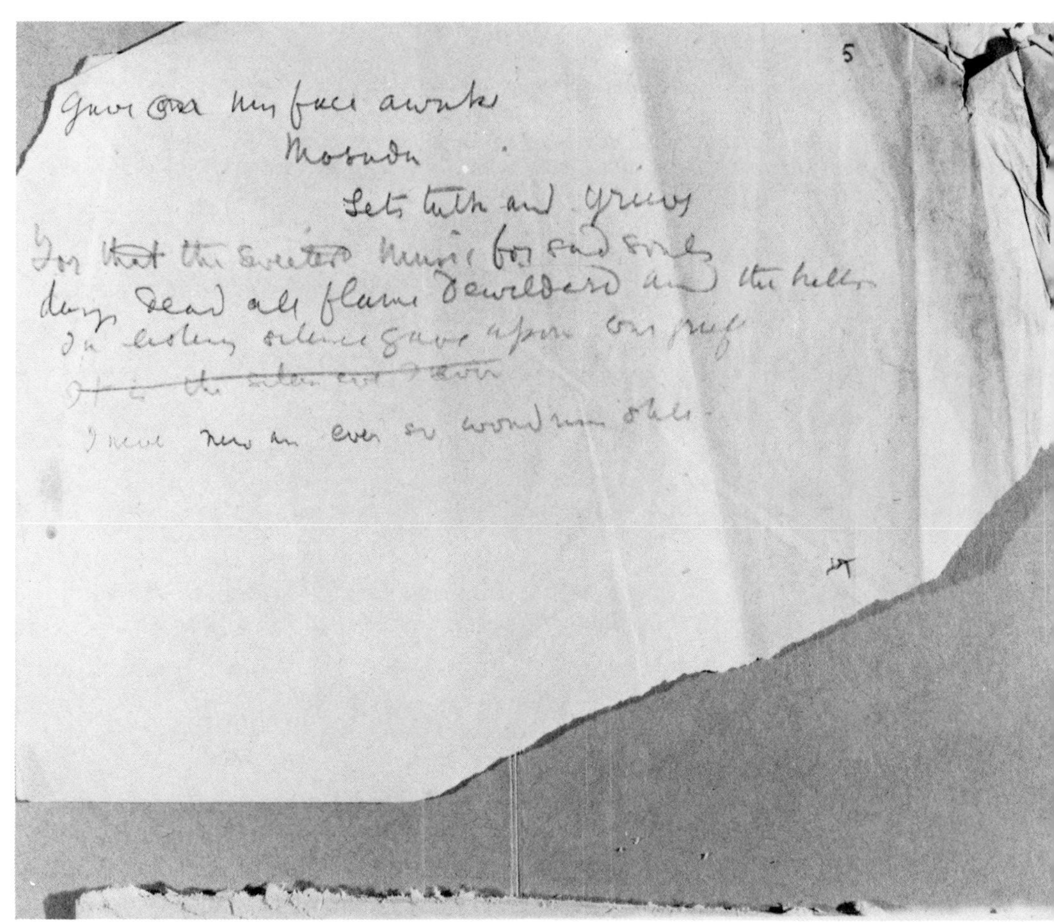

{on
1 *[?gaze] {on my face awake*
2 *Mosada*
3 *Lets talk and grieve*
4 *For that the sweetest music for sad souls*
5 *days dead all flame dewilderd and the hills*
6 *In listening silence gaze upon our grief*
7 ~~*It is the [?silent] eve I ever*~~
I never new an even so wondrous still

This fragment of scene 3 appears on a torn and charred sheet of light green paper. Problems in placing it and the verso are discussed in the headnote to TCD 3502/3.

1 Yeats may have written "gave" for "gaze" here and in l. 6.

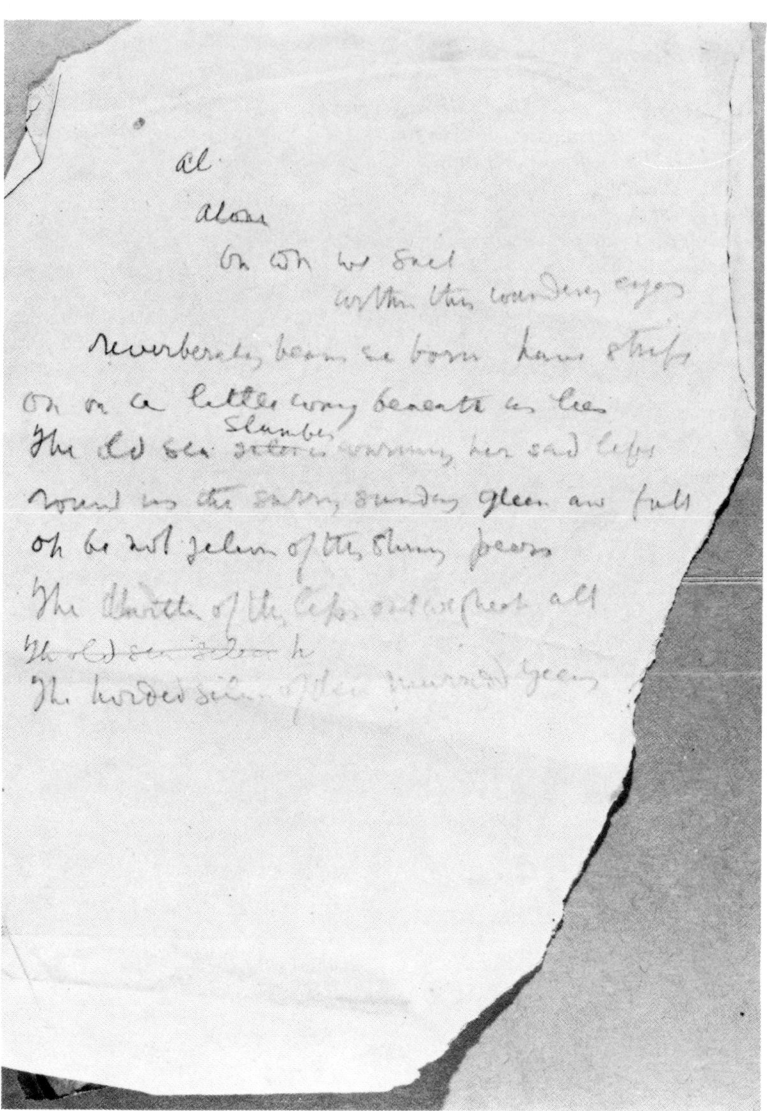

[TCD 3502/3,6v] [VP 3:78f?]

1 *Al*
2 *~~Alone~~*
3 *On on we sail*
4 *within thy wandering eyes*
5 *reverberating beams se born have strife*
6 *On on a little way beneath us lies*
slumber
7 *The old sea ~~silence~~ warming her sad life*
8 *round us the [?sarry] [?sunding] gleam and [?full/?fall]*
9 *Oh be not jelous of thy shining peers*
10 *The [?] of thy lips outweighest all*
11 *~~The old sea silen~~ h*
12 *The horded silence of their [?murriad] years*

The Island of Statues

MANUSCRIPTS, WITH TRANSCRIPTIONS AND PHOTOGRAPHIC REPRODUCTIONS

The surviving manuscripts of *The Island of Statues* preserve the evolution of that work in exceptional detail, extending all the way from rough draft through printer's copy. The earliest version is at Trinity College Dublin, together with the *Mosada* materials; the middle versions belong to the collection of Michael B. Yeats now in the National Library of Ireland; and the printer's copy is in the possession of King's School, Canterbury. The manuscripts are transcribed in approximate chronological order, as follows:

MS TCD 3502/2, a notebook of which foliated pages 13^{v}–30^{v} comprise the earliest draft of the play

MS SB 23.2.199–276, a notebook containing ''The lady of tuneful guile—a fairy tale in two acts,'' together with several loose leaves

MS SB 23.3.1–61, a notebook containing ''The Island of Statues an Arcadian fairy tale'' and dated August 1884, together with one loose leaf; the entire scene 3 of act 2 is cancelled in this version

MSS SB 22.3.44–45, 23.3.68–80, and 23.3.115–146, which represent later versions of parts of act 2: the first is a single loose leaf containing versions of two of Antonio's speeches in act 2, scene 2; the second is part of a notebook and represents most of act 2, scene 3; the third is part of a different notebook and offers a complete version of scene 3

The King's School manuscript of ''*The Island of Statues,*'' which is on forty-nine numbered leaves and constitutes the printer's copy of the *Dublin University Review* version.

The notebooks are identical to those used for the *Mosada* drafts: maroon stamped with the oval device of ''W. CARSON BOOKSELLER & STATIONER'' and consisting of lined pages measuring approximately 19.8 cm by 15.7 cm. The loose leaves enumerated above vary in description, as do the bound ones comprising the printer's copy; details are given below in the notes to the respective versions. The loose leaves in the notebooks generally appear to be slightly earlier or later versions of the draft contained in the respective notebook, and I have thought it best to transcribe them together with the notebook in which they now appear.

To facilitate identification, each page of transcription includes a top left set of brackets indicating the manuscript page, with those from the collection of Michael B. Yeats noted according to their arrangement in the microfilm archive in the library of the State University of New York at Stony Brook. Thus [TCD 3502/2, 16] refers to foliated page 16 in the notebook labelled 3502/2 in the Trinity College library; [SB 23.2.206] refers to page 206 of volume 2 of the hard copy derived from reel 23 in the Stony Brook archive; and [KS 2] refers to the leaf numbered 2 in the King's School manuscript. The conversion table in Appendix Two gives the National Library of Ireland equivalents for the Stony Brook numbering. The placement of the occasional pages missed in the filming for Stony Brook is indicated in notes to those pages. The second set of brackets at the top of each page indicates the scene and line numbers to which the page corresponds in *The Variorum Edition of the Poems of W. B. Yeats,* ed. Peter Allt and Russell K. Alspach (New York: Macmillan, corrected 3d printing, 1966). Thus [VP 1,1:9–26] indicates lines 9–26 of act 1, scene 1, of *The Island of Statues.*

First Version: Rough Draft

The earliest draft of *The Island of Statues* is found in notebook TCD 3502/2, which contains in order: a draft of *Time and the Witch Vivien,* with the last page possibly belonging to a different work; two early versions of scene 3 of *Mosada;* and the *Island* draft. Because the later draft SB 23.3.1–61 is dated August 1884 by Yeats, and because the most probable date for the second version of *Mosada* is June 7, 1884, it seems reasonable to assign this notebook containing the earliest drafts of both dramas to sometime before June 7, 1884.

The title for his new work gave Yeats considerable trouble, as the changes in later versions show; the present draft lacks a title altogether, although it does have a "Dramatis Personae" page. The draft itself shows that even at this stage Yeats had a clear conception of a symmetric structure of two acts, each with three scenes. Otherwise, the draft is so rough that correlation with the final version is problematic. Yeats was apparently intent on setting down an initial conception rapidly, with most of the play not in the eventually dominant iambic pentameter but rather in approximate meters or in prose, at times amounting only to a broad synopsis of the action and a few rough lines of dialogue. The character later known as Naschina is called Evadne in this draft.

The version is written in black ink. Unlike his general practice of using only one side of the page for the *Mosada* draft in the same notebook (as well as later notebook versions of both plays), Yeats here used both sides, with the exception of the verso of page 16. Accordingly, the transcriptions employ the superscript letters r and v to indicate recto and verso.

Dramatis Personæ

Almintor — a hunter

Thernot } Shepherds
Clorin }

Evadne a Shepherdess

Antonio a page

~~and the~~

An Enchantress

and two sleepers

[TCD 3502/2, 13v]

Dramatis Personae
Almintor — a hunter
Thernot } shepherds
Clorin }
Evadne a shepherdess
Antonio a page
~~And [?the]~~
An Enchantress
And two sleepers

14

Scene (morning – before
the cotage of Evadne
~~a bush in the centre~~
Enter Thernot on ~~one~~ side
Clorin on the ~~side of the bush~~ [on]
They both ~~song~~ [have] lute
Clorin (ascend)
~~Evadne will soon come forth.~~
'Tis morning the sheep are on the hills
O will ~~[illegible]~~ welcome her with song
(sits down on seat)
Thernot
I will welcome sweet [Evadne] with lute play
I ~~have bring the lute been more~~ [and a song] sweet
than shepherd pipes
~~Clo~~
Clorin (who has been tuning his lute)
sing to or the verse of his song)

1 Scene (morning—before
2 the cotage of Evadne
3 ~~a bush in the center~~
4 Enter Thernot on ~~one~~ side
{i oth
5 Clor{cn on the ~~side of the bush~~
have
6 They both ~~cary~~ lutes
7 Clorin (aside)
8 ~~Evadne will soon come forth~~
9 Tis morning the sheep are on the hills
10 I will [~~?cel~~] welcome her with song
11 (sits [?] on sid)
12 Thernot
Evadne
13 I will welcom sweet with lute play
and a song
14 ~~I have [?brung] the lute being more~~ sweet
15 ~~Than shepherd pips~~
16 ~~Clo~~
Clorin (who has been tuning his lute
17 sings [?] [?or] the verse of his song)

---

3 Yeats may have followed the spelling "centre" for the last word of this line.

Thernot

(Clorin here what does he
With his crab owl [?] players,) I'll sing
and ~~star~~ shame him into dumbness
Sing a verse or two

Clorin (aside)

here is this sparrow voiced Clorin
I will over throw him with melodies
~~[?]~~ mock war and sweet Evadne to
~~Sing a few more verse~~
Shall hear ~~His~~ his fall —
Sing a few verse

Thernot
Clorin here what does he
a lut
With his crak ~~voice~~ playing Ill sing
And ~~sha~~ shame him into dumbness
Sing a verse or two
Clorin (aside
here is thus sparrow voiced Clorin
I will oer throw him with melodies
~~war~~ ~~mock~~ war and sweet Evadne to
~~sing a few more verses~~
Shall hear ~~his~~ his fall—
Sing a few verses

Lines 2–11 are cancelled by a large, wavy line. It is possible that "sing" in ll. 5, 10, 12, and elsewhere in the manuscript could be "say".

[TCD 3502/2, 15^{r}] [VP 1,1:30ff.]

are you Thernot
here
v
~~O~~ sparew soice ~~do you~~ [~~?sing~~] ~~singer~~
al
is that you can do
hear me and rest in [?dumness]
(sing a few verses)
Clorin
I ~~am~~ do not rest in [?dumness] that is a
l
sike the scaping together of wo reeds
sweet welcom for Evadne that—
hear [?me] a brut you heart
(sing a few verses)
Thernot
he he ha
Clorin
well

At the top of the page the message "Don't forget that we expect you at the Studio for lunch today at 1-30" is written in pencil in another hand and cancelled in ink.

8 "scaping" is presumably intended to be "scraping", and "wo" to be "two".

Thorn

Ah what a voice

Clorin

O what a thing is envy

And how it ~~broubel~~ troubeleth ~~to~~ Thernot

Thernot

~~but~~ keep silence you with the cracked voice new to ~~sing~~ ~~your~~ voice let me

(sing many verses)

(during which ~~Clorin~~ Thernot shows signs of supreme rage)

Thernot

— I'll drown his speeches now —

The ~~Sings~~ both sing together but different songs growing louder and louder as they draw near to each other with signs of rage

1 Thern
{A
2 {ah what a voice
3 Clorin
4 O what a thing is thy envy
5 And how it ~~troubel~~ troubelet ~~T~~ Thernot
6 Thernot
with the cracked ~~y[?~~]
7 ~~W~~ keep silence you new to [~~?sing~~] voic
8 let me
9 (sing many verses)
Thernot
10 (during which ~~Clorin~~ show sings
11 of suprest rage)
12 Thernot
13 Ill [?draw/?drown] his squeeker now—
14 ~~sings~~
15 The both sing [?together] but different
16 songs [?grown/?growing] louder and louder
17 As they draw near to each other with [?signs]
18 of rage

---

10 "sings" was presumably meant to be "signs".

Enter Evadne

Evadne

O what a noise my head spins round

Clorin

I came but ~~that~~ to sing to you ~~ere~~ you
the fair morn before you went
to seek your sheep [illegible] these [illegible]
Crack voices [illegible] ~~came to~~ [illegible]

Thernot

I came most sweet Evadne to save
from discord your sweet ears
And greet them with soft melody

~~Discord~~

Clorin

discord my song that broke once
or the time a nightingale's small heart
for envy — discord? I will prove
[illegible] smaller than violet [illegible]
[illegible] once again [illegible] it is [illegible]
~~Any one but Thernot be a [illegible]~~

1 Enter Evadne
2 Evadne
3 O what a nois My head [?spins] round
4 Clorin
to
5 I came but ~~that~~ sing to ~~you as~~ [?go/?yo]
6 this fair morn before you went
{b
7 to seek your sheep {aut then this
this Thernot
8 cracke voiced thing ~~came to~~
9 Thern
10 I came most sweet Evadne to save
11 from discourd your sweet ears
12 And greet them with soft melody
13 ~~Discord~~
14 Clorin
15 discourd my song that broke once
at a small
16 ~~one~~ time a nighting gale's ~~poor~~ [?heart]
17 for envy—discord? I ~~will~~ pound
{to {s
18 {[?] peices {mmaller than violet leav
19 [?As] [?] once again say it is discrod
20 ~~Any one but Thernot hes a bro~~

17

Thernot

with you

Cloris

Any one but Thernot he's a brother

musician (Enter) here sir!

(an arrow passes thro the air)

Thernot and Cloris

to gather cry

Robbers and fly —

Evadne

O miracle of courage

Enter

Alminter and Antonio

Alminter

So The heron ~~passed the~~ way fly you

Antonio

You missed I think it flies

quite steady

Alminter sees Evadne

Thernot
will you
Clorin
Any one but Thernot he's a brother
musician (a horn sound)
(An arrow pass thru the aire)
Thernot and Clorin
to gather cry
Robbers and fly—
Evadne
O miracls of courage
Enter
Almintor and Antonio
Almintor
See The heron ~~passed this~~ way fly [?you/?yon]
Antonio
You missed I think It flies
quite [?steady]
e
Almintor seeing evadne

---

15 "See" is written in the left margin and apparently was added later.

19 The mark transcribed as "e" above "evadne" may be a loop intended to capitalize the original, lower-case "e".

O most fair ~~Sphespe~~ shepherdess Evadne
Antonio (bowing)
~~I most~~ (and mimicking Almintor)
fair shepherdess Evadne.
Almintor
Thy flock awaiteth thee on the hills
May I drive them for thee
Evadne
No thou ~~most~~ thou ~~bes~~ ruff hunter
I am weary of you
~~You bring me leo~~ leopards
~~thou~~ a leopard
What canst thou do worthy Evadne
lov
You: ~~[illegible]~~ me shot with your great
bow a ~~herons brest~~ a pole cat
~~dappled hide bright feath from~~ brim
brow
Anton

[TCD 3502/2, 17^{v}] [VP 1,1:118–150]

O most fair ~~Spherpe~~ shepherdess Evadne
Antonio (bowing)
~~O most~~ (and mimicking Almintor)
fair shepherdess Avadne
Almintor
Thy flock await the on the hills
them
May I drive for thee
Evadne
[?tho]
No thou ~~most~~ [~~?beg~~] ruff hunter
I am weary of you
~~You bring me leaperds~~
~~[?then] a leapards~~
What canst thou do worthy Evadne
lov
You b[?]t me shot with your great
bow a ~~herrns brest~~ a pole cats
~~dapleed hide brigt [?feathers] from~~ [?various]
bird
Antonio

18

I and he made you a cloak
O ~~Silver Skin~~ cap of a silver sk
Of the skin of a silver ?

Evadn

So be it this I could with
a bow and arrow Thernot
and Colin too could do this man
Could they not Antony

Anton

Antonio's my name

Evad

Yea they ever could do this you
all alike a cowardly forest pest
This will do but wound you
upon a long and dangerous ~~quest~~
as knights to please their ladies do
Ay not for an hundred thousand
Evadne then [illegible] hunts

Exit

1 I and he made you a cloak
[?lynx]
2 O ~~silver skin~~ of a silver [?lynx] sk
of the skin of a silver [?Lynx]
3 —Evadn
4 So bee It thus I could with
5 a bow and arrow Thernot
6 and Chlorin ~~g~~ could do this [?much]
7 Could they not Antony
8 Antonio
9 Antonio's my name
10 Evade
c
11 Yes they [?even/?ever] [?{ sould] [?do/?did] this you
12 all alike a cowaldly forest peop
13 This will do but would you
14 Upon a long and dangerous quest
ladies
15 As knights to please ther do
16 No not for an hundred thousan
17 Evadne thou uncouth hunter
18 Exit

---

6 "Chlorin" is misspelled, but the exact letters are difficult to decipher.
14 Here and elsewhere in the manuscript Yeats may have written "j" for "g" in "dangerous".

Anton
Well uncouth hunter what ails you
now
Almintor
What shall I do Antonio
(Exit)

[TCD 3502/2, 18^{v}] [VP 1,1:168–169]

1 Antonio
2 Well uncooth hunter what ails you
now
3 Almint
4 What shall I do Antonio
5 (Exit)

19

Another ~~part~~.
The wood
Almintor and Antonio
Almintor
My page as I have told you I'm
resolved to go upon a ~~very~~ distant
dangerous quest from which
few men return My loved [illegible]
calls me but a hunter ~~[illegible]~~ rude
a sort of ~~[illegible]~~ forester ~~then~~ Therefore
~~of~~ or ~~forester~~ rustic clown I go
~~to bring~~ to bring to her the famous flower
that if any man shall give his ~~lady~~
love ~~he with~~ he's seen always beauteous
to her and she have fifty years
of youth before age comes
Antonio
None ever from this quest return
It's there all are changed to stone

~~Another part~~
The wood
Almintor and Antonio
Almintor
{a
My page {is I have told yo I'm
resolved to go up on a ~~very distan~~
dangercous quest from which
few men return My loved Avadne
calls me but a Hunter ~~ruff~~ rude
a sort of ~~Archer~~ forester ~~ther~~ Thernot
hunter
~~of~~ or ~~forester~~ Clorin I go
the
~~To bring~~ to bring to her famous flowe
that if any man shall give his ~~lady~~
love ~~he will~~ [?he'd] seem alway [?beautiful]
to her and she have fifty year
of youth before age comes
Antonio
None ever from that quest returns
{t
Tis they all are changed to s{oon

This page begins scene 2 of act 1.

Almintor
You know the story then
how or in ~~t~~ the forest depths
there is a lake with an Island
where the flower grows.
And how how to the ~~border~~ of the
lake the swans come and ~~sing~~ before
they die and all strange they are come
And how there is a living boat
that takes a man across to the
Enchanted Island where the flower
grows
Antonio
And from whence ~~no~~ no man
return
Almintor
Tis dangerous across the placid border
Antonio — Ay
Almintor
and I have come here to this

[TCD 3502/2, 19v] [VP 1,2:32–49]

Almintor
You know the story then
How on an ~~island~~ the forest depths
the is a lake with an Island
Where the flower grows
And how how to the border of the
lake the swams come and sing before
th die and all [?stray] they [?are] [?come]
and how there is a living boat
that take a man acros to the
Enchanted Island where the flower
grows
Antonio
And from whence no man
returns
Alminto
Tis [?dangerous] away to please Evadne
Antonio— Ay
Almintr
and I have come here to this

---

4 "the" is presumably intended to be "there".
8 "th" is presumably intended to be "they".

20

hollow in the forest among
the hazel bushes, to wait
for for the enchanted sign that
a man must follow
It came they say at evening
out of the air and leads a
man to the enchanted bower that
spreads wide magical wings
and skims over the water like
a wild bird alighting rushing in
a bright bow beheld in the water
Fro Yu ~~[illegible]~~ every now · you sky
then ~~and~~ the cam com the
a ~~[illegible] from~~
from the air a voice
eri follow
Almintor
heard you a sound
Antonor
~~Almintor~~ I did Sad like the

hollow in the forest among
the hazel bushes to wait
for for the enchanted son that
a man must follow
It come they say at evening
out of the air and leads a
Man to the [?Enchanted] boaat that
spreds [?wide] magical wings
and skims over the water like
a wild bird alighting raising in
a bright bow [?behind] it the waters
~~Tio~~ Tis ~~nearly~~ evening now you stay
here and no [?care] [?can] no
~~A voice from~~
from the air a voice
[?cries] follow
Almintor
heard you a sound
Antonio
~~Almintor~~ I did sad Like the

---

3 ''son'' is presumably intended to be ''song''.
13–14 These two lines are squeezed into the same lined space of the notebook.

friend here is a dream
(the voice sings
a song whose chorus is
follow follow follow
Almintor goes toward the voice
slowly away
Antonio
~~Away the the voice~~
he, O here voice far away borne
him alone with its follow follow
I'll never see him more
see he ~~he~~ leaps on his bow with the
red feather arrows —

friend here in a [?dream]
(the woice sings
\ a song who's {c
shorus is
follow follow follow
Almintor goes [?fades/?fore] the voice
slowly away
Antioh
~~O~~
~~[?Away] the the voice~~
[?] o [?] voice far awa lures
him allon with its follow follow
I'll never see him more
See he ~~he~~ left me his bow with the
red [?fetherd] arrows—

7 The word transcribed as "Antioh" may be "Anto oh".

21

Scene 3 —

~~My [illegible]~~
&
~~Autumn~~

Scene 3 —

The home of the enchanter
many flowers are in groups in
pots of diverse and wondrous
shapes along the walls
two ~~old~~ men ^long^ beards of
enormous length are stooping
as if in the act of pulling a flower
but with ^a^ movement
Enter Almintor
Twas here the singing stopped
did ever man see such an ocean of
many coloured bloom before ~~[illegible]~~
and Colonnades covered and halls

—~~scene~~ 3—
~~My pa~~
~~A~~
~~Antonio~~
Scene 3—
The home of the enchantress
many flowre are [?ranged] in
pots of diverse and wondrous
shapes alon the walls
with
two ~~old~~ men beards of
enormous length are stooping
if in the act of pulling a flower
a
but with movement
Enter Almintor
'Twas hear the singing stoped
did ever man see such an ocen of
many coloured blow before [?]
and [? ?] and hall

---

6 The second word may be "house" rather than "home".
16 "ocen" may be "ocerd" as a misspelling for "orchard".

I have ~~too~~ gone wander up
and down and no one
flower out shine the rest
supremely which then is the enchanted
flower how may one choose
I will address on of the old men
whose beards ~~sweep~~ on the ground flowing
over these antiquated dream
father how shall one know the flower
no answer tis strange as I
came ~~many the~~ through the island
full many I have seen with low
bend others and are even silent
father will you speak
Silent too
Stone Stone
They all are stone then it is true
If I choose wrong I shall be ~~made~~ changed also
to stone

I have ~~wa~~ gone wander up
and down and no one
flower out shines the rest
supremely which then is the Enchanted
flower. how may one choose
I will adress one of the old men
        beards { s
whose   { [?]weep on the ground flowing
over their antiquated dress
father how shall one no the flor
No answer tis strang as I
Came ~~mong the~~ through [?the/?this] Island
full many I have seen with low
                are
beard thus and were silent
father will you speak
   Silent two
      Ston stone
They all are stone then it is true
      { c   changed
If I { shoos [?rongh] I shal be ~~made~~ also
to stone

22

But if I cannot retn again
for none of those fail may for
the magic boat sped again over the
water I mas chose
I with blessings choor and may
fate guides fate and all sylvan
gods that preside over Naxos guide
me

he plucks a flower and is changed
into stone

End of Act 1

1 But yet I cannot retu again
2 for none of those fail may for
            boat
3 the magic sped again over the
4 water I mus chose
5 I will [?blessing] choos and may
6 fate guide   fate and all sylvan
      th
7 gods preside over [?hunters] guide
8 me
9   he pluck a flow and is changed
10   into stone

11   End of Act 1—

Act 2.

~~Evadne and Antonio~~

Antonio sits on a stone seat

Enter Evadne —

~~So the [illegible]~~

Enter Antonio and Evadne

Evadne

My gentle Antonio

I will go after disguised as a shepherd ~~[illegible]~~ not despair

Antonio

None ever have returned from the quest

Evadne

But then I shall die

~~Antonio~~

You made him go

Now that he has not returned

If I am changed to stone

I shall be near him

Antonio [illegible]

Act 2.
~~Evadne and Antonio~~
[?E/?to] ~~Antonio sitting on a~~ tree [?stump]
~~enter Evadne~~ —
~~So he he~~
Enter Antonio and Evadne
Avadne
My [?pretty] Antonio
after discised as a shepherd
I will go ~~di~~∧& not dispute
Antonio
None ever have returned from the [?quest]
Ewadne
But here I shall die
~~Antono~~
~~you made him go~~
Now that he has not returned
If I am changed to stone
I shall be near him
Antonio

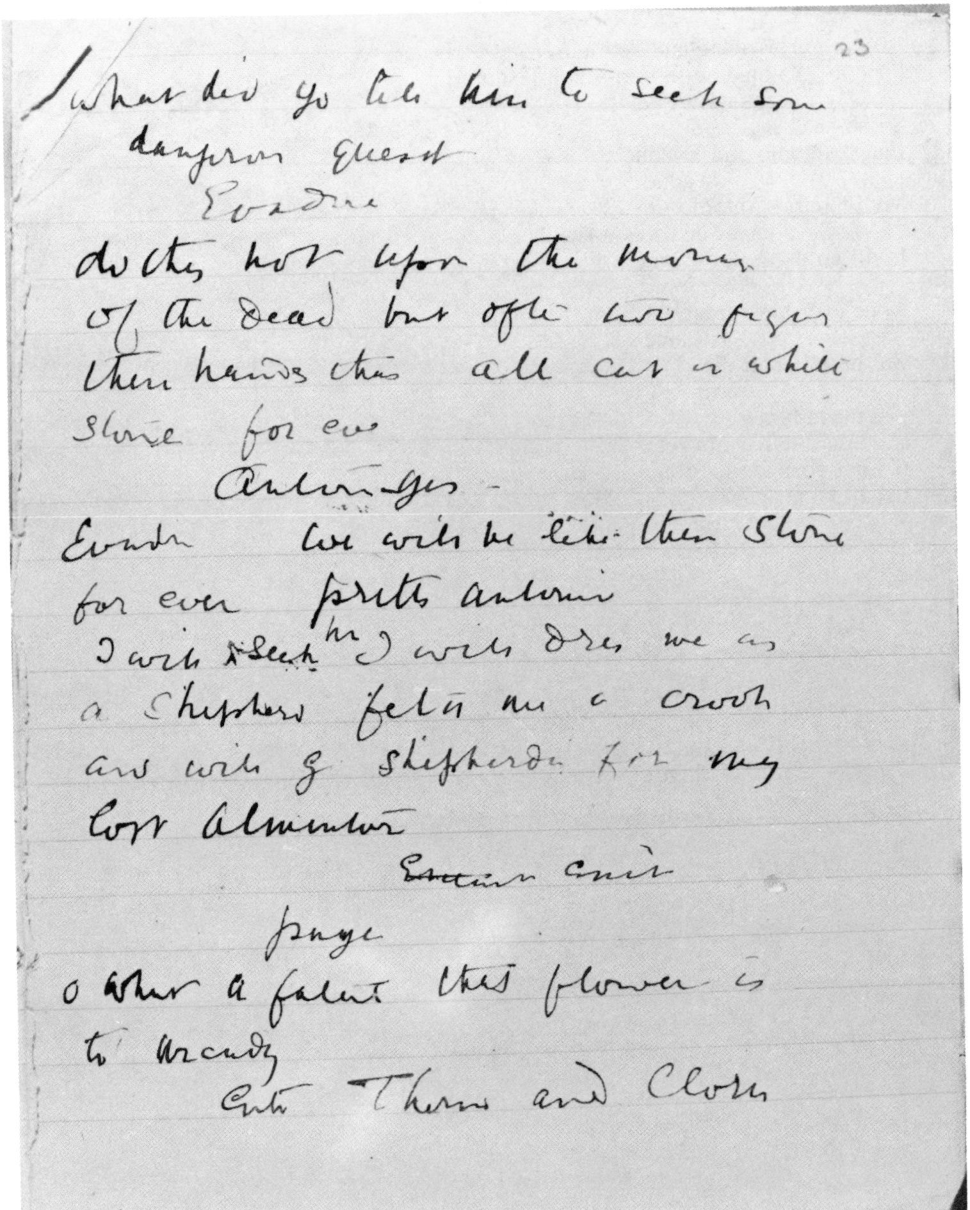
23

/what did yo tell him to seek some
dangerous Quest
Evadne
do they not upon the money
of the dead but ofte two figures
their hands thus all cut in white
stone for ever
Antonio-ges -
Evadne we will be like them stone
for ever pretty antonio
I will ~~seek~~ no I will dress me as
a shepherd fetch me a crook
and will go shepherding for my
lost Almintor
~~Evadne~~ exit
Page
O what a falent this flower is
to Arcady
Enter Thernot and Colin

[TCD 3502/2, 23^{r}] [VP 2,1:6–29]

What did yo tell him to seek some
dangerous quesst
                    Evadne
do they not upon the [?morning]
of the dead but often two figur
their hands thus all cut in white
stone for ever
                    Antonio—yes—
Evadne   We will be like these stone
for ever   pretty Antonio
            [?him]
I will seek I will dres me as
a shepherd fetch me a crook
and will go shepherding for my
lost Almintor
                                        ~~Exeunt~~ exit
                    page
O what a [?   ] that flower is
to Arcady
                Enter Thernot and Clorin

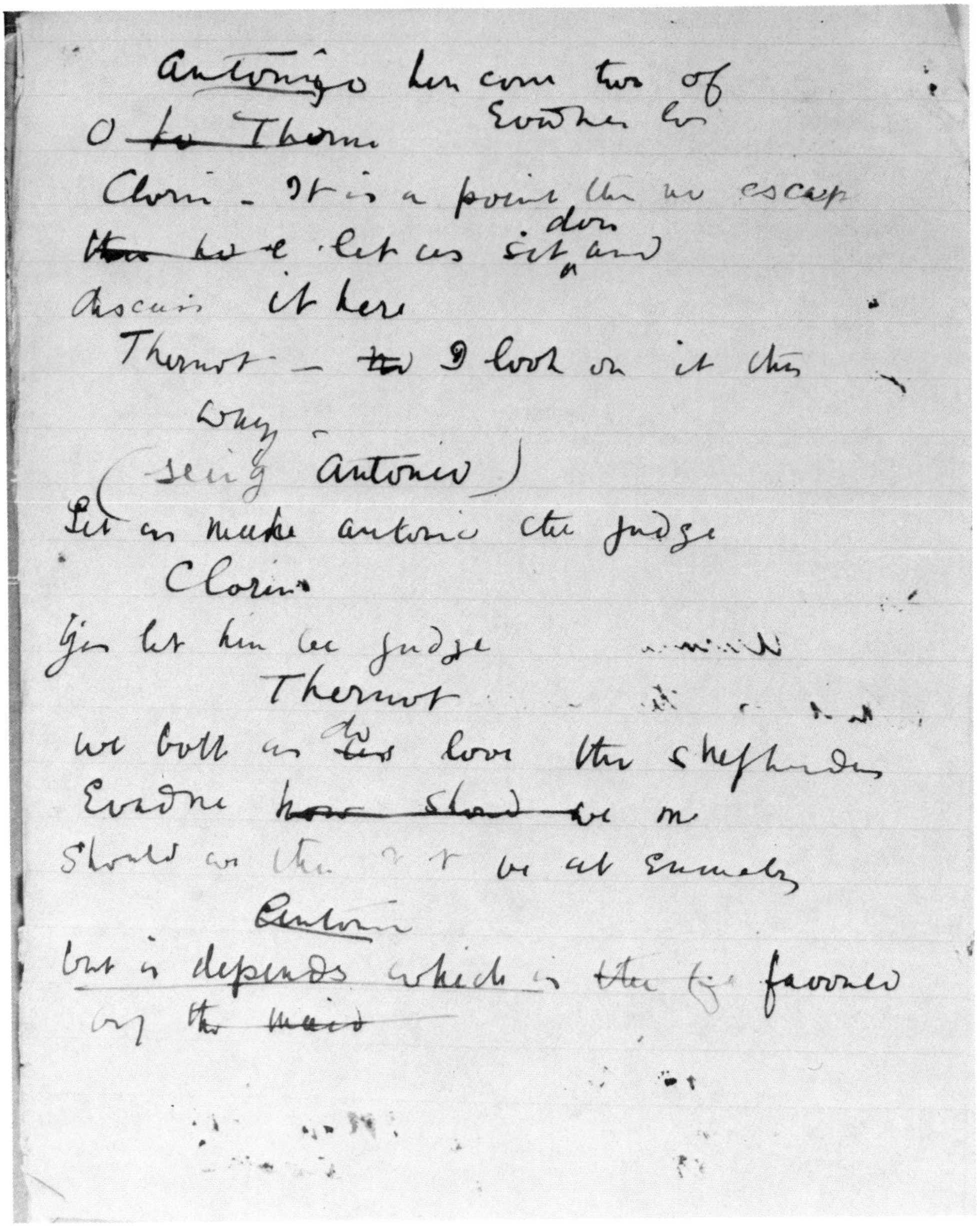
Antonio has come two of
O ~~to Thorm~~ Evadne lo
Clorin — It is a point that we escape
~~tha ho~~ e · let us sit down and
discuss it here
Thernot — ~~tw~~ I look on it this
way
(seeing Antonio)
Let us make Antonio the judge
Clorin
Yes let him be judge
Thernot
We both as ~~two~~ do love the shepherdess
Evadne ~~how should we~~ in
Should we then [illegible] be at enmity
Antonio
but it depends which is the [illegible] favoured
of the ~~maid~~

1 Anton{i / yo} here come two of
Evadne s [?lovers]
2 O ~~ho Therno~~
3 Clorin—It is a point then no escap
down
4 ~~then no e~~ let us sit∧and
5 discuss it here
6 Thernot—~~no~~ I look on it this
7 way—
8 (seeing Antonio)
9 Let us make Antonio the judge
10 Clorin
11 Yes let him be judge
12 Thernot
do
13 We both us ~~us~~ love the shepherdess
14 Evadne ~~how should we~~ m
15 Should we then not be at Enmity
16 ~~Antonio~~
17 ~~but it depends which is~~ ~~the fa~~ favored
18 by ~~the maid~~

1 "Evadne's [?lovers]" is written underneath the rest of the line but higher than l. 2. The line under "Antonio" may be intended as a cancellation mark.

24

~~Cos~~

~~Dos~~

Does not the code of honour
Say we should be enemies
that is the point perplexing us
you being

Antonio

Squire to Almintor

Thernot

Should be learned on these things

Antonio

~~Which is the favour one~~

Thernot

~~Why what who have not spoken~~

~~yes~~ Antonio

Yes you ~~should~~ according to
all honourable laws ~~be~~ laws
You should fight

both fight

Antonio

with ~~swords~~ / Both with
swords

1 ~~dos~~
~~Dos~~
Does not the code of honour
2 Say we should be enemies
3 that is the point perplexing us
4 you being
5 Anton
6 squire to Almintor
7 Thernot
8 Should be learned on these things
9 Antonio
10 ~~Which is the favou one~~
11 ~~Thernot~~
12 ~~Why [?] who have not~~ spoken
13 ~~yet~~ Antonio
14 Yes ~~you should~~ according to
15 all honourable [?~~war~~] [?] laws
16 You should fight
17 both—fight
18 Antonio | Both with
19 with swords | swords

5–6 Both "Antonio" and "Almintor" are misspelled, but the exact letters are difficult to decipher.

So a thing wept out one by

a death

Both

a death

Antonio

But some one comes

Enter Evadne

to Antonio

Look I am well disguised

~~Anton~~

Clown ~~and~~

Who is this

~~Antonio~~

Evadne

A ~~young~~ shepherd of Peregot

new to these parts.

Antonio

~~[illegible]~~ Remember the match we have talked

about ~~to~~ her to him.

So a thing wipt out only by
a death
Both
a death
Antonio ~~s~~
But some one comes
Enter Evadne
to Antonio
Look I am well discized
~~Antonio~~
Clorin ~~and~~
Who [?is] this
~~Antonio~~
Evadne
A ~~youth~~ shepherd [?a] Perigot
new to these parts
Antonio
~~We~~ w [?refer] the matter we have taked
About ~~to her~~ to him

Act Second – the shepherds gorge

~~Colin~~

Thernot ~~fair~~ good Thernot

we both do love a maid

Evadne

Evadne

I saw the maid short freckled

Some what curving in the nose

Both – no

She is more bright & ~~[illegible]~~ than

morning

Evadne

Opinion differ

well the question

Antonio

Is this should ~~the~~ ~~[illegible]~~ this

~~For~~ not be enemies ~~fight~~ for both cannot

be loved by the same ~~freckled~~

short ~~cur~~ freckled curve nosed

Evadne Should you [illegible]

not fight

[TCD 3502/2, 25r] [VP 2,1:65–69]

1 let Perot the shepherd you judge
2 ~~Colin~~
3 Thernot ~~fair~~ good Thernot
{v
4 we both do lo{ee maid
5 Evadne
6 Evadne
7 I no the maid short freckled
8 Some what curving in the nose
9 Both—no
10 She is more butiful ~~that~~ than
11 morning
12 Evadne
13 [?Opinions] differ
14 well the question
15 Antonio ~~is~~
16 Is this should ~~the [?not] [?die]~~ they
be enemies
17 ~~For~~ not ~~fight~~ for both cannot
18 be loved by this same ~~freckled~~
19 Short ~~cur~~ freckled curve nosed
20 Evadne Should ~~you~~ they
21 not fight

Evadne
Yes to the death
~~Clorin~~ Shepherd
farewell > fight to death
to Antonio so ~~an~~ do I not
look well in this shepher [?]
let is go
Antonio farewell
Evadne
but Think you will they fight
~~Fight not they~~
Colin
Fight not [?they]
exeunt

---

3 ''Shepherd'' may be intended as an insertion in the following line.
10 The ''but'' was apparently added later.

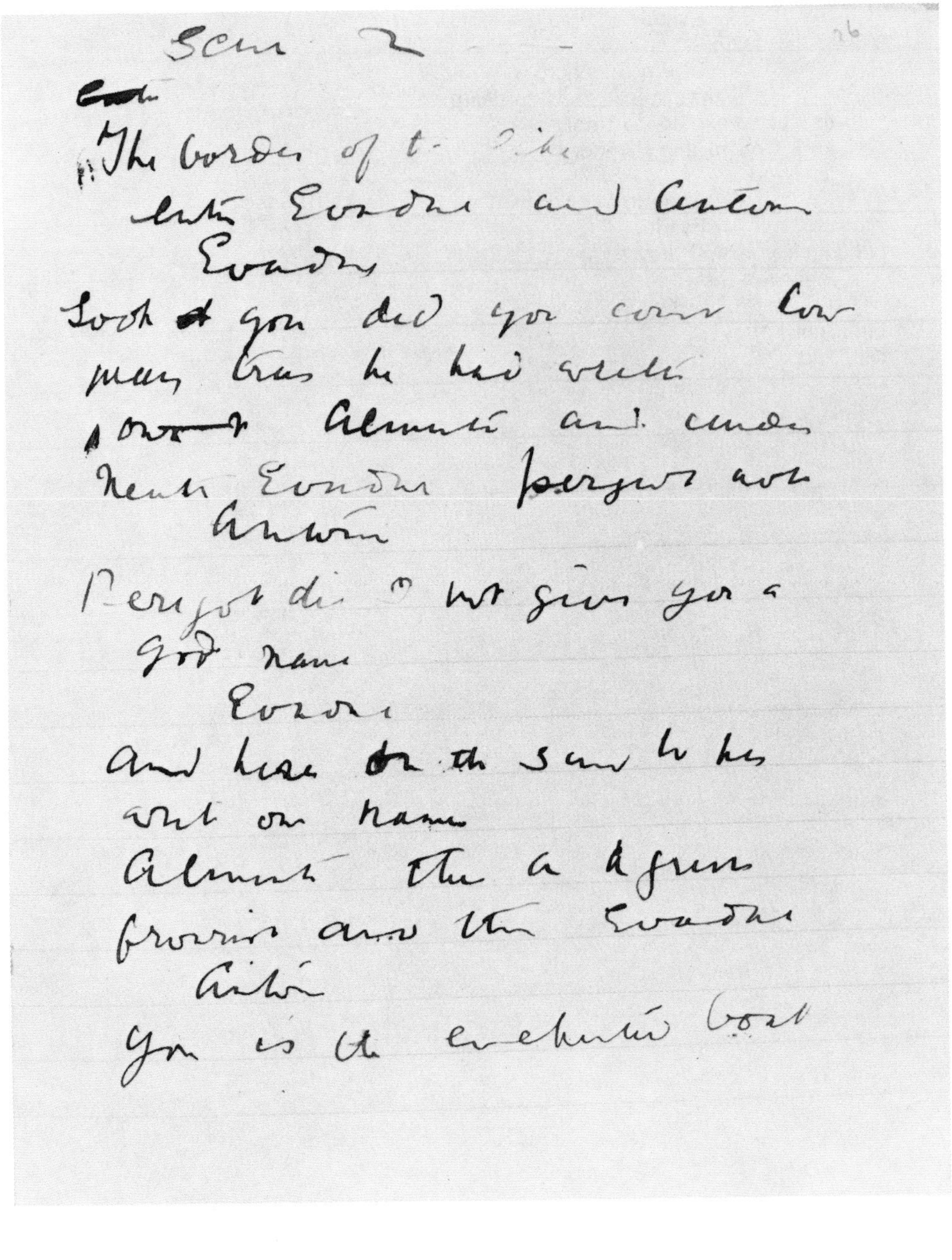

Scene 2 —

The border of the lake

enter Evadne and Antonio

Evadne

Look you did you come how

many times he had called

Almintor and wonder

near Evadne Perigot and

Antonio

Perigot did not give you a

good name

Evadne

And here are the same to his

not our name

Almintor the a green

frowning and the Evadne

Antonio

Yon is the enchanted boat

Scene 2—
~~enter~~
The border of the lake
enter Evadne and Antonio
Evadne
Look ~~at~~ you did you count how
many trees he had written
~~our n~~ Almintor and under
Neath Evadne pergiot not
Antonio
Perigot did I not give you a
good name
Evadne
{ o
And here { [?]n th sand he has
writ our names
Almintor then a a great
frourish and then Evadne
Antonio
Yon is the enchantéd boat

19 The stress mark over the "e" of "enchantéd" may be intended as the cross of the "t".

Evadne

farewell I will return soon or
not at all

Antonio there is that sad
voice out of the air again

(the song dies echoes follow)

Evadne

I must go alone farewell

(Exit)

Almintor gone Evadne gone
never to return a curse is on me
but here come Cloris Colin and
Thernot let us be merry a bit
just to ~~mock~~ anger sadness

enter Colin and Thernot
with swords at play

we have got swords Antonio

Antonio

are both of you alone
I who am the ancient

evadne
fara well I will return soon or
not a tall
Antonio there is that sad
voic out of the air again
w
(the song [?]ith its chorus follow)
Evadne
I must go alone farwell
(exit)
Almintor gone Evadne gone
Never to return a woe is me
ha here come ~~Clor~~ Colin and
Thernot let [?us] be merry a bit
anger
just to ~~mock~~ sadness
enter Colin and Thernot
with sword play
We have got swords Antonio
Antonio
are both of you alive
O where is the ancient

6 Yeats left several words in this line unfinished.

courage of S. [?] 27

Full doubtless you have come
here to fight

Colin

We are sheep strayed

Thernot (aside to Antonio)

I would have fought but Colin is
a Colin coward –

Antonio.

I'll see all fair

Thernot

No it is late we would be
belated and caught by the night

Antonio

No by all shepherd gods I
being squire to Almintor swear this
honour requires ye to fight
draw your swords.

Colin draws his slowly

(aside to Antonio

[TCD 3502/2, 27^{r}] [VP 2,2:56–62]

courage of shepherds
[?but] doubtless you have come
here to fight
Colin
No a sheep strayed
Thernot (aside to Antonio)
I would have fough but Colin is
a born coward—
Antonio
I'll see all fair
Thernot
No It is late we would be
belatend and [?caught] by the nigh
Antonio
No by all shepherd gods I
[?As]
~~being~~ squire to Almin sware that
honor requires ye to fight
draw your swords
Colin drawhs his slowly
([?ascid] to Antonio

6 Yeats left "Antonio" substantially unfinished.

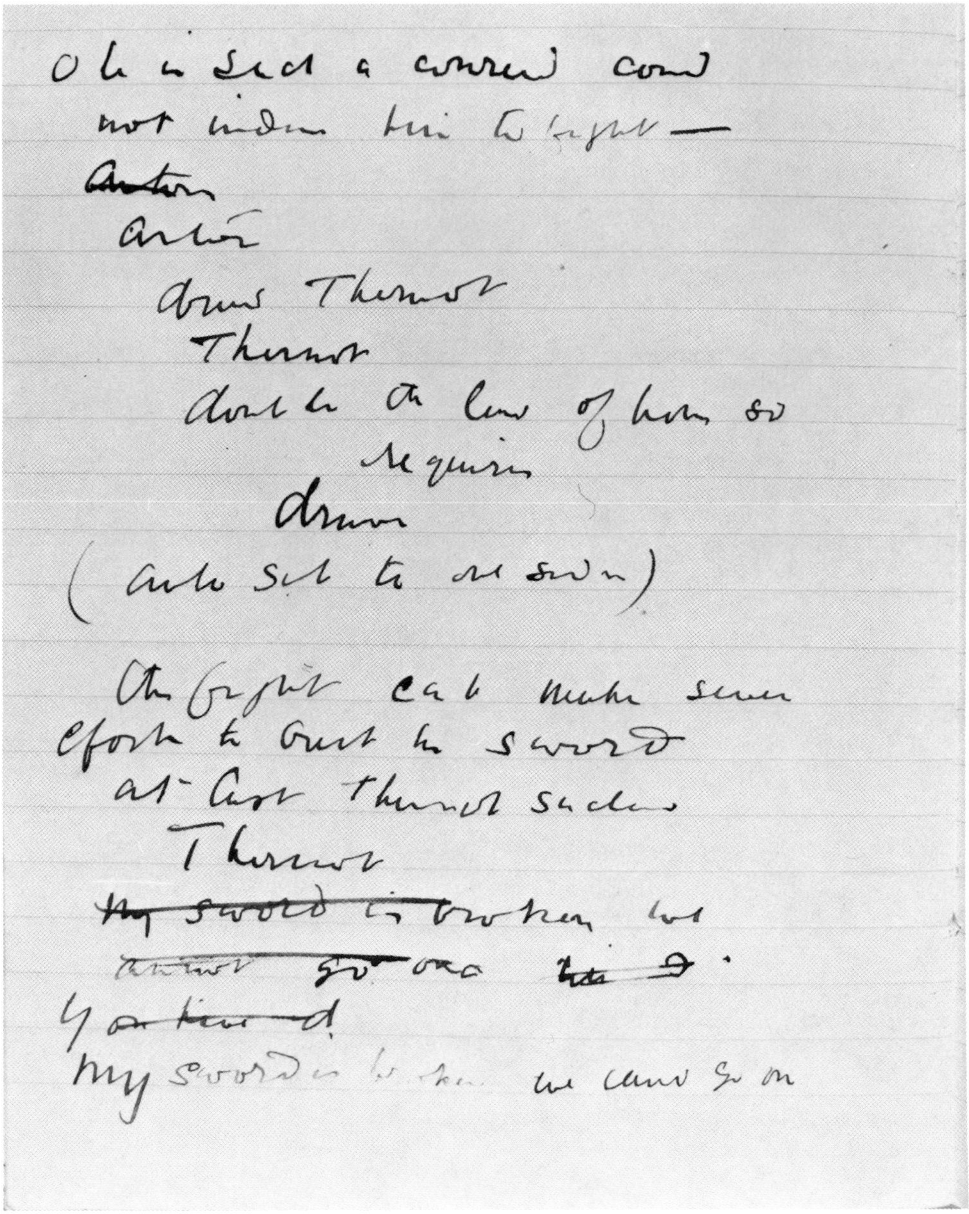

[TCD 3502/2, 27v] [VP 2,2:62–68]

[?Oh/?O he] is such a coward could
not [?induce] him to fight—
~~Antonio~~
Antonio
draw Thernot
Thernot
[?doubtless] the law of honor so
requires
draws
(Anto sit to one side)
They fight each make sever
efort to break his sword
at last Thernot [?sucheeds]
Thernot
~~My sword is broken~~ we
~~cannot go on~~ ~~We I~~
~~You have d~~
My sword is broken we cannot go on

[TCD 3502/2, 28^{r}] [VP 2,2:end of scene]

I am disarmed by an accident
Antonio and ~~The~~ Clorin
Clorin expect denunciation as a
coward—and [?thus/?then/?they] go —
[?] [?sce]—

Same as scene ~~B~~ of act 1 –
The old men still kneels
~~and the longbeards sits~~
Enter the enchantress
and Evadne
Enchantress
Good you return again you are young
1000 years I have not had pity
But you are good
Evadne
~~To~~ Give ~~the~~ Almintor life
Enchantress
I cannot once changed all stone
I have no power over them
~~But~~ he who touches
But if a mortal touch them on the lips
with the enchanted flower
They wake But none can find that flower
among them there

{3
Same as scene {4 of act 1—
The old men still kneeling
~~and the longbeards [?sil/?sitt]~~
enter the enchantress
and Evadne
Enchan
Good you retu again you are yong
1000 years I have not had pity
But you are young
Evadne
[~~?~~] give [~~?my~~] Almintor life
Enchantress
I cannot once changed into stone
I have no power ove^{r} them
~~But he~~ who touches
But if a mortal touch them on the lips
with the enchanted flower
The wake But none can find the flower
among these [?thorns]

Erodne

O what a world of flowers
how shall I chose
Enchantress

I have

I would gladly tell them but when
the flower is pulled I die
Erodne

~~As and~~ with thy never
as me and with I never
could I of I chose son
Enchantress.

(this one / has been here this
since Belyon had rule
this one since tiron was first
besieged) —
Erodne
I will pull on thy char

Evadne
O what a world of flowers
how shall I chose
Enchantress
I ha

I would gladly tel thee but when
the flower is pulled I die
Evadne
~~[?Ay] and will~~ thy never
Ay me and will I never
wake If I chose rong
Enchantress
this one has been here thus
since Bilyon had rule
this one since tiroy was first
besejud—
Evadne
I will pull on by [?chance]

[TCD 3502/2, 29^{v}] [VP 2,3:34ff.]

Enchan
Stay fair youth go back
do not chose I tel you but
I'die
Evadne
Give Alminto lif
Enchan
I cannot go back again
I led you here by long and twisted ways
to keep your for a time from here
I who have no pitied for a thousand
years
Evadne
I chose
Enchan
stay I will show yo its [?place]
And I will die I could not
see you changed to stone fair youth
Here are a thousand one all stone

30

then I have slain I will die
what ~~ill~~ is it to die for
I do not know I have lived
a thousand look you here is
the flower ~~place~~ I was doom-
(lie down)
and when you pull it I die
What are thats ue
yet pull it not I love you far
yount ~~sleep here a little~~
ah you will pull it I am
~~dying~~ gone
Evadne pulls the flower
Tt Almintor and the old men
awake
1 old man
I have slept
2 old m
(heard)

[?these] I have [?stone/?shone] I will die
what ~~ist~~ is it to die for
I do not know I have lived
A thousand look you here is
the flower ~~pluck~~ I will down
(lies down)
and when you pull it I die
What [?ere] that be
yet pull it not I love you fair
yout ~~stay here a little~~
ah you will pull it I am
~~dying~~ gone
Evadne pulls the flower
~~Th~~ Almintor and the old men
awake
1 old man
I have slept
2 olm
beard

1 old man
My beard
Almintor
Clondon
Evadne
You have slept years old men
1 old man
Is Babylon that was triumphant
2 old man
And does Ulysses wander still
I was his shepherd and I left him
When she touched this land
Evadne
~~A thousand~~ hundreds years ago Babylon fell
Hundred of years Ulysses is dead
Both old men
O wonderful
Almintor
My Evadne the world and thee
once more

[TCD 3502/2, 30^{v}] [VP 2,3:278–323]

1 old man
My beard
Almintor
Evadne
Evadne
You have slept years old man
1 old man
Is babylon that was [?triumphant]
2 old man
and does Ulyses wander still
I was his shipmate and I left her
When she touched this land
Evade
~~[?]~~ hundreds of
A ~~thousands~~ year ago Babiln fell
hundred of years Ulsyes is dead
Both old men
O wonderful
Almintor
My Evadne the world and thee
once more

It is particularly difficult to distinguish "man" from "men" on this page.

Second Version: "The Lady of Tuneful Guile"

SB 23.2.199–276 (NLI 30,328) includes a notebook containing a complete draft of the play up through the eventual line 291 of the *Variorum Poems* numbering, three pages on two loose leaves completing the play, three more pages on loose leaves giving earlier versions of passages in that draft, and an additional title page. The existence of the loose leaves that carry earlier versions suggests that Yeats drafted part or all of this version separately before transcribing it into the notebook, which itself contains heavy revision. The exact period of composition is unknown but cannot be later than the August 1884 date affixed by Yeats to the subsequent version of the play.

The present draft displays Yeats filling out the play to approximate its final form, with the action substantially complete and at least a rough form of most of the dialogue in place. It begins as a reasonably fair copy but soon turns into a working text that Yeats revises substantially as he proceeds. He sometimes inserts passages out of the proper order, apparently as they occur to him; for example, in act 1 an additional part of the exchange between Thernot and Colin in scene 1 stands between scenes 2 and 3 of the notebook, while in act 2 the song "A man has a hope for heaven" from the eventual scene 3 appears here only inside the back cover of the notebook and on the facing verso. Other important lines, like the song of the voices which eventually opened the final scene, are altogether absent from the text at this stage.

The version is mostly in black ink, with one loose leaf and occasional corrections in pencil. Yeats began the notebook using only the rectos, but soon began to employ versos both for reworking passages and sometimes for continuing the text itself. Because the Stony Brook numbering already assigns a separate number to each page of leaves written on both sides, I have added a superscript r or v to indicate recto and verso; thus SB 23.2.211^{v} indicates the verso of the page of which SB 23.2.210^{r} is the recto.

The transcriptions begin with the three detached pages that contain earlier versions of passages, proceed through the notebook until it breaks off in scene 3 of act 2, continue that act on the loose leaves to its conclusion (together with the alternate title page on the verso of one of them), and then return to the notebook for the draft of "A man has a hope for heaven" inside the back cover.

The loose leaves comprising SB 23.2.199–204 are all of the same unlined white paper, but their dimensions vary slightly because of tearing; they measure 18.4 cm by about 22.7 cm. The leaf SB 23.2.276 is of a different kind of unlined white paper measuring approximately 22.6 cm by 18.1 cm and is folded once.

all the dancers' singing
joy and and love are one excellence
ever ranging ever singing
[illegible]
is the [illegible] song of with loud possession
Colin
O O no it is not so
Love [illegible] and [illegible] and sadness
[illegible] soul of all excellence
Sadness sow heart of deepest joy
[illegible] the sun love [illegible] possession
of the song and [illegible] lover a [illegible] weary [illegible]
of change the severer of the gods
[illegible] Olympus
Love then [illegible] and clean
Came in answer to this word
Lest a man in earth pleasure
Should forget how earth he trod
Men had labor and had leasure
and laugh over the summer sod
moved a day with cadence measure
and when [illegible] Cyprus was
and the [illegible] years leave lover

day
1 All the dawning is singing
2 joy and and love are one existence
3 ever ringing ever ringing
4 ~~singin~~
5 is the ~~music~~ song ~~of~~ with loud persiten
6 Colin
7 O Oh no its not so
love ~~song~~ and ~~sou~~ and sadness
8 ~~sadness~~ soul ~~of all~~ existence
soul
9 sadness ~~heart~~ of deepest joy
[?] the singing long
10 [~~?means~~] ~~the [?buruden] and~~ persistence
~~and how to~~ loves a ~~toke~~ wary wear the joy
11 ~~of the song~~ ~~and~~ [—?—] [?the] [?yo/?go]
12 of change the sevent of the god$
13 ~~sent from~~
[?] Olympia
14 love then [~~?abused~~] and [?treason/?treasure]
his
15 came in answer to ~~their~~ nod$
16 lest a man in [?earthy] pleasur
17 Should forget how ere he trod
18 Men had labour and had leasure
19 and lovely oer the summer sod
a {y
20 moved ~~hou~~ da{w with caden measure
21 and when oer [—?—] [?then/?them/?their] Cypris wave
22 and the pointed yew leave [?bower/?hover]

This page is the first of four made by folding a single loose leaf in half. Only pp. 1 and 3 of the leaf (SB 23.2.199–200) have writing on them; they contain an earlier draft of SB. 23.2.210, l. 9, to SB 23.2.212, l. 3.

8 Yeats may have omitted the final "s" of "sadness" at the end of the line here and again at the beginning of l. 9. "love" is written in the left margin.

10 Yeats omitted one or more letters at the end of "persistence", but the exact spelling is difficult to determine.

15 The "ir" of "their" is written over the "r" of "ther". The "s" of "nods", like that of "gods" in l. 12, is cancelled by a vertical line.

21 The cancelled word appears to begin with "th".

1 Murmer softly oer his grave
will maid
2 ~~Would~~ the lips of ~~loved~~ and lover
3 Thern

1 *as when the stars in heaven shake*
wide
2 *~~and~~ the woodlands dim and dreary*
3 *~~of [?]~~*
wake
4 *to the phantom [?] ~~brake~~*
5 *of the shadow hounds of faery*
who while stars above
6 *~~while above the stars~~ are blinking*
the
7 *and ~~the~~ winds there life renewing*
lone [?woods]
8 *and the ~~wood~~ [~~—?—~~] ~~forest~~*
[?wrinkling]
[?shadowy]
9 *go the ~~phantom~~ [?faer] pasing*
10 *~~on~~ on I fly or [?] and dreary*
11 *ocean hill and [~~—?—~~] hill*
12 *and wander hollow*
fawns
13 *As the shadow ~~hound~~ of faery*
~~singing~~
14 *And my song is ever follow*
15 *A soaring [?shadow] singing ever*
16 *driven on oer hill and hollow*
17 *singing on and singing ever*
18 *worn and mortal rise and follow*

Written in pencil, this loose leaf appears to be a rough version of the Voice's song at the end of act 1, scene 2.
6 It is unclear whether there are one or more cancellation marks deleting "while . . . above".
8 There are additional letters at the end of "[?woods]", perhaps making "woodland".

The lady of tuneful guile—
a fairy tale
in two acts

W B Yeats—

[*?*]

Line 4 is in blue pencil or crayon, and l. 5 is in ordinary pencil.

Scene 1—
~~A forest~~—before the cottage
of the shepherdes Naschina
It is morning enter Thernet
with a lute

Thernet

Maiden come forth the woods are waiting thee
Tis morn how high the dawn burns over head
Tis morn, thy sheep are browsing in the vale
Tis morn, like old mens eyes the stars are pale
Tis morn, through the air love thoughts are winging
Tis morn and from the dew drenched woods I sped
To welcome the ~~M~~ Naschina with sweet
singing

(sits down ~~and~~ be on a tree stem
and begins tuning his lute)
~~Co~~—enter Colin with a lute—

Colin

Naschina where fore lingereth thou for see

16 The final dashlike mark is well below the level of the line.

The Island of Statues Manuscripts, Second Version
[SB 23.2.207[r]] [VP 1,1:20–31, 64–67]

{d
Naschina, dawn the crimson bu{t hath spred
Naschina crimson petals oer head
Naschina hear my music pours for thee
~~The o~~
a quenchless grieving of love melody
(sits and begins to tune his lute)
Thernet (who does not see Colin)
(Sings)
Come forth for in a thousand bowers
Blossoms ~~of~~ ope their dewy lips
On the lake the water flowers
Floating are like silver ships
The hand of dawn the foliage fingereth
And the waves are leaping white
Thou alone O maiden lingereth
While the world is rolled in light
Colin
What hear with thy cracked voice to mar the morn
shepherd
hear me and^hearing me grow dumb

[SB 23.2.208r] [VP 1,1:37–41]

Colin sings
Come thou maid with burning hair
reds the dewy mountain heather
a thousand ~~bur~~ birds are singing there
Joy and sadnes both to geather
In there song is ever blending
Come thou come and to this string
rending
Though my love sick heart is ~~rending~~
Note a sad note will I sing
Thernet
I am not dumb I'd sooner in the fold
Be dumb to hear the creaking of the gate
(sings)
In mine heart thine image ever
Sitting is o maiden fair
'Fore mine eyes a burning river
Is the glory of thine hair
Once I saw the ever after
O my love I had assurance
From the long and wondering laughter

---

5 "geather" may be "gather".
9 Yeats wrote "Note" for "Not" at the beginning of the line.
14–17 The vertical line in the left margin is in pencil.

Of the river songs endurence
For the nymphs and nyads cry
down among the wildering billows
Loud thy name as back they [?~~lay~~] lie
on their wan and watery pillows
Colin
I'll silence this dull singer
sings
~~come~~
wherefore maiden lingreth thou
failing
Oer the trees the moon is ~~fading~~ ~~waning~~ [?~~paling~~]
~~And her clear and silvery~~
shining dappled
And her ~~clear and silver~~ brow
dawn bewildered's ~~failing failing~~ paling paling
Come—I've loved the lonly glade
And have squandered all my sorrow
Fore the stars began to fade
or the buds new lustre [~~ba~~] borrow
and thou
Come ~~thou~~ my ~~love~~ ~~sick~~ heart is rending
for
~~To give~~ the plesure will I sing

1–5 The vertical lines in the left margin are in pencil, or possibly black crayon.
11–19 These lines are cancelled by a diagonal pencil line, presumably intended to include ll. 10 and 20 as well.

[SB 23.2.210^{r}] [VP 1,1:36–37, 63–78]

Merry songs melodious blending
With the lyric viol string
                    Thernet (sing [?loud]
I'll quench his singing with louds song
Come forth for in a thousand bower
blossoms ope their dewy lips
{ o
{[?]ver the lake the water flowers
Floating are like silver ships
All the dawning day is singing
joy and love are one existance
ever ringing ever ringing
is the song with loud persistence
                    Colin (~~s~~
~~Love's the soul~~
hear [?waiting] [?thee] [?thy] Colin weepest
Love and sorrow one existence
                         the
Sadnes soul of ~~all~~ ~~of~~ ~~y~~ joy deepest
Iis the burden and persistance
Of the song that never sleepest
Love from heaven came of yore
As a token and sign

15–16 These two lines are squeezed into the same ruled space of the notebook.

The Island of Statues Manuscripts, Second Version
[SB 23.2.211^{v}] [VP 1,1:82–85, 91–92]

1 The moon has gone with sicle bright
2 Slowly slowy fadeth she
3 Weary of reaping the barren night
~~shuddering~~
4 ~~and the~~ [~~?writhing~~] ~~moonlight sea~~
The barren and the shuddering sea

5 Colin
6 ~~lonely~~ is the heart of the [?dawn]
[?these] [?rivers] are
over crimson vapour singing
7 ~~around~~ them ~~shuddering~~ ~~raiment~~ [?fling/?fiery]
8 ~~Colin~~
9 ~~Come for the day is wandering~~ now
high [?hazeld]
10 ~~Over the hill with the [?oaky]~~ brow

The first passage is an interpolation and the second a rough draft for part of the facing page SB 23.2.212^{r}, which continues SB 23.2.210^{r}. Although Yeats does not indicate their exact placement, ll. 1–4 would follow l. 5 on the facing page, and ll. 5–10 are apparently a rough draft of ll. 6–10 there.

4 Yeats apparently first cancelled ''[?writhing]'' and substituted ''shuddering''; then he cancelled the entire line and wrote a new version underneath it.

6–7 The exact placement of the words at the end is unclear.

9–10 These lines are cancelled by a single curved line looping back at the right.

1 ~~Of its death~~ singing oer and oer and oer
2 of its death and change malign
3 Thernet ([?standing]
4 ~~N~~
5 With louder song I'll drown his song
6 (sings)
7 ~~Far awide the dawn is singing~~
8 round her crimson raiment flinging
9 ar and wide the dawn is winging
10 and the clarion-rivers singing
11 Colin (standing
[?dawning]
12 ~~loud for the morning cryath~~
~~and fore the~~
loud for the morning cryeth
13 ~~and my soul in waiting dyeth~~
and my soul in waiting dyeth
14 ever dyeth ever dyeth
15 Thernet
16 ~~Far awide the vapours~~ satter
the
Far marning vapours shatter
s
17 as the leaves in Autumn {ccatter

Yeats later rearranged the order of these passages. The preceding page contains a draft of ll. 6–10 and an interpolation to follow l. 5.

8–9 These lines are squeezed into the same lined space of the notebook.

all the world is singing singing
~~Colin~~
~~Come as to~~
All the world is ringing ringing
Colin
[~~?save~~] lift
~~wake~~ my soul from deepest night
Thernet
↑ Back the shadows creep aghast
Colin
Music of my soul and light
Come Naschina thou my light
Thernet
↓ Stricken all the night is past
~~Colin~~
They approach one anoth while singing
with angry gestures

Lines 8 and 13 are relocated by crossed arrows in the left margin.

3 Yeats may have begun another letter after the word "to".

10–11 These lines are squeezed into the same lined space of the notebook. Line 10 appears to be added later, and Yeats may have intended to cancel l. 11.

1 enter Naschina
2 with her crook
3 [~~?Nas~~]
4 Naschina
5 ~~My~~
6 ~~Cease your mad singing~~
7 ~~my~~
~~with~~
8 ~~cease~~ ~~your mad singing~~
{g
9 you ~~send brain a spining with your~~ son{gs
10 ~~That grow in clamour with the light~~
11 Colin
12 ~~that grew~~
13 ~~That [?ger]~~
you
14 ~~That~~ grew in clamour louder [?and] more strong
15 Till all my brain was spining with your song
16 Colin
17 I fan had been the first of singing things
18 To welcome thee before the lumenous wings
19 Of shore ward sweeping waves had lost the glow

---

10 The cancellation mark curves downward in the right margin.
17 There may be an ''s'' at the end of ''singing''.

                                                                                                   {i
                                                                                                 w{ald
1 of ~~down~~ dawn [~~?whos~~] upon their wan ~~white~~
                                                                             wildering snow
2 But yonder thing ~~reed~~ yon broken reed yon srow
3 yon shepherd ([?pointing]
4 ~~would fain your~~ Thernet
5   ~~Came~~ ~~yo~~ Came your spirit to beguile
6 with singing sweet as ere on lake lulled isle
7 beat wave's winged feet but yonder shepherd vile
8 all clamour clothed
9   Colin
10   Was't clamour when I sung
11 whom men have called Arcadia sweetest tung
12 All mischiefs on the man who shall repeat
               word   might him
13 That ~~thus~~ for ~~low~~ I∧(cast ~~him~~ at my feet
14 ~~and give~~ his spirt to the [—?—] winds
15   Thernet
16   ~~wo~~ ~~[?you/?yon]~~ ~~[?arts]~~
17   (~~starting back~~)
18 Then [?I] ~~I repeat~~

1 The "ir" of "their" was added later.
14 The illegible word is cancelled by both a straight and a wavy line.

1 Colin
2 ~~[?Stay] all but you on yonder hill~~
3 ~~W[?] feed a [?young] flocks~~

4 ~~Nay all~~
~~Nay all but~~ [?you/?yon]
5 ~~st~~
6 ~~Colin~~ Thernet
7 [~~?stay ?stay~~]
8 ~~you will [?would] if~~ I
9 ~~Colin~~ [?on/?N]
10 if I should then
11 Colin
12 ~~Colin~~ I might
13 (horn is heard)
14 ~~A [?wandering] men~~
a horn go
15 some ~~A robber troup of wandering men~~
in [?] ~~green wood~~
16 ~~thru the forest deep with sword and~~ bow
17 So and spear
much Thernet
18 ∧O ~~sorely I fear me~~ wandering go

15–18 The placement of the corrections in the manuscript is confusing. The line numbering of the transcription follows the lined spaces of the notebook.

1 an arrow passes thru the air
2 Thernet
3 Robbers Robbers let us fly
4 (~~exit~~)
5 (exeunt Thernet and
6 Colin) →
7 (There gone) corageous miracles
8 Enter Almintor and Antonio
9 The [?sunlit] shown
10 ~~And [?showned] among~~ the
[?] ~~leafy~~ s
11 Upon his wings in yonder ~~gloom~~
green abys
12 I sent an arrow
13 Antonio
14 And I saw you miss
15 ~~This heron~~
16 And far away the heron ~~soar~~ soars I wis

---

7 "There gone" is relocated to the right margin by an arrow, probably to complete l. 3 metrically.
16 There may be a second "s" at the end of "wis".

~~C~~
Almintor
Nay for his fly days are don

---

winding
A horn some troup of robers ~~wandering~~
goes
near by with subtile tread tred and bended
bows
And swinging swords ~~fly~~ (an arrow passes)
fly
Thernet fly
—exeunt Thernet and Colin—
Naschina—So they are gone
Corageous miracles
(enter Almintor and Antonio)
Almintor
The sunlight shone
Upon his wings in yonder green abyss
I sent an arrow

Lines 4–15 of this page and ll. 1–6 of the next contain a revision of the previous page and a half.
6 The uncancelled "fly" is raised by an arrow to its proper place in the line.

Antonio
And I saw you miss
and far away the heron soars I wiss
a fluttering white star
{ys
Almintor nay nay his da{ys
is oer
of flight ~~are done~~
(seeing Naschina)
Most fair of all who graze
~~Yong sheep in many a southern facing~~ lair
~~Of all clear browed ar Arcadians fa~~ most fair
~~Naschina hail~~
~~Page~~
~~Naschina hail ([?mimics] Almintor)~~
[~~?No/?Na~~]
Naschina hail
There [?sheep] in in arcady ~~Nashina hail~~
~~Page (mimicking Almintor~~)
Naschina hail
Page
Most fair of all who graze
{ l
There sheep in arcady Naschina hai{ [?]

---

5 At the end of the line Yeats first wrote "days", then wrote a large "y" over the "ys", and finally added a new "s".

10 Yeats may have written "farr" for "fair".

Naschina hail
                    Almintor
                Yon southern facing vale
~~Thy sheep~~
    [?richly]
Will feed with dewy gras thy sheep
~~there~~ all night
~~For~~ ~~oer it~~ all ~~night~~ long the heavens weep
~~There all night long the lady of the deep~~
    [?oderous]
In ~~drowsy~~ silemce of there sleep
There all night long ~~thus~~ [~~?faintly~~] the moon
                                        the white
  pale
~~far~~ wild
~~sick~~ ∧lady of the deep pours down her light
There all night long the heaven is bent
Oer breezes heavy with the lylack sent
There all night long a fountain sings
        and
And crys fluttering wide its wan wild wings
and singes all day long to its own heart

    When dawn about her fling
                            {c
Singing her raiments {srimson glow

16–17 These two lines are relocated by a line which ends at the right margin of l. 8 but which is probably intended to indicate a replacement for the cancelled portion of ll. 5–7 on the facing page SB 23.2.221r.

You grew in clamour louder and more strong
Till all my brain was spining with your song
Colin
I fain had been the first of singing things
thee
To welcome / ~~when-dawn-with-whirly-wings~~
~~Sat ready to be gone upon the flow~~
idle
~~Of streams~~—But yonder thing, yon noise, yon crow
Yon shepherd
Thernet
Came your spirit to beguile
With singing sweet as er'e round lake lulled isle
Moan summer waves But yonder shepher vile
All clamour clothed
Colin
Was't clamour when I sung
Whom men have called arcadia s sweetes tongue
(the sound of a horn is heard)
A horn—some troup of robbers winding goes
Near by with subtile tred and bended bows

At this point Yeats began reworking SB 23.2.214ff. into more advanced form.

5–6 The cancellation of the latter part of l. 5 and all of l. 6 is done with repeated, linked diagonal lines in pencil; "Of streams" in l. 7 is cancelled separately. Lines 16–17 from the facing verso are probably intended for insertion here.

fly
an arrow passes
Thernet
fly
—exeunt Colin and Thernet—
Naschina
shepherds
So these braves both are gone
corageous miracles
{e
{Anter Almintor and ~~his~~ Antonio
talking togeath
Almintor
The sunlight shone
Upon his wings in yonder green abys
I sent and arrow
Antonio
And I saw you miss
[?and/?as] Far ~~aw~~ a way the heron soars in wis
~~Nay~~ ~~nay I didn't~~

17 The "and" or "as" was apparently added later in the margin.

1 Almintor
2 Nay, nay I did not miss his days
3 Of flight are done
4 (Seeing Naschina~~)~~ and bowing low)
5 Most fair of all who graze
6 There sheep in Arcady Naschina hail
7 Naschina hail
8 Antonio (mimick him)
9 Most fair of all who graze
10 There sheep in arcady Naschin hail
11 Naschina hail
12 Alminto
13 ~~O may I drive thy sheep~~
Ill drive thy wooly sheep
14 If so I may unto a dewy vale
~~silent~~ and weep
15 Where all night long the heaven weep
dreeming in there oder laden sleep
~~there [?] oder~~ ~~dewy~~
16 In oderous silence ~~of their sleep~~
lonly
17 Where all night long the moon the white
18 Sick lady of the dee{p / d} pours down her light
brooding
19 Where all night long the heaven is bent

1 Oer breazes heavy with the lylac sent
all flame like from hollow
2 ~~And there~~ high gushing ~~mong~~ the ~~mossy~~ stones
3 All day and night a lonly fountain sings
~~like some mysterious [?thing] with wide white [?wings]~~
4 ~~And cries and flutters wide its shuddering~~ wings
moans
5 And there to its own heart for ever ~~sings.~~
6 Naschin
7 I'd be alone
8 Almin
9 We two by that pale ~~found~~ fount
woe
10 Un mindful of its ~~grief~~ will twine a ~~crown~~ wreath
11 As fair as any that on Ida mount
12 Paris for Oenone made and down beneath
13 ~~The~~ shall brows thy gentle sheep
14 Naschina Be gone Be gone
{A
15 For all on whom {arcadean suns have shone
16 Are all alike a cowardly race Your love
17 to prove what can ye do what things above
bring
18 sheep guiding or the ~~shooting~~ some strange bird
19 or some ~~str~~ small beast most wonderfuly furd
sad
20 or^ ~~gathering~~ sea shells where little echo's sit

The tip of the arrow between ll. 1 and 2 indicates the placement of an insertion from the facing page SB 23.2.224v:

~~And mong the~~
And mong the stunted ashes drooping rings.

A line without an arrow may have misplaced the insertion at first.

4 The cancellation of the line "And cries . . ." is in pencil.

5 "own" is misspelled, but the exact letters are difficult to decipher.

9–13 These lines are marked by a vertical line and question mark on the facing page; the question mark is in pencil. Yeats may have placed an apostrophe between the "I" and "d" of "Ida".

15 "Arcadean" has an extra letter, which is difficult to decipher.

Such paltry quests me thinks [illegible] little worth

Antonio

And the great grey lynx [illegible] skin

Naschina

Indeed I think

that I myself could shoot a great grey lynx

with bow and arrow [illegible] well as you

[illegible] could colin. also do

Colin and Thernot [illegible]

Antonio is it so

Antonio

Antonio my name

(Naschina turns to go)

Stay, [illegible] sweet Naschina stay

Naschina

Your all the same

[illegible] of courage of the woodland folk

I'm weary [illegible] shall [illegible] and hunter toys

To prove his love a knight with lance in rest

with circle round the world upon a quest

Such paltry quests me thinks nead little wit
Antonio
And the great grey lynx~~s [?grey] lynx~~ skin
Naschina
{k
[~~?~~] [?Indeed] I thin{g
that I myself could shoot a great grey lynx
~~methink could Colin~~
with bow and arrow ~~and Co I and us~~ well as you
~~and~~ {C me think could Colin also do
~~Could~~ {~~colin and Thernet like wise~~ do
Antony ist so
Antonio
Antonio my name
(Naschina turn to go)
Almintor
~~quite~~ stay ~~stay f~~ sweet
~~Stay shepherdess~~ ^ Naschina stay
~~Antonio~~ Nasch
Your all the same
{q
hearts {suenched of courage by the woodland joys
shell
Im weary [?] your ~~hides~~ and hunter toys
To prove his love a knight with lance in rest
Will circle round the world upon a quest

On the otherwise blank facing page SB 23.2.226v the following two lines, which open Naschina's speech in later versions, appear opposite ll. 15 and 16 of the present page:

Hear where men know the graceous wood land joy
{J
{Toys brother fear dwells ever in each brest

Untill he ~~sou~~ [?found/?faced] a dragon shiny scaled
from morn ~~those~~ the twain until the evening palled
the
[~~?And~~] ~~war~~ or else he'd ~~search~~ seek enchanter
old
~~alone~~
who sat ~~alone~~ in lonly [?night/?might] all maled in gold
~~and they would fight in~~
~~in cavern deep and they would fight~~
And they would war ~~mong~~ mong wondrous [?elfin] sights
Such will I love the suddering forest lights
green do
Of ~~clear~~ Arcadia hide not a trow
t
Such [?] Not uncooth hunter [?]hou ~~wiss~~
art such (exit)
Antonio
And whither uncouth hunter now
Almintor
~~Ay~~ ~~whither boy~~ ~~ay ay~~ ay [?bo]
ay
Antonio
Lets see if that same Heron slid
dead
down or if you missed I know you did
exit Antonio Alminto following

---

15 Some of the letters are missing from the end of "Almintor".

18 The otherwise blank facing page (not included in the Stony Brook filming) has "~~Why not~~" written opposite this line.

~~Anoth~~
A forest Valley
followed by Antonio
enter Alminto ~~and Antonio~~
Antonio
And whither uncouth hunter [?now/?how] so fast
My strength all gone ay so you pau at last
Almintor
Here is the place the hill encircled wood
{a
here grow th{et shy retiring sisterhood
The pale enemonies we seached all day
and found
Antonio
'Tis well another mile of way
I could not go (they sit don)
Almin
Lets talk & Lets be sad
~~Here on the gras~~
here in the shade
Antonio
~~Y~~ Why Why

12 Several letters are missing from the end of the speaker tag, but it is difficult to determine them.

1 Almintor
2 For what is glad
the murmer of yon
3 For look you ~~look~~ you sads ~~the voice~~ ~~of laden~~
bees
The and
4 ~~And~~ wind goes sadly [~~?thr~~] the gras and trees
5 reply like moaning of enprisioned elf
6 The whole wolds sadly talking to its self
7 In yon far lake that is where points my hand
8 The waves lament there life out on the sand
9 ~~The bird~~
{t nestle
the birds {ahat ~~hover~~ in leaves
10 ~~deep bosomed in the leaves the birds~~ are sad
11 poor sad wood rasadists
12 ~~Antonio~~ Anto
13 Nay they are glad
14 Almintor
15 All wrapsedy hath sorrow for its soul
{i
16 Anton{eo
17 Yon lake that fills with song the whole
18 Of this wide ~~f~~ vale embossomed in the air
19 ~~What sorrow in his~~
is sorrow in his song or any care

10 There is a mark above the "ds" of the uncancelled "birds" that may be the start of another letter or else an apostrophe.

14–15 These two lines are written within the same ruled space of the notebook.

17 "lake" is probably an error for "lark"; Yeats may still have had l. 7 in mind.

bird yon
does not yon∧quivering bird rejoice
Almintor
I hear the whole sky sorrow in one voice
Antonio
~~Nay nay he's glad~~
Nay nay Almintor yonder bird is glad
Alminto
Tis beautifull and therefore it is sad
~~For gief and beaty wander on there way~~
~~And whisper in each others ear alway~~
Antonio
~~and and~~
have done this frasing and tell why in truth
Thou has Almintor grown so full of ruth
~~Almint~~
~~and why art~~ [?]
and wherefore have we come
~~and why are we now~~ here
Alminto ~~To here a song~~
A song to here
An
A song from whence
~~from whence~~ whom an [?when/?where]

8–9 These lines are cancelled in pencil, or possibly in black crayon.
19–20 These lines are crowded within the same ruled space of the notebook.

Almintor
Over the willows seer
Out of the air
Anton
and when
Almintor
yonder the
When ~~the [?patient]~~ sun goes slanting down
over the crown of the willows brown
~~Antonio~~
O boy Im bound upon a dangerous quest
you heard? upon
For so she willed ~~as you have heard~~. The brest
from of
Of yonder lake ~~upon~~ who's banks alway
The high trees gaze across the water grey
a
And nod to one another lies ~~an isle~~ small
~~And busky isle~~
green isle where neither leaf of blossom withered
fall
For there great enchantress lives
Antonio and there
There grows the goblin fower all her care

1 ~~O well I know that favrit shepherd~~ tale
by
2 ~~Which~~ many saught It is ~~an~~ a favrit tale
3 how all who saught were doomed to ever fale
4 Almintor
5 I seek the bloom ~~you never shall return~~
6 Antonio
7 You never will return
8 Almintor
9 I seek the bloom for her that I may earn
blowm
10 Her love to [?whowse] [?care] hath that comes truth
before
11 ^Unthought on and strange years of youth
a
12 Beyond [~~?old~~] mortal time
13 I wait the song
14 That calls
15 Antonio
16 O evil starred
17 Almintor
18 It comes along
19 The wind at evening when the sun goes down
20 over the crown of the willows brown

11 "before" is written partly in the left margin.

See yonde sinks the sun yonder a shade
Goes flickering in reverberated light
Yon yon do you not see
Antonio
I see the night
Slow footed gathering oer the empty glade
—a voice sing—
When the tree was oer appled
for mother eve s sinning
I was at her wining
oer the grass light endappled
~~I wander~~
~~oer the~~
I wandered and trod
Or the green eded sod
And I sang round the trees
As I sing now to the tree
Arise from the hollow
~~The green leafy hollow~~
and ~~ff~~ follow and follow

9–10 Arrows in the right margin indicate the interchange of "sinning" and "win[n]ing".
12–13 The wavy "X" within a circle at the right margin is in pencil.
12–14 The illegible diagonal word or phrase at the right is written and cancelled in pencil.

away great
an there in the ~~way of~~ pard~~ize~~ ise
As I wandered unesen
glad was her
~~Hope~~ ~~full~~ in mien
you
I saw her as now arize
Before her I trod
Oer the green eden trod
And I [?sang/?sung] round the tree
As I sing now to the
From the green hollow
Arise then and follow
—exit Almintor—
The voice sing dying away
And I [?sang/?sung] round the tree
As I sing now to the tree
green
~~arise~~ From the ~~grean~~ hollow
~~Arize thou and follow~~
come
Come follow me follow
[?Antonio]
~~A woe~~ a ~~A woe is me I never see him~~ more

that
Ill follow to border of ~~sullen~~ sea
Him never ~~never~~ mor no mor n more Ill I [?see]
exit

The owl has gone from where she flew
Flickering under the white moon shine
She sleeps with owlets three and two
~~Sleeping.~~
Sleepily are closed their dewy eyes
For the dawn the foliage fringeth
And the waves are leaping white
Thou alone O maiden lingerest
While the world is rolled in light

Echo

What art thou come croaked voice to mar
the morn
Near me and shepherd hears, we grow dumb
Woolly ~~sheep~~ flock all [illegible] meet
By the singing rivers edge
Tread and tread their cloven feet
By the ruddy river sedge
O [illegible] comes the light in Glendin[illegible]
Come then come and [illegible]
Though my love [illegible] is ruddy

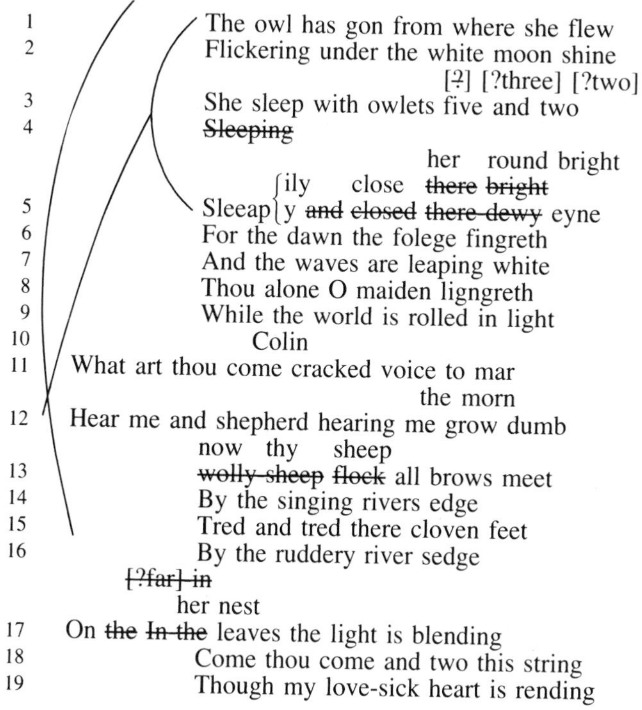

1 The owl has gon from where she flew
2 Flickering under the white moon shine
[?] [?three] [?two]
3 She sleep with owlets five and two
4 ~~Sleeping~~
her round bright
{ily close ~~there bright~~
5 Sleeap{y ~~and closed~~ ~~there dewy~~ eyne
6 For the dawn the folege fingreth
7 And the waves are leaping white
8 Thou alone O maiden ligngreth
9 While the world is rolled in light
10 Colin
11 What art thou come cracked voice to mar
the morn
12 Hear me and shepherd hearing me grow dumb
now thy sheep
13 ~~wolly sheep~~ ~~flock~~ all brows meet
14 By the singing rivers edge
15 Tred and tred there cloven feet
16 By the ruddery river sedge
~~[?far] in~~
her nest
17 On ~~the~~ ~~In the~~ leaves the light is blending
18 Come thou come and two this string
19 Though my love-sick heart is rending

Before progressing to scene 3 of act 1, Yeats devoted this and the following page to revising the singing match between Colin and Thernot at the start of scene 1. Although the vertical lines in the left margin lack pointed arrows, their intent seems to be to rearrange the lines on this page in the following order: ll. 13–16, 6–9, 10–12, 1–5, and 17–19. That rearrangement agrees with the final form of the passage.

3 The cancelled, illegible mark is probably a numeral, perhaps "3" or "5".

1 not a sad note will I sing

2 ———*I am not dumb I'd sooner in the fold*
3 ———*be dumb to here the creaking of*
the gate—

4 *sings*

{and [?~~to~~]{e
5 *[?] woodland {oer valley ~~oer~~ se{es*
6 *awaken awaken to new born lustre*
{t {o
7 *a new day {[?]roop of {[?]f wasp and bee*
[?rond]
8 *hang on the side of the ~~round~~ grape*
cluster

dull
9 *over head the ~~white~~ stars sicken*
10 *oer valley ore hill and ore sea*
11 *so doth the soul of the shepherd [?stricken]*
wearily
12 *in ~~[?wating] and~~ watch for the*

5 The final "e" of "see" is written over "es". Yeats may have written "vales" or "valey" for "valley".

Scene—The pallace of flower
pillared
far into the distance rech halls
and corrodor where the flower grow
of men
~~old~~ figures are standing ~~about~~
imovable to to the ground there
long beards reach through
the [?corridors] at times floats wandering
faery music
enter Almintor
me useless
Woes∧that ~~that~~ on a ~~bootless~~ quest I go
For how may I the sacked flower {now / [?]}
Among this flowery pomp a woe is me
~~Woe that I [?eer] have crossed the [?singing] sea~~
bot
that ere in fairy I crossed the sea
Woe sigh and
~~We~~ that I heard the ~~fairy~~ water ~~siging~~ sing
Beneath the fairy frigate fairy wing
For he who shall not find the sacred bloom
Shall neer return Why have I crossed the gloom
[~~?thy/?the~~] ~~harmonie~~
With that song {[?lea] / [?gui]ding} where ~~the~~ remotest woods

---

This page begins scene 3 of act 1; it moves directly from the opening stage direction to Almintor's entrance after l. 21 of the published text.

2 Yeats appears to have written one or more additional letters at the end of "into", perhaps repeating the "to".

nurish the sorrorw in dim
~~dwell in there sorrow and there~~ solitudes
vast greeness where eternel rumour dwells
And hath his home through many folded dells
I passed ~~th~~ by many cavern of dim stones
~~Where~~
And heard the viewless echoes on their thrones
[?] lone regenents of the wood deep muttering
[?then]
And new murmers came new utterings
[?song]
~~in~~ in from goblin waters swaying white
Who mock with patent laughter all the night
and then I saw the boad
Of that vast wood ~~ay woes is me that~~ eer
living wide winged upon the water's float
And sitting down between the living win{g / [?]s}
It ~~bo~~ ~~bore~~ bore me swiftly where the white sand ring
This lake embossomed isle—But how to find
is
The flower that ~~lies~~ so heavy to my mind
~~I have no signs—I will [?address] this weared~~
~~Who standeth here—O thou who's~~ beard
exit and then
again Enter

14 Letters are missing in "where" and "white", but it is difficult to determine which.

1 O where to seek I will adress this weard
2 old man who standeth
3 —O thou whos beard
4 Like a river of moon light sweeps the ground
enchanted
5 Where is the ~~fairy~~ flower to be found
6 For all these thousand thousands are as one
7 And fairer that the others [?then/?there] is none—
8 No answer (goes over and touch the old man)
~~th~~
9 ~~As ^ these~~ he is
10 ~~as [?a ?stone]~~ as the others he is cold
11 congealed to stone because in heart [?ore/?are] bold
12 long centuries ago he saught the sacred bloom
13 And with all others found an equall doom
risketh all in chance
14 such may I find who ~~must the hazard choose~~
15 ~~For there is no return~~
16 All shepherd gods but chiefly pan down glance
17 From thy deep withered brow and guard me now
18 (He ~~picks~~ pulls a flower and [?immediately]
19 becomes stone

1 The faught and then the deep [?earth]
2 gathered them
3 ~~each one a taper or unbafled~~ stars
shining clear {s some
4 each ~~fairy flower~~ a{n unbafleed star
5 and ~~bright petaled is as~~ some
6 ~~unbafleed~~ star

4 "ground", like "found" in the next line, may lack an "n".
6 Yeats apparently started to form another letter at the end of "For" and then stopped.

SB 23.2.242v is on the verso of a torn and otherwise blank leaf and faces ll. 3–7 of the following recto in the notebook.

red
green and gold and
1 The evening gleams are ~~g[?]~~
Upon white stars
2 ~~Above~~ the lake [?when/?where] flickering ~~stars~~ tread
are
3 Flowers an hundred thousand round me ~~flow~~
~~A blinding sea of ever [?burning] [?shining] *glow*~~
4 In ~~one vast sea of ever shining~~ show
5 The skies more dim thou burning like a shild
6 of gold above these men whose lips wer seald
7 Full long ago and into stone congealed
It is a wonder deep how man
8 And O the wonder ~~of the thing~~, each came
sank down
low the sun ~~the~~ sun
9 When ~~slanted down~~ ~~eac~~ in clotted flame
10 ~~beyond the trees~~
11 beyond the the lake ~~the lake~~ who smallest wave
[?with] burdened
rolling trees
12 With ~~crimson~~ fire beyond the high ~~bur~~ turbaned
~~clinging~~ ~~par [?]~~ s[?]
13 with ~~rolling~~^mist each ill starred wandere cam
just when the sun beams wane
14 As I to chose ~~the flower of his bane~~
15 Chose rong and so was stone as I unless
{s
16 {come god pro[?] ~~how long in [?such] str[?]~~
in this green wilderness
17 how ~~long have I in this green~~ wilderness
among the flower meny
18 ~~gone to and fro~~ how ~~men~~ men have I
19 called to here where the pilgrim wavelets ply
20 About the isle [?shining] in each man veins

9 A mark which may represent a "g", a "y", or a comma appears at the end of "slanted".

1 was life to find for all my calling games
2 another man of stone as I shall be
3 Unless some [?pitying] god shall succor me
4 In this my choice (stops as If to plu a
5 flow [?put] s[?] again)
6 Some god migh help if so
7 Twere better that aside I throw
8 all choice and give to chance for guiding chance
9 ~~come~~ some cast of die or let some arrow
glance
{b
10 For guiding of the gods The sacred {gloom
thru the purple
11 ~~To seek not hopeless have I saught the gloom~~
crossed
12 To seek not hopeless have I ~~saught~~ the gloom
13 With that song guiding where harmonic woods
the panthers in dim
14 Nourish ~~dim sorrows~~ ~~in their~~ solitudes
15 Vast greeness where Eternal rumour dwells
by
16 and hath his home, ~~through~~ many folded dells
17 I passed by many caverns of dim stones
unseen
18 and heard the [~~?viewless~~] Echos on their [~~?stones~~]
Thrones

On the otherwise blank facing verso the phrase "each one around is stone" appears opposite l. 2.
18 "their" is misspelled, but the last three letters are difficult to determine.

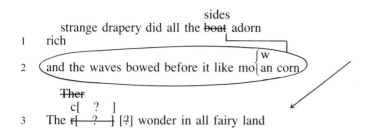

sides
strange drapery did all the ~~boat~~ adorn
rich

w
and the waves bowed before it like mo{an corn

~~Ther~~
c[?]
The ~~r[?]~~ [?] wonder in all fairy land

This verso contains insertions for the facing recto SB 23.2.247r.

2 This line is opposite l. 7 of the facing page, where the couplet of ll. 1–2 on the present page will go in future versions. The arrow indicates that l. 3 on the present page will then follow.

lone regents of the wood deep muttering
and then new murmer came new utterring
In song from goblin waters swaing white
mocking with patient laughter all the night
boat
Of those vast woods and then I saw the ~~bo~~
living wide winged upon the water float
[?~~buoyed~~]
~~borne on the foam as in a silver hand~~
and sitting down between each living wing
It bore me softly where the shallow sand
bind as within a gurdle or a a ring
Nay this my quest
The lake Imbossomed isle ~~Nay not beguiled~~
shall not so hopeless prove some god may rest
Upon the wind and guide mine arrows course
From yonder pinnacle above the lake
Ill seend mine arrow now my last [?resource]
~~The neere~~
and where It falls I will the nearest flower take
(he goes out fitting and arrow to his bow)

---

3 Yeats may have omitted either the "b" or the "l" from "goblin".

5 Yeats cancelled the first two letters of "boat" because he ran out of space at the right margin and then wrote the entire word above and slightly to the left of the cancellation.

7 See the previous page for insertions at this point.

13 There may be another letter at the end of "mine".

1 A voice
2 Ficklle the guiding his arrow shall find
3 Some ~~spi~~ goblin my servent on wings that
are fleet
4 That nestles alone in the whistling wind

go {his
5 ~~Shall~~ pillot the course of {[?this] arrow descet
6 [~~?raise~~]
where the winds oer
7 ~~rouse~~ from ~~the~~ lake ~~that is~~ dapple
rouse rouse
8 ~~with breeze~~ [?guiles] in [~~?thy~~] soul still dwell
9 As ~~the~~ wasps on the side of the apple
or
10 ~~As~~ the echo's that [?burrow] in a shell
11 (The arrow falls)
12 Enter Almintor
the arrow
13 Tis here ~~it~~ fell the breezes laughed
{p
14 Around the fethery ti{[?] unto the shaft
statue
15 This flower is most near ~~old~~ O thou
a
16 Who's beard moonligt river is who's brow
17 is stone old sleeper this same after noon
18 [?Oer] [?Much] Ive talked I shall be silent soon

7–10 In addition to individual cancellations, the entire passage is cancelled with an "X". The separate cancellations of "the" in ll. 7 and 9, and of "[?thy]" in l. 8, look more like dark squares than individual lines.
17 Yeats may have written "sleepor" for "sleeper".

1 If rong my choice as silent as thou art
2 (in a louder voice)
3 All shepherd gods but chiefl pan my part
4 Now take and guard lest evil chance or guile
5 Should me enchant congealed to [?] stone
6 Echo stone
7 Almintor
8 Peace Eho art thou echo or some lone
9 propetic voiced familiar of the isle
10 chooses and is changed to stone
11 a voice sings
12 Now spred the fickle wing of life
13 And flee the mansion of the strife
love and ~~take~~ and go
14 Now take up the staff ~~of love~~
the way of thy wanderings [?no] men know
15 ~~What man may tell of thy feet that~~ rove
{O
16 Now spred thy fickle wings {of life
[?short/?show] the senses of thy strife
17 ~~The world with living men is rife~~
18 ~~And now take up thy staff o love~~
now
19 ~~And~~ love take now thy staff and go
20 Thou art a figure made of snow

14 Yeats may have written something in the left margin, and he may also have written "thy" for "the".
16 Yeats probably wrote "O" over "of", but the order is difficult to determine.

far {a
Come forth The morn {is from the pyre
{D {ne
Of sad queen {dido sho{[?wn] the lapping fire
unto the [?wanderers/?wandering] ships or as day fills
The brazen sky, so burn the dafadils
from
As when ~~upon~~ ~~high~~ on the cloud
oer muffled peek
Enone saw the fires of [?troia] [?leap]
so
And laughed [~~?~~] [?] so along the [?parly] rills
In lemon tinted lines So burn the daffodils
As argive [?Clytemnestra] saw out burn
flagrunt
The ~~flagrunt~~ signal of her lords return
~~is~~
~~[?A] [?fiery] heralds up~~
Clear [?shine] s[?] on the herald hills
In vale and dell so burn the dafodills

Of all fair things my music [?flows/?pours] for thee
a quenchless grieving of love melody

Before proceeding to act 2, Yeats composed this page; except for the last two lines (which are present in earlier form on SB 23.2.207r) it contains the earliest surviving draft of what became Colin's opening speech in the first scene. An arrow in the left margin relocates ll. 5–8 after ll. 9–13.

1 Act 2—
2 ~~A~~ The wood
Naschina
3 Enter ~~Almintor~~ and Antonio
4 Naschina
5 ~~And I wil~~
6 And In a shepherd's dress Ill seek
and seek
7 Untill I find him ~~out~~ What a weary weak
8 My ~~pretty child~~ since he was gon tas been
9 Tell oer again how unto you was seen
10 his passage oer the lake
11 Antonio
12 When we two came
13 From out the wood Then like a silver flame
doloures
14 We saw the ~~goblin~~ lake and near at hand
prow
15 A boats ~~keel~~ gratted on the shallow sand
then [~~?~~] twice
16 ~~And~~ loudly ~~then~~ the living wing flapt wide
17 And leaping to their feet the chos cried
each other answering and
18 ~~up standing on their throne~~s between each wing
white
19 he [~~?slat~~] sat and then I heard the ~~sad~~ lake sing
20 beneath the prow and then as some wild drake

---

17 Yeats apparently wrote "a" after the "e" in "their" but then dotted it. He presumably intended "chos" to be "echoes".

half lit so flapped the wing across the lake
~~And leeping to ther feet the Echos~~ cried
~~Up standing on the thrones where always~~ they abide
~~called~~
~~And cried to one another oere the whistling tide~~
But see I make you sadder shepherdess
Nasch
old
Nay grief in feeding on ~~fresh~~ grief grows less
Antonio
grief needs much feeding then Of him Ill swear
a deel we've said and not a whit more rare
Do come your weeping fits
~~Naschina farewell Ill done~~
~~My travelling dress and then return anon~~
look you so straight
{i
{as the mansion of the kingfisher and deep
No other bird may enter ~~in~~ there
Antonio
Well
Naschina —Late
very late grave sorrow came to weep

Lines 2–4 are cancelled individually with a wavy horizontal line in pencil. Lines 3–4 are a revision of ll. 17–18 on the previous page.

9 "swear" is misspelled, but the exact letters are difficult to decipher.

and naught but
~~more of~~
within my heart ~~no other~~ sorrow now
can enter ~~thear~~ there
Almintor
See or yon tangled brow
of hill two shepherds come
Naschina
Farewell Ill done
shepherd cloak
my ~~travelling~~ ~~dress~~ and then return anon
Exit
Enter Colin and Thernet
Thernet
Two men [?ho] who love one maid
Hav have ample cause ~~of~~
Of war Of yore two shephers where we pause
Faught once fore self sam reason on the hem
Of the wide woods
Colin
And the deep earth gathered them
~~We mu~~

The wavy marks through ll. 2–4 are rubbings from the pencil cancellations on the facing verso and not cancellations for this page.

12 Yeats reached the margin with ''maid'' and then wrote ''Hav'' at the left of the next line before moving to the right to complete l. 12.

17 Yeats salvaged this line from the projected insertion to act 1, scene 3 on SB 23.2.242v.

1 Thernet
2 ~~We must~~ ~~sw~~ we must get swords
3 Colin
4 ist only way—O see
5 is yon the hunter Sir Almintor s page
6 Let him between us judge for he can gage
7 And measure out the ways of Chivalry
8 Thernet
9 Sir page Almìntor's friend and There fore learned
in
10 Such like things we humbly pray the lend
rs
11 Thine ea{ [?] and judge
12 Antonio
my popinjay
[?wel] ~~feather~~ head
13 well ~~grashopper~~ what ~~ist~~ now
14 Colin ~~Thernet~~ Must we two fight
15 These things we ask judge thou
16 each came one morn with welcoming of song
17 ~~And found the other there~~
~~together to~~ where nod the long
[?met] ~~unto~~ her door for [?the/?this] ~~where~~
18 ~~each~~ ~~came and~~ met ~~and then not after long~~
19 ~~each [?ode] of have treasured for himself alone~~
20 ~~And for his [?lonly/?lowly] joy a peble stone~~
~~on~~ in
21 o ~~which her [?sandels] of the morn first trod~~

9 The letters of the last word have been crowded together at the right margin of the page and are not wholly distinct; "ne" may be missing altogether.

14–15 These two lines are crowded within the same ruled space of the notebook; l. 14 may have been added later.

~~same~~
same thing
and these ~~things~~
~~For these^ down where the long waves nod~~
within the wood [?nigh] ~~as~~ wave
~~unto the shore fain had we faught but the~~ waves [?bringing]
The ~~brown weed burden so the sword~~ brings fear
To us
~~Ther~~
and shoor ward waves nigh had we faught
waves bring
The brown weed burden so the sword brings fear
To us
Thernet
Tell us for wise thou art in such like thing
being Almintor s page judge for you hear
~~We love one maid for this~~ our
We love Naschina both
~~Colin~~ Antonio
Whom loves she best
~~Thernet~~ Colin
cares
She [~~?eaves~~] no whit for either but hath blest
Another with her love

---

1 Some letters in the "these" to the left of the caret are overwritten, but they are difficult to decipher. Yeats's pen apparently ran out of ink as he was writing the uncancelled "same".

2 "wood" lacks either an "o" or a "d".

7 One or more letters may be missing in "brings".

Enter Naschina disguised as a shepherd
Colin
~~strange to this place~~
~~here coometh one that is~~ Whom art thou speek
As the see furrows on a sea tost shell
Sad histories are lettered on thy cheek
(Naschina seems embarresed)
Antonio
Tis who loveth well
~~It is~~ the shepherd Guarimond ~~who loves to dwell~~
centers
In the deep ~~eitidals~~ of the secret woods
hords
Old∧miser ~~stores~~ of grief to tell and tell
Young Guarimond he tells them oer and oer
by
To see them drowned ~~in~~ those vast solitudes
With their unhuman ~~grief~~ sorrows
Naschina
Cease no more (of this)
agile
↓Thou hast an ~~nimble~~ tongue
Colin
Thy grief
What is it friend?
Antonio

7 The parenthetical stage direction is squeezed into the same ruled space of the notebook as the speaker tag.
10 Nothing is written above the caret after "Old".
16 The "n" on "an" is very small and apparently was added to the "a" when Yeats changed the following "nimble" to "agile".

He lost the favourit chi{ e / [?]f }
and only sheep he loved of all his flock
Colin
Than [?thy/?this] grief shepherd greater is the stock
of mine I like you and I know not why
{ s / [?] }o will you ju{ d / nge } must Thernet yon and I
fight for this thing we love one maid
Naschina
Her name
Colin
Naschina tis
Naschina
I know her well a lame
dull witted thing with face red squirrel brown
Antonio
A long [~~?brom~~] brown grashopper of maids
Naschina
~~page~~
peace ~~sir~~ *sir*
Thernet
Tis clear that you have seen her not—The crown

15 "Antonio" may be misspelled.
18 The cancellation marks and new words "page" and "sir" are in blue crayon or pencil.

Of flickering sunlight round yon lonly fir
Is not so fair or joyous as she is
Naschina
{ye
~~No~~ There is no way but that {we fight I wis
If <u>her</u> ye love
Thernet
Aye ~~Yes~~ Colin we must fight
Colin
aye
~~Yes~~ we must fight
Antonio and Naschina are going
Tell me Antonio might
The get them swords and both or either fall
Antonio
No no when that shall be then men may call
that
Unto their feet the stars ~~at~~ sit alone
whirling
each one at gaze up his ~~circling~~ thron

And boy saw you when through the forest we
~~we two ca~~
two came His name and mine on many a tree
Carved here beyond the lakes slow muffled tred
In sand our name's are also to be read

The line across the page before ll. 17–20 indicates the end of scene 1 and that those lines should come after the relocated final couplet on the facing page SB 23.2.259r.

7 In both ll. 7 and 9 the cancellation line through the opening "yes" and the new word "aye" are in blue crayon or pencil.

15 The crossing of the "t"s makes "that" appear to be cancelled.

16 "at" may be "a" and a cancelled beginning of another letter.

Another part of the wood
Through knotted and twisted trees
under
The lake is seen shining ~~in~~ the
red evening
Enter Naschina and Antonio
Antonio
Behold how like a ~~fl~~ flet of fiery bees
The light is dancing oer the knotted trees
In busy flakes reshining from the lake
the
Through this night vested place red beems brake
Naschina
From the deep earth unto the wrinked sky
All thing lie quiet in the eaves wind eye
Antonio
Yonders the sacred Isle for which we came
The a sheet of
∧~~th~~ white wave wrap it in ~~this silver~~ flame
Naschin
The air is still above and still each leaf
some (clenched)
As ~~is a he~~ soul in [~~?forced~~] and tearless grief

2 The "ed" of "knotted" appears to have been added later, and a "t" may be missing.
10 "Through" is misspelled, but the exact letters are difficult to determine.
15 The first letter of "Yonders" is so badly formed that it almost resembles a "W".
18–19 These two lines are circled and relocated with an arrow to follow l. 14. The last four lines on the preceding page would in turn follow them. The new order agrees with the final version.

And yon a hudling blacknes draweth nigh
blinding
Tis that strange boat against the ~~bly~~ sky
Naschine Naschina
Boy antonio if I die full soon
As if I find him not I shall—This boon
Then grant Tis very very quiet hear
So bid them carry me to this quite near
When I am dead to bury me and build
near to me
A white stone statue ~~over me~~ and guild
It not and cut no name when I am dead
crown
And put no blossom ~~wreat~~ around the head
A white lone thing of sorrow let it stand
between the dead lake and the dead lake sand
Antonio
{e
The boat I almost hear—you he{ad me not

Lines 3–15 are cancelled by an "X" of which the bottom right section consists of two wavy lines; an additional diagonal cancellation line extends from "Naschina" in l. 3 to just before "Tis" in l. 6.

2 The new word "blinding" and the cancellation mark through "bly" are in blue crayon or pencil.

10 Yeats may have written "deed" for "dead" at the end of the line.

1 Antonio Boy If I return no more
{ id
2 Then b{ [?uild] them raise my statue on the shore
{r
3 Hear where the {sound waves come hear let them build
it
4 ~~Hear~~ facing to the sea and no name guild
{A dumb
5 {a white ~~lone~~ thing of tears here let it stand
lonly {the
—Between the forest and {[?] sand
6 ~~Between the dead lake and the dead lake sand~~
7 Antonio
here
8 The boat is almost ~~hear~~, you heed me not
9 Naschina
let to
10 And when the summers deep ~~unto~~ this spot
{T
{the arcadeans
11 Let ~~maiden~~ come and let the stone be raised
12 As I am standing now as thou I gazed
thus in marble white
13 —One hand brow shading—far into the night
14 And one arm pointing—let the stone be white—
15 And once a year let the arcadeans come
16 And neath it sit and of the woven sum
{re
17 Of human grief he {ar let them moralize
18 And let them tell sad histries till their eyes
19 Are dim with tears

2 The "o" of "shore" is written over another letter.

4–6 These lines may be deleted by a single diagonal blue crayon or pencil stroke.

8 Yeats may have written "head" for "heed".

13 The phrase "thus in marble white" is written in purple ink.

18 "And" may be written over the start of another word, and "their" may be misspelled.

n
1 Antonio (poi{ [?]ting

a
2 ~~You must be gon~~ the faery boats { [?]t hand
3 You must be gone the rolling grans of sand
4 Are neath its prow and crushing shells
5 Naschina (going)
6 And let the tale be dolouros each one tells
7 (exit)

k
8 Far through the mist the boat and maiden sin{ g
down [?there] [?on] ~~blue~~ cold
9 ~~Upon~~ the flickering lake the ~~cold~~ stars blink
(and red)
10 In quires of green and gold and blue
quivering
11 pearcing the water through and through
[?the] ther [~~?your~~]
12 ~~The~~ sentenals of night who keep ~~the~~ watch
13 oer grief I drink new sorrow from the beems
their cold (starting)
14 Of ~~your~~ ~~pale~~ eyes—where yonder lylac blotch
d l
15 Above the e{ gge and pulsing water g{ reams
re mayhap som mirth
16 Once mo{ or those shepherds come, ~~some~~
I f
17 { lll have O absant one tis not { Ior dirth
say
18 Of grief—and if they Antonio laught

11 There may be an "s" at the end of "water".
13 "oer" may be either "ore" or "on".

Say then "a popinjay before griefs shaft
Pierced through"
a voice from without Antonio
enter
Colin and Thernet
Thernet
we have resolved to fight
Colin
anon to fight
~~Thernet~~
Antonio
O wonderful
{ T
{ [?]hernet
And we have swords
~~Colin~~
Antonio
O night
Of wonders, ~~eve~~ eve of prodagies
Colin
draw draw

Antonio (pointing at Thernet)
He'll
~~He [?strives]~~ to break his sword
Colin (drawing his sword)
raised is the lions paw
Colin and Thernet fight—
Antonio
Ceese Thernets wounded cease They will not heed
~~How fearce they~~ are
fearce thrust—a tardy blossom hath the seed
but heavy fruit How swift the argument
—crash swords— ~~well [?foiled]~~
Of those steely tongues Well thrust well ~~sent~~ bent
Aside
~~A bur~~
(A distant Burst of music) ~~crosses~~
~~the lake~~
This music told Almintor end
And of
~~It~~ Naschina's now it tells rend rend
her with rushing
O heart—~~The~~ dirge ~~The derge~~ ~~In~~ ~~their white~~ arms the waves
Cast on the sound on on—This night of graves
r
—The spinning stars—The toiling sea—whi{ [?]ls round

---

1 "pointing at Thernet" is underlined (or perhaps crossed out) in blue crayon or pencil.

~~peace~~
sinking —~~still~~ cease—ceas
1 My ~~dazled~~ brain—~~still~~ [~~?sink~~] ~~swords~~
heard ye yon sound
cease ceas
2 The dirge of her ye love ~~your dumb~~ again
3 (the music's burst is echoed)
4 The echos fling upon my weary brain

The labour and the cadence of their pain
5 ~~The sound pouring down there cadent pain~~
6 exit
7 (The scen closes on Thernet and
8 Colin still fighting)

3–4 These two lines are squeezed into the same ruled space of the notebook.

Scene—
Island
The ~~pallace~~ of flowers
Far into the distance reach shadowey
ways burdened with the fairy
flowers — ~~old men [?stand]~~
{ b
{ [?]earded figures of stone are seen
them
[?among] ~~flower~~ There also is
{A
the statue that once was {almintor
over all in the distance ~~is a blue~~
[?faltering]
~~evening~~ ~~sky flecked with a few ^ stars~~

---

tinctured
a citron ~~coloured~~ sky where [?falter]
a few stars—
Enter Naschina disguised as a shepherd
And the enchantres the fameliar of the
Isle
The enchantress
O youth
By this my vine hung staff I s[?]
{or
I pity thee return again f{ar fair
And ~~very~~ yong thou art and where fore I

The first four pages of this version of scene 3 differ so substantially from the final version that correlation by line numbers is not feasible.

whove pited none so pity thee I know not why
save that wour yong and by my staff I sware
~~yo~~
My staff with Ivy bound that you are fair
~~Antonio~~ *Naschina*
Where is the flower lady
Enchantress If I tell
I die by old decree Nay seek it not
Sit here—~~a graceous s~~
The shade is graceous in this spot
and I will tell thee old world fairy tales
~~Wh~~ About the sorrows of the nighting gales
~~What is [?] it dwells withing this ruddy~~ shell
~~Held~~ [?]
~~There~~ ~~are~~ with*in* the portal of this shell
Naschina
The phantoms of dead waves
Enchantress
~~then~~
and ~~and~~ I will tell
There pent up secrets and why they toil

But if ~~where~~ I show where is the fairy flower

---

7 At least one letter may be missing at the end of "Enchantress".

12 This line has a horizontal line above it that curls downward in the right margin, the intent of which is unclear. The horizontal line that begins below l. 12 and extends down the left margin is in pencil.

13 The line beginning "There are" is crowded into the same ruled space of the notebook as l. 14.

16 "Enchantress" is misspelled, but the exact letters are difficult to decipher.

And it be pulled Then by the sacred coil
                    u   the self same
Of the slow sea snake { apon ~~that very~~ hour
I ~~must~~ die
                    Naschina
                    ~~I cannot~~
          Then wake the sleepers from their sleep
Of stone
                    Enchantress
          No No I cannot for they keep
Seeled hearts untill some mortal touch ther lips
With that strange flower [?thou] light as some bee sips
                    wake
~~that wake~~ They'll ^ and some will murmer of old loves
          comrades
          ~~armies~~
and some of ~~comrades~~ now for ages dust
Seek yon O youth within these shining groves
Some comrade dear and sad whom find you must
Or die   What is love for breathing fairy breath
I know love not at all I have heard say
                    of change and
It is a whispering thing ~~the friend of~~ death
     The [?clinging] friend give oer quest [?]
~~What [?]~~ ~~The unknon one~~ ~~forget thy~~ ~~friend~~ yet stay
Upon this isle forget thy hopes and fears
Forget the world and its [~~—?—~~] embattled years

---

6 The "lee" of "sleepers" is written over something else.
7–8 These lines are squeezed into the same ruled space of the notebook.
12 Yeats omitted either the "e" or the "r" at the end of "murmer".

1 ~~Here come the winds from where they~~ rent
2 ~~upon the far off hills thir honeyed scent~~
3 ~~and here the writhing wave is [?still]~~
4 Here all sweet odours by the winds are brought
these
5 ~~Winds~~ gentle as the moth like wings of [?thought]
are
6 And here the writhing waves is still~~ed~~ and calm
7 In sleep each burdenened oer with poppy balm
and
8 And hope ~~or~~ memery grown still as these
{a
9 Scarce stir or trouble by these shuddering se{es
10 ~~Almintor~~ Naschin
11 I choose the sacred flower (by chance)
12 ~~Naschina~~
s
13 Enchantres ~~stay~~ stay
~~unto~~
14 not there ~~with eyes upon~~ the ~~burning~~ way
15 But yon a pillar tall and grey
16 rears high its lenght and hanging ~~fo~~ from its head
17 There is a flower like a ruby red
18 and laping flame see shepherd I have told
~~wer~~ worlds
19 yet take it not [?than/?thou] all the wide ~~wold~~ gold
20 Be not its worth—your silent and quite still

---

6 The small "s" at the end of "waves" appears to be added later, probably when "is" was changed to "are" but left uncancelled.
11 "by chance" is circled and relocated to the beginning of the line.

~~Ay~~
Be not so silent—woe is me you will
take it and when the busy wings are furld
there
Of [?fairies] [?they] are dead indeed ~~ther~~ ~~our~~ life
is a little dreem reard up within a world
Of sleep tis pleasent here the wave have strife
{ t
And toil about us shepherd sit { [?]hou here
and the ill give my ivy staff the fear
O goblin all and I will bring the fruits
[?hidden]
far nurishéd about the [~~?sheltering~~] ruits
in [?and]
~~of~~ the deep wood ~~a~~ ~~full~~ many a wide eyed band
Of the pied tiger [?kittens] from thy hand
[?touch] crown
will I make feed but ah you ~~reach~~ the brown
of the *my*
high pillar thus upon knees [?] down
I kneel to the O let me live on still
~~For~~ I I know not what death is for Ive seen fill
The round of months and seen the summers fling
thou
There scents two ~~hundred~~ years An evil thing
It is I only know—your eyes are wet
my
Ay you will spare to me poor life yet

The page following this one is torn out of the notebook; no writing remains on the stub.
5 "is" may have been added later.

1 a~~n~~ moment stay
2 Naschina
3 Blood from the snapt [?stem] drips
4 Enchantress
5 I fade (dies)
6 Naschin
7 blue pallor creeps acros her lips
8 And dwells upon her cheek so round and full
9 Cruel her life her death most pity full
[?]
(1 s[~~—?—~~] s[?])
10 (To Almintor)
11 Almintor wake for light as some be sips
12 The ~~sta~~ sacred flower lies upon thy lips
13 Almintor (wakes)
shook
14 an hour long nap—twas—warm scarce cirling ~~shook~~
15 The falling hawthorn bloom
16 Naschin
17 knowest thou me look
18 (~~[?start/?spirit] [?song]~~ (far [?song])
19 [?proceeds]
20 Naschin and Almintor stand apart
21 Whispering [?during] the song

7 There may be a "u" in "pallor".
8 Either the "u" or the "n" is missing in "round".
15 Yeats may have written "hawhorn" for "hawthorn".
Lines 20–21 are crowded together at the bottom of the page.

Naschina
Sea farer wake for lit as some bee sips
The sacred flower lies upon thy lips
(1 Sleeper wakes)
Have I slept long
Naschina
long year
T awaked Sleeper
With hungry heart ~~doth~~
doth still the wanderer rove with his ships
I saw him from sad dido s shore depart
Enamoured of the waves impetuous lips
Naschina
These twain are dust
—wake light as a bee sips
The sacred flower lies upon thy lips
Wake sleeper wake

This page is the recto of the last leaf in the notebook. The previous, facing page SB 23.2.272^{v}, all in pencil, contains a sketch of a head, a large black square, and possibly a heavily cancelled and now illegible insertion for SB 23.2.273^{r}.

6 Here and in l. 13 Naschina's name is not spelled out fully.

1 —2 sleeper awaking—
2 was my sleep long
3 Naschina ~~yea~~
[~~?full~~]
4 ~~years~~ long years
5 Sleeper
6 a [?] rover I who comes from where mens ears
new {r
7 love storm and stained with mist the ~~red~~ moons flai{rs
8 doth still the man who*m* each stern rover fears
9 The autere arthur rule from Uther's chair
10 Naschina
11 He is long dust—wake light as some bee sips
12 The sacred flower lies upon thy lips
13 3—Sleeper—
~~Was my~~
14 ~~I Have I long slept o youth~~
15 Was my sleep long o youth
16 Naschina long long and deep
17 Sleeper
18 Youth as I came I saw god pan he played
19 And [?othen] pipe unto a ~~litt~~ listning fawn

The two loose leaves consisting of this page and the next three continue act 3, scene 2 from the end of the notebook and provide an alternate title page and cast of characters. 23.2.204 and 203 are opposite sides of the same leaf, as are 23.2.202 and 201.

7 The "s" of "moons" appears to have been added later, probably at the time that Yeats changed "flairs" to "flair".

8 The "m" at the end of "whom" was added later in pencil.

1 eyes to unused would weep
2 he [?] dwell [?witin] the forest shade
~~populace~~ shadows the
3 and rule the ~~people~~ ~~shadows~~ of ~~the~~ eve and dawn
4 Naschina
5 long dust he is—wake light as some bee sips
6 The sacred flower lies upon thy lips
7 Sleeper awake
8 Sleeper ([?awaking/?awakes])
{ h
9 {[?]ow long my sleep
10 Naschina
11 unnumbered
12 Are the years of fairy sleep
13 Sleepe
14 While I slumbered
15 How In Troea passed the years away
{th still
16 Do{st It^hold the Achaean host at bay
walls
17 Where rise those ~~towers~~ ~~above~~ magestical above
18 The windy plaines a fair haired maid I love

The missing parts of ll. 1–2 have been torn away, but enough remains to suggest that the missing word between "to" and "unused" in l. 1 is probably "grief". Not enough remains of the word immediately before "eyes" to be deciphered.

4 "Naschina" may lack the final "a" here and may lack one or more letters at the end of l. 10.

dust
eeper Woe's me
1 Sleepe
Be thou our king o youth
Naschina
~~Nay long beard~~ see
let thy king bee
Yon archer he who hath the halycons wing
High fixéd like a [?glad] [?thought] on his crest
—all the awakend sleepers to Almintor
Clear browed Arcadian thou shalt be our king
Naschina
~~Almintor love full werthy was thy quest~~
O my Almintor werthy was thy quest
Sleepers
Clear browed arcadian though shall be
our king.

The top left corner of the page is torn away, and with it part of the first two lines of text, presumably including an "Sl" before "eeper" in l. 2.

16 There is a red checkmark passing through "shall be" and "king"; its intent is unclear.

~~Na~~
Naschina
A drama of Archady

Characters

Naschina	—	a shepherdess—
Colin	—	shepherds—
Thernet	—	
Almintor	—	a hunter—
Antonio	—	a little boy—

Scene—Archadia

From the shade vested hollow
arise thou and follow
(1)
one on the island dies
and soon where the white waves call
on poplar
~~neath~~ the sands away neath the ~~willo~~ grey
two with the blue blade fall
~~But~~ a man has a hoped for heaven
~~But~~ soulles a spirit dies
as a leaf that is old and withered and cold
When the wintry vapours rise
2
Son shall our wings be stilld
and the tale of our laugher done
So let us dance where the [?flamy/?flaming] lance
of the barley shoots in the sun
S let us dance on the fringed waves
wisest
and shout at the ~~dreaming~~ owls
in their downy caps and startl the naps
of the dreaming water fowls

This page is the inside back cover of the notebook. The first two lines belong to the song at the end of act 1, scene 2; the remainder is a draft of the song at the death of the Enchantress in act 2, scene 3, separately published as "Song of the Faeries."

and fight for the back sloe [?berry/?berries]
for soulles a spirit dies
as a leaf that is old and [?withered] and cold
when the wintry vapours rise

These four lines form the last stanza of the song on the preceding page of transcription and are found at the bottom of the last page of the notebook, facing the inside back cover. At the top of the page are two names in pencil (probably "Jules Dalou" and "A W Bowcher") not included in the transcription.

Third Version: "The Island of Statues"

The third version of *The Island of Statues* consists of one loose leaf and an entire maroon-covered notebook identical to the others used for this work and *Mosada*. Inside the front cover the notebook is dated August 1884. By now Yeats had an advanced draft of the entire verse drama, though scene 3 of act 2 continued to trouble him. He cancelled the entire version of the scene in this notebook, and would create two more alternate versions of it (transcribed in the following section) before the final printer's copy.

In an effort to produce a visually appealing copy of this advanced manuscript, Yeats employed two colors of ink—purple and black. He used purple for speaker tags, stage directions, and the like, and turned to black for the dialogue itself. The transcriptions render both colors in the same type style because they do not pertain to different stages of composition; the special cases of the title page and the rare accidental variations from the basic pattern are indicated in notes. The pencil corrections and insertions, of course, appear in italic. Yeats's occasional line counts in blue pencil are indicated in notes.

Yeats at first wrote only on the rectos of the notebook pages, leaving the versos blank or reserving them for occasional corrections, insertions, or line counts. But by the time he reached the final scene, he realized that the notebook lacked sufficient pages to continue in that manner and began using both versos and rectos. Because the Stony Brook numbering already assigns a separate number to each page of leaves written on both sides, I have added a superscript r or v to indicate that a given page is a recto or a verso. Even with the shift to both sides of pages, Yeats just barely managed to fit the play into the notebook; the final lines appear inside the back cover.

The single loose leaf is written in pencil on unlined white paper measuring approximately 22.2 cm by 18.1 cm and is folded once. It contains a version of Almintor's lines near the end of act 1, scene 1, intermediate between those on SB 23.2.225 of the previous draft and SB 23.3.16 of the present one. As do the loose leaves in the notebook containing the previous draft, this one suggests that Yeats revised all or part of the verse drama on separate sheets between making the notebook versions.

1 *long ere and arrow whised*
or sword left
sheath
2 *The shepherd Pari for Oenone made*
~~courts~~
arm
3 *Singing of ~~arms~~ and battles some old stave*
4 *as sleeps dark water in a*
murmerous glade
5 *dreeming the live long sumer in*
the shade
6 *dreaming of speed or of the*
pluméd wave
7 *Naschi*
8 *I weary of ye all so get ye gone*

1 W B Yeats
2 August
3 1884
4 *10 Ashfield Terrace*
5 *Harolds Cross*

SB 23.3.1r (transcribed first on this page) is a loose leaf placed within the notebook whose transcription follows. It is a slightly earlier version of ll. 12–19 on page SB 23.3.16 of the notebook.

SB 23.3.3 (transcribed second on this page) is written inside the front cover of the notebook. Lines 1–3 are in purple ink; ll. 4–5 are in blue pencil or crayon.

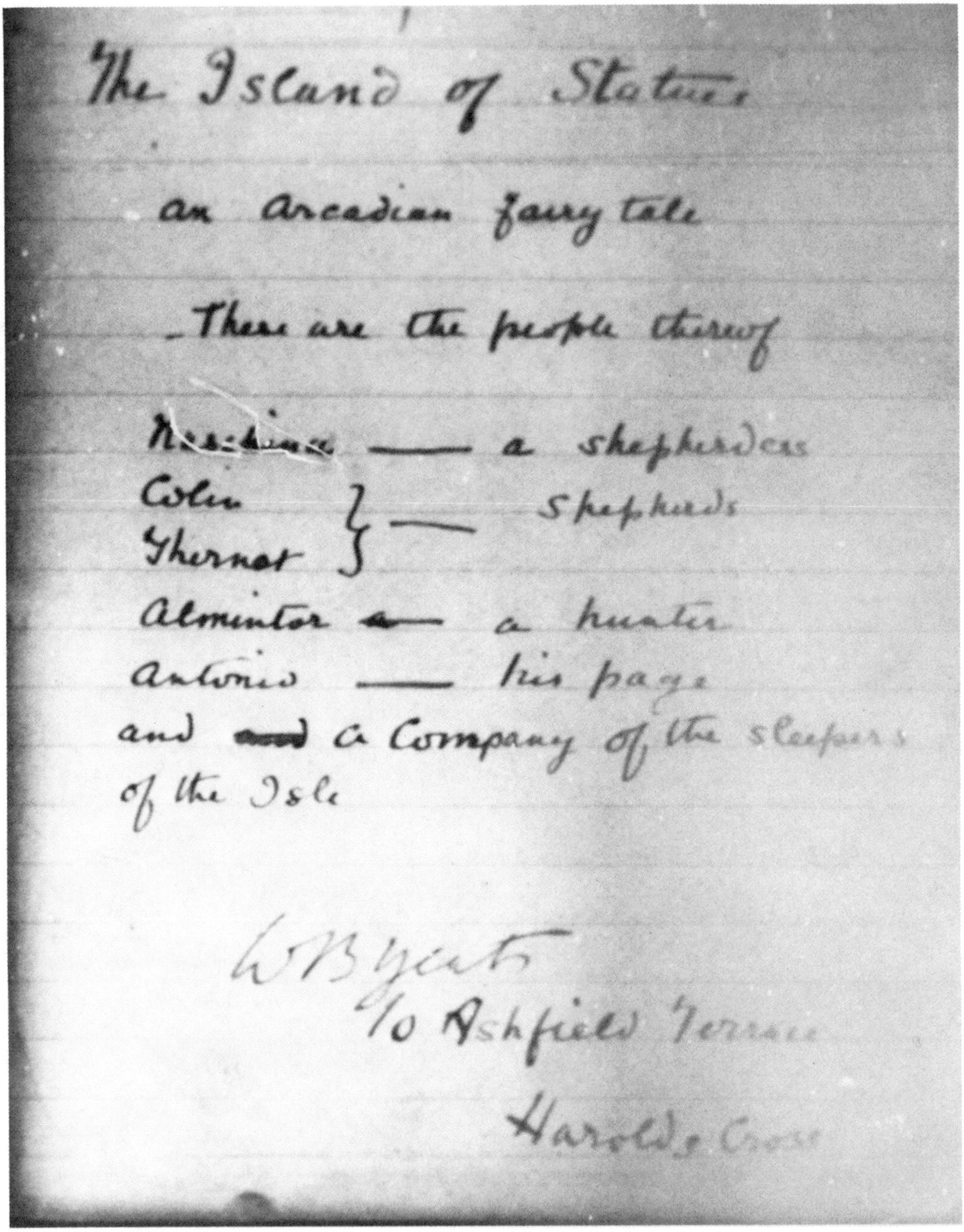

The Island of Statues

an Arcadian fairy tale

These are the people thereof

Naschina — a shepherdess
Colin }
Thernot } — shepherds
Almintor — a hunter
Antonio — his page
and ~~and~~ a Company of the sleepers
of the Isle

W B Yeats
10 Ashfield Terrace
Harolds Cross

[SB 23.3.4^{r}]

The Island of Statues

an Arcadian fairy tale

—These are the people thereof

Naschina —— a shepherdess
Colin
Thern{o / et} } —— shepherds
Almintor ~~a~~— a hunter
Antonio —— his page
and ~~and~~ a Company of the sleepers
of the Isle

W B Yeats
10 Ashfield Terrace
Harolds Cross

Lines 1 and 11–13 are in purple ink, as are the four long dashes between the names of the characters and their occupations.

ACT 1.
Scene 1.
Before the Cottage of Naschina it
is morning
Enter Thernot with a lute
Thernot
Maiden come forth the woods are waiting thee
Within the drowsy blossom hangs the bee
'Tis morn, Thy sheep are wandering in the vale
'Tis morn, the dawn light burneth gold and ~~re~~
red
'Tis morn, like old men's eyes the stars are pale
And in the oderous air love dreams are winging
'Tis morn and from the dew drenched wood I sped
To welcome thee Naschina with sweet singing
Sitting on a tree stem he begins to tune
his lute enter Colin upon the
other side abstractedly
Colin
Come forth the morn is fair as from the ~~fire~~ pyre

As indicated in the headnote to this notebook, speaker tags, scene descriptions, and the like are in purple ink (here, ll. 1–6 and 15–18). This feature of the manuscript will not be noted separately again except in a rare instance when Yeats accidentally diverged from the pattern.

10 Yeats reached the margin with ''re'', cancelled it, and wrote the entire word ''red'' immediately below.

Of sad queen Dido shone the lapping fire
Unto the wonderer's ships or as day fills
The brazen sky so blaze the dafodills
As Argive Clytemnistra saw out burn
{a
The flagrant sign{ail of her lords return
A far clear shineing on the herald hills
In vale and dell so blaze the dafodills
As when from on her cloud oer muffled [~~?she~~]
steep
OEnone saw the fires of Troyea leep
the
And laughed so so along^bubbling rills
In lemon tinted lines so blaze the dafodills
come forth
Come forth:^my music pours for thee
A quenchless geiving of love melody
Thernot (sings)
Now thy sheep all brousing meet
By the singing waters edge
Tred and tred their cloven feet
On the ruddy river sedge
For the dawn the foleage finereth

And the waves are leaping white
{er
Thou alone o lady ling{reeth
While the world is rolled in light
Colin
~~Wh~~ Shepherd to mar the morning hast thou come
Hear me and shepherd hearing me grow dumb
(sings)
The owl has gone [~~?frorn~~] from where she flew
Flickering under the white moon shine
She sleeps with owlets ~~th~~ two and two
Sleapily close her round bright eyne
O'er her nest the light is blending
Come thou come and two this string
Though my love sick heart is rending
Not a sad note will I sing
Thernot
I am not dumb I'd sooner silent wait
Within the ~~creaking~~ fold to hear the creaking
gate

14 The "o" in "Thernot" may be written over an "e", which was the spelling in earlier drafts.

17 Opposite this line on the otherwise blank facing verso is the (line) number 50 followed by a short horizontal line, both in blue pencil.

(sings)
The
~~O~~ woodland and valley and sea
a waken awaken to new born lustre
A new day's troup of wasp and bee
Hang on the side of the round grape cluster
blenching
~~Withering~~ high the dull stars sicken
Morn bewildered and the cup
young
Of the tarn where ~~dull~~ waves quicken
Hurls {ir
~~Casts~~ the{re swooning lustre up
Colin
I'll silence this dull singer
((sings)
O more dark thy lustrous hair is
Than the peeping pansies face
And thine eye more bright than faries
Dancinging in some moony place
~~See I tell~~
and thy ~~head~~ neck*s* a poised lily
See I tell thy beauties oer
As within a cellar chilly

18 The "s" at the end of "neck" was added later in blue pencil.

                    e
1 some old mis~~a~~r tells his store
memories of [?thee] [?keep]
2 ~~and thy memorys I keep~~
3 till all else is empty chaff
till
4 ~~and~~ I laugh when others weep
                    all
5 weeping when ~~an~~ other laugh
6   Thernot
7 Ill quench his singing with loud song
8   sings wildly
9 Come forth for in a thousand bowers
10   Blossoms ope their dewy lips
11 Oer the lake the water flowers
12   Floating are like silver ships
13 All the dawning day is singing
14   Joy and love are one existance
15 ever ringing ~~ever~~ ringing ringing
16   with unfaltering persistance
17   Colin (sings)
Alone ~~th~~   I weep
18 ∧in Waiting thee ~~thy Colin weepest~~
19   Love and sorrow one existance
20 ~~Is the burden and p~~

1 The cancellation of the ''a'' in ''misar'' and the new letter ''e'' are in pencil.
2 The cancellation and new line are in blue pencil.
4 The cancellation and new word ''till'' are in blue pencil.
18 ''Alone in'' is written in the margin and apparently was added later.
20 The ''p'' at the end is unfinished.

most deep
Sadness soul of joy ~~the deepest~~
Is the burden and persistance
sleep
Of the songs that never ~~sleepest~~ — *x*
Love from heaven came of yore
As a token and a sign
Singing o'er and o'er and o'er
his
Of ~~its~~ ^ death and change malign
Thernot
yon
With fiery song Ill drown ~~this~~ puny voice
(sings leeping to his feet)
The moon has gone with sicle bright
Slowly slowly fadeth she
weary of reaping the barren night
the *desolate*
and ~~The barren~~ ~~night and the~~ shuddering sea
Colin (standing)
Loud for ~~the~~ thee the morning cryeth
And my soul in waiting dyeth
ever dyeth ever dyeth
Thernot (sings)
{h
Far the morning vapours s{catter

---

1 "deep" is written over another spelling, perhaps "deeep".
3 The "x" in the right margin is in pencil.
17 Opposite this line on the otherwise blank facing verso is the numeral 100 in blue pencil.

[SB 23.3.11[r]] [VP 1,1:90–98]

As the leaves in autum scatter
Colin (sings)
In the heart of the dawn the rivers are
singing
Over them crimson vapours winging
Thernot (sings)
All the world is singing singing
All the world is ringing ringing
Colin (sings)
rayless
lift my soul from ~~hopeless~~ night
Thernot (sings)
Stricken all the night is past
Colin (sings)
Music of my soul and light
Thernot (sings)
Back the shaddows creep aghast

They approach one another while
singing with angry gestures

Enter Naschina
Naschina

O cease your singing, wild and shrill and
loud

On my poor brain thy busy tumults crowd

Colin

I fain had been the first of singing things
To welcome ~~the~~ when of the owlets wings ~~[illegible]~~
and troubled eyes. came mornings new born glow
~~With her first light the [illegible]~~

But yonder thing, you idle noise, you crow
You shepherd

Thernot

Came your spirit to beguile
With singing sweet as e'er round Lake Calladisle
Moan summer waves – But yonder shepherd vile
All clamour clothed

Colin

Was't clamour when I sung
Whom men have called Arcadia's sweetest tongue
(The sound of a horn is heard)
a horn – some troop of robbers winding goes

enter Naschina
Naschina
  {c
O {sease your singing, wild and shrill and
loud
On my poor brain thy buisy tumults crowd
Colin
I fain had been the first of singing things
o'er
when ~~on~~ the owlets wings
To welcome ~~thee when quivering morning rings~~
came
and troubled eyes ~~shone~~ mornings new born glow
~~With her first light the waters [?chimeing] flow~~ —
But yonder thing, yon idle noise, yon crow
Yon shepherd
Thernot
Came your spirit to beguile
With singing sweet as e'er round lake lulled isle
Moan summer waves. But yonder shepherd vile
All clamour clothed
Colin
Was't clamour when I sung
Whom men have called Arcadia's sweetest tongue
(The sound of a horn is heard)
A horn — some troop of robbers winding goes

The verso facing this page contains an illegible list in blue pencil of items numbered 1 through 6 on the left and renumbered as 1 through 5 on the right.

2 The speaker tag appears to have been added later; it is squeezed into the same ruled space of the notebook as l. 3.

13 Yeats inadvertently began another letter at the end of "With", probably an "s".

The Island of Statues Manuscripts, Third Version
[SB 23.3.13^{r}] [VP 1,1:111–116] and [SB 23.3.14^{r}] [VP 1,1:117–127]

Near by with subtile tred and bended bows
(an arrow passes)
Fly—
Thernot
Fly—
(Colin and Thernot go)
Naschina
So these brave shepherds both are
gone
Courageous miracles
Enter Almintor and Antonio
talking togeather
Almintor
The sunlight shone
Upon his wings, in yonder green abys
I sent an arrow
Antonio
And I saw you miss
And far away the Heron soars I wis

Almintor
Nay, nay I did not miss, his days
Of flight are done
(seing Naschina and bowing low)
Most fair of all who graze
There sheep in Arcady Naschina hail
Naschina hail
~~Nas~~ Antonio (mimicking him and
bowing lower)
Most fair of all who graze
There sheep in Arcady Naschina hail
Naschina hail
Almintor
I'll drive thy wooly sheep
If so I may unto a dewy vale
Where all night long the heavens weep and weep
dreaming in their soft odour laden sleep
where all night long the lonly moon the white
sick lady of the deep pours down her light
where all night long the brooding heaven is bent

Oer breezes heavy with the lylac sent
and mong the stunted ashes drooping rings
like gushing
all flame ~~like~~^from the hollow stones
all day and night a lonly fountain sings
and there to its own heart for ever moans
Naschina
Id be alone
Almintor
We two by that pale fount
Unmindful of its woe's will twine a wreath
As fair as any that on Ida's mount
long e'r an~~d~~ arrow whized or sword left sheath
The shepherd Paris for Oenone made
Singing of arms and battles some old stave
as sleeps dark water in a murmerous glade
Dreaming the live long summer in the shade
Dreaming of speed and of the pluméd wave
Naschina
there is none
[~~?every/?even~~] ~~one~~
I weary of ye, ~~all so get ye~~ gone
of all
~~For~~ all on whom arcadean suns have shone
Sunstains his soul in courege or in might

2 On the facing page SB 23.3.15v opposite this line is the numeral 150 in blue pencil.
17 The accent on "plumėd is in blue pencil.
17–19 On the facing page opposite these lines is the following insertion in blue pencil:
Antonio
Naschina wherefore are your eyes so bright
With tears
19–20 The cancellation, comma, and substitute phrasing are in blue pencil.
21 This line in blue pencil was squeezed on to the bottom of the page.

poor race of leafy Arcady
~~are all alike, a cowardly race~~—your love
To prove what can ye do what things above
Sheep guiding or the bringing some strange bird
or some small beast most wonderfully firred
or sad sea shells where little echos sit
such questing I methink*s* needs little wit
~~Antonio~~ Antonio
And the great grey lynx's skin
Naschina
me-
In sooth ~~I~~ think*s*
That I my self could shoot a great grey lynx*s*
With bow and ~~arrow~~ arrow—I and well as you
Could Colin e'n or Thernot also do
(Naschina is going)
Almintor
Stay fair Naschina stay
Naschina
Here where men know the graceous woodland joys
Joys brother fear dwells ever in each brest
songs wood land
I'm weary of your ~~shells~~ and ~~hunters~~ toys
^ ^ ^

Opposite ll. 1–5 on the otherwise blank facing verso is the following, difficult-to-decipher passage in blue pencil:

Antonio
~~Naschin~~
~~Or songs ye bring of home at eve before~~
~~The far off lonly [?thoughtful] of his [?flock]~~
~~The shepherd sees the morning [—?—] pass~~
~~Flapping his [?dew] be [—?—] wings along his [—?—]~~

1 The cancellation line and new wording are in blue pencil.

6 The "s" at the end of "methinks" was added later in blue pencil.

8–13 This passage is cancelled by four diagonal lines in blue pencil.

12 Yeats seems first to have misspelled "arrow", then to have corrected the spelling, and finally to have cancelled it and rewritten the word.

20 The cancellation lines through "shells" and "hunters" are in blue pencil, as is the word "songs" and caret under it.

To prove his love a knight with lance in rest
Would
~~Will~~ circle round the world upon a quest
Unti~~l~~l he'd found a dragon shiny scalled
From morn the twain until the evening palled
Would old
~~Will~~ war Or else he'd seek enchanter ~~bold~~
Who sat in lonely might all mailed in gold
And they would war mong wond'rous elfin sights
Such will I love the shuddering forest lights
Of green Arcadia do not hide I trow
Such one — not uncooth hunter thou
Ar't such (goes)
Antonio
And whither uncooth hunter now
Almintor
Ay boy
Antonio
Let's sea if that same heron slid
Down dead or if you missed I know you did
Antonio goes Almintor following

---

1 The "k" of "knight" may have been added later.
2 The cancellation and new word "Would" are in blue pencil.
5 The cancellation and new word "Would" are in blue pencil.
9 In writing both "Of" and "do" either Yeats's pen slipped or he began a different initial letter and then wrote over it.
18–19 Opposite these lines on the otherwise blank facing verso SB 23.3.18 is the following, written in blue pencil:

193—
202 counting stage directions
and Dramatis Persona Etc

Scene 2
A remote forest valley—
Enter Almintor followed by
Antonio
Antonio
hunter
And whither uncooth ^why so fast
I'm weary out—Aye so you pause at last
Almintor
Here is the ~~the~~ place the cliff encircled wood
Here grow that shy retiring sisterhood
The pale enemonies—we've searched all day
And found
Antonio
le
Tis well another mi{[?] of way
I could not go (they sit down)
Almintor
Let's talk and let's be sad
Here in the shade
Antonio
Why why

Lines 6 and 7 are cancelled by a wavy line in blue pencil.

1 Almintor
2 For what is glad
3 For look you sad's the murmour of the bees
Yon goes
4 ~~The~~ wind ~~goes~~ ~~g[?]~~ sadly and the grass and trees
5 reply like moaning of emprisoned elf
6 The whole world's sadly talking to it's self
the waves
7 In yon far lake that is where points my hand
beat out their lives lamenting on the sand [~~?s~~]
{ir
8 The waves lament the{re life out on the sand
9 The birds that nestle in the leaves are sad
10 Poor sad wood wrapsadists
11 Antonio
Nay 're
12 Nay they ~~are~~ glad
13 Almintor
14 All wrapsody hath sorrow for its soul
15 Antonio
16 Yon lark that fills with song the whole
17 O this wide vale embossomed in the air
song
18 Is sorrow in his ~~soul~~ or any care
19 doth not yon bird yon quivering bird rejoice

---

4 The word cancelled after "goes" may be "go's".

7 The phrase "that is where" is partially surrounded by straight and curved horizontal lines whose purpose is unclear, but one may be an awry cancellation of "that is" and another may relocate "where" earlier in the line.

8 Yeats did not cancel the original wording "lament their life out on the sand", although he presumably meant the new wording "beat out their lives lamenting on the sand" to replace it.

16 A line from the otherwise blank facing verso indicates the insertion of "eager" after "Yon".

Almintor
I hear the whole sky's sorrow in one voice
Antonio
yonder
Nay nay Almintor ~~yon brown~~ bird is glad
Almintor
'Tis beautiful and therefore it is sad
Antonio
Have done this phrasing and say why in truth
Almintor thou hast grown so full of ruth
And wherefore have we come
Almintor
A song to hear
Antonio
~~A song~~ from whence and when?
Almintor
Over the willows seer
Out of the air
Antonio
And when?

Almintor
When the sun goes down
Over the crown of the willows brown
perilous
O boy I'm bound upon a ~~dangerous~~ quest
For so she willed—you heard? Upon the brest
Of yonder lake from off who's banks alway
The poplars gaze across the waters grey
And nod to one another lies a small
green isle where never leaves or blossoms fall
great
For there the ~~fair~~ ^ enchantress lives
Antonio
And there
groweth the goblin flower all her care
By many saught it is a forest tale
seek are
How all who ~~saught~~ ~~were~~ doomed to ever fail
Almintor
That flower I seek
Antonio
never
and will know
~~You never will~~ return *? !*

On the facing verso SB 23.3.23, the numeral 50 in blue pencil is placed opposite l. 15 of SB 23.3.24 by a diagonal line. The verso also contains the following two lines in ink with pencil corrections, marked for insertion after l.15:

[?saugt] the
some say that all who ~~saught~~ ~~that~~ island lone
are
~~were~~ changed forever into moonwhite stone.

7 The "s" was apparently added to "water" later.

15 The two lines from the facing verso are marked for insertion after this line. Yeats may have first written "fale" instead of "fail".

19 The punctuation marks at the end, like the cancellation and new wording, are in pencil. The question mark may be cancelled.

Almintor
I seek that bloom for her that I may earn
him who
Her love—To ~~whom e'r~~ hath that bloom
comes truth
And [?] elfin wisdom and ~~strong~~ long years of youth
Beyond a mortal's time—I wait the song
that calls
Antonio
O evil starred
Almintor
It comes along
The wind at evening when the sun goes down
Over the crown of the willows brown——
{y
See yonder sinks the sun {aonder a shade
{ng
goes flickeri{ing in reverberated light
yon yon do you not see
Antonio
I see the night
Slow footed gathering oer the empty glade

14 Yeats may have written "go'es" for "goes".

A voice sings
From the shade vested hollow
Arise thou and follow
Almintor
sad fairy tones
~~Tis thus they ever seem~~
Antonio
Tis thus they ever seem
singing v
As some dead maidens ~~voice heard~~ in a dreem
The voice sings
~~When Th~~ When the tree was o'er appled
For mother Eve s wining
I was at her sinning
Oer the grass light endappled
I wandered and trod
{E
Oer the green {eden sod
And I sang round the tree
As I sing now to thee
Arise from the hollow
and ~~flol~~ follow and follow

the { r
And away in g{ [?]een paradize
As I wandered unseen
Glad was her meen
I saw her as you now ~~arize~~ arise
Before her I trod
{ er
O'{ [?] the green eden sod
{ g
And I san{ [?y] round the tree
As I sing now to thee
forth
From^the green hollow
Arise thou and follow
exit Almintor
The voice sings dying away
And I sang round the tree
As I sing now to thee
shade
From the ~~shaddow~~ ~~shadow~~ vested hollow
arise worm and follow
~~Worm and mortal rise and follow~~
Antonio
will
ÌH follow for this evil starred ones sake
fairy
Unto the border of the (dolerous)^lake
(exit)

15 The cancelled "shaddow" has an additional cancellation mark through its second "d".

19 Opposite this line on the otherwise blank facing verso are a mark < and the numeral 100 in blue pencil. Yeats may have used the spelling "faery" rather than "fairy" here, as he does elsewhere.

Oh learned is each monk hood mind
wisdom
And full of ~~learning~~ is each bloom
As [?clothed] in ceremonius gloom
He hears the story of the wind
That dieth slow with sun sick doom

These lines in pencil appear in the notebook opposite Almintor's speech at the beginning of scene 3 on the facing recto SB 23.3.29. The pencil "X" at the left margin of the second line of his speech there may indicate that these lines should be inserted at that point; eventually, they became the second speech of the First Voice.

3 "clothed" appears to have one or more extra letters, but they are difficult to decipher.

5 The "w" of "slow" is unfinished.

1 Scene 3. In the twilight
2 Far into the distance reach shaddowy
3 ways burdened with the fairy
4 flowers As though stooping
5 to some flower figures are standing
6 imovable Through the air at
7 times floats wandering music
8 Enter Almintor
9 Almintor
10 The evenings gleams are green and gold and red
along the lake—The crane has homeward fled
11 X ~~Upon the lake where white stars flickering tread~~
{l and flowers around in clustering thousands are
12 ~~F~~{ ~~rowers an hundred thousand round me~~ are
13 each shining clear as some unbaffled star
14 The skies more dim thou burning like a shield
mouths
15 Of gold above these men whos ~~lips~~ were sealed
16 [?Tall/?Full] long ago and into stone congealed
17 And o the wonder of the thing each came
18 When low the sun sank down in clotted flame
19 Beyond the lake who's smallest wave was burdened

After writing "Scene 3" in purple ink, Yeats (presumably mistakenly) switched to black ink for "In the twilight" before reverting to the customary purple for describing settings and the like in this manuscript.

1 Yeats clearly meant "twilight". He may have written "thilight", or else "thelight" with an "i" added later.

11 The pencil "X" (which is in the left margin) may indicate insertion of the five lines on the facing page. The cancellation mark is in pencil.

15 The caret is in pencil.

With rolling fire, beyond the high trees turbaned
with clinging mist, each ill starred wanderer came
As I to chose beneath days dying flame
each one around is stone as I shall bee
Unless some pitying god shall succour me
In this my choice
                    (stoops as if about to choose some flower)
                              Some god might help if so
May hap
^'Twere better that aside I throw
                                        {c
All choice and give to chan{ae for guiding chance
Some cast of die or let some arrow glance
Fror guiding of the gods. The sacred bloon
To find not hopeless have I crossed the gloom
With that song guiding where harmonic woods
Nourish the panthers in dim solitudes
vast greenness where eternal rumour dwells
And hath his home — by many folded dells
                                   caves of dripping
I passed, by many ~~caverns of wet~~ stones
And heard the unseen echo's on their thrones
lone regents of the wood deep muttering

9 Part of ''May'' extends into the left margin.

And then new murmers came new uttering
In song from goblin waters swaying white
Mocking with patient laughter all the night
Of those vast woods and then I saw the boat
living wide winged upon the waters float
Strange draperies did all the sides adorn
And the waves bowed before it like moan corn
        winged   of
The ~~strangest~~ wornder ~~in~~ all fairy land
It bore me softly where the shallow sand
binds as within a girdle or a ring
The lake embosomed isle—nay this my quest
Shall not so hopeless prove some god may rest
Upon the wind and guide mine arrows course
From yonder pinacle above the lake
Ill send mine arrow now my last resource
~~And where it falls the nearest flower~~
The nighest flower where it falls Ill take
                (goes out fitting an arrow to his bow)

8 Yeats may have used the spelling "faery" for "fairy" here, as he does elsewhere.
11 The "s" in "isle" appears to be added later.

50 ———

He was our [?anchien] god If I speak low
~~If I speak low~~ and not to clear
knew
How will the [~~—?—~~] god ever know
but that I called on him

The numeral and elongated dash in l. 1 are in blue pencil. The mark at the right margin of ll. 3–4 indicates the insertion of ll. 2–5 at the end of Almintor's speech on the next page, which faces this one in the notebook.

4 There is a mark under the correction that may be a caret or another letter.

A voice (sings)
Fickle the guiding his arrow shall find
Some goblin my servent on wings that are fleet
That nestles alone in the whistling wind
go pilot the course of his arrow's deceet
The arrow falls
enter Almintor
Almintor
'Tis here the arrow fell the breezes laughed
Around the feathery tip, unto the shaft
This flower is most near. statue o thou
Who's beard ~~who~~ a moonlight river is__Who's brow
Is stone old sleeper this same afternoon,
Oer much I've talked__. I shall be silent soon,
If rong my choice, as silent as thou art
O graceous Pan take now thy servents part
he pulls a flower and is changed
to stone
a voice sings
sleeping lord of archery

---

10 The mark after "tip" may be a blot rather than a comma.
12 The punctuation between "is" and "Who's" is unclear.
14 The punctuation between "talked" and "I" is unclear.
16 Lines 2–5 on the preceding verso SB 23.3.32 should be inserted here.

No more a roving shall't thou see
                                        her
The panther with ~~ther~~^yellow hide
Of the forests all the pride
Or her ever burning eyes
                              a   { n
When she ~~doth~~ in caver{ ns lies
guarding oer her awful young
Where their sinewy might is strung
In the never lifting dark—
No thou standeth still and stark
That were wont to move for ever
But a mother panther never
Oer her yong so eagerly
did her lonely watchings take
As I in guarding lest you wake
Sleeping lord of archery

End of Act 1 __

15 The otherwise blank facing verso has the numeral 77 and a dash, both in blue pencil, opposite this line.

ACT 2
scene 1.
The wood
enter Antonio and Naschina
Naschina
I in a shepherds dress will seek and seek
{Until
{[?] I find him—what a weary week
gone
My pretty child since he was^'t as been
Tell oer again how unto you was seen
His passage oer the lake
~~Antonio~~
Antonio
When we two came
these
From ~~the~~ wood~~s~~ ways—Then like a silver flame
We saw the dolerous lake and near at hand
The boats prow gratted on the shallow sand
Then loudly twice the living wings flapt wide
And leaping to their feet the echo's cried

---

14 After writing ''the'' as the second word, Yeats may have tried to add ''se'' at the end before cancelling it and writing ''these'' above it in pencil; the ''s'' of ''woods'' is cancelled in pencil.

1 each other answering and between each wing
2 He sat and then I heard the white lake sing
3 ~~Beneath~~
Curving beneath the prow, as some wild drake
4 Half lit—so flapt the wings acros the lake
5 But see I make you sadder shepherdess
6 ~~Nasch~~
7 Naschina
8 Nay grief in feeding on old grief grows less
9 Antonio
feeding
10 Grief needs much^then. Of him I'll sware
11 A deal we've said and not a whit more rare
{f
12 Do come your weeping {sits
13 Naschina
14 Look you so straight
15 Is the mansion of the kingfisher and deep
16 No other bird ~~but he~~ ~~can~~ may enter there
17 Antonio
18 Well

---

6 "~~Nasch~~" is in black ink; presumably, Yeats cancelled it when he realized that he had not changed to purple for a speaker's name.

15 The "f" of "kingfisher" is written over the "g".

Naschina
Late
very latey ~~grave~~ sorrow came to weep
within my heart and naught but sorrow
now
can enter there
Antonio
See oer yon brow
Of hill two shepherds come
Naschina
Farewell I'll done
My ~~M~~ shepherds cloak and then return anon
Enter Colin and Thernot
Thernot
Two men who love one maid—have ample cause
Of war__Of yore two shepherds where we pause
Faught once for self same reason on the hem
Of the wide woods

---

3 Yeats first wrote "late" and then added a "y", perhaps intending "lately". The word "grave" is cancelled by a separate diagonal stroke through each letter.

1 Colin
2 And the deep earth gathered them
3 Thernot
4 We must get swords
5 Colon
6 Is't the only way? O see
7 Is yon the hunter sir Almintor's page
8 Let him between us judge for he can gauge
9 And measure out the ways of chivalry
10 Thernot
11 Sir page Almintor's friend and therefore ~~lear~~
learned
12 In such like things—prey let thine ears
be turned
13 Prey hear and judge
14 ~~Colin~~
15 ~~Must we two fight judge~~ thou
16 Antonio
17 My ~~poping~~ popinjay what now?

---

11 There is a purple "y" between the first two letters of "Almintor". Yeats may have written "trerefore" for "therefore".

14 "Colin" is written in purple ink and cancelled in black.

Colin
This thing we ask—must we two fight—judge thou
Each came one morn with with
welcoming of song
Unto her door for this where nod the long
And shoreward waves night had we faught
waves bring
The brown weed burden so the sword brings fear
To us
Thernot
O
~~Tell us for~~ wise are't thou in such like
thing
now
being Almintor's page—∧judge ~~for~~ you here
~~We love one maid~~
We love Naschina both
Antonio
Whom loves she best
{Co
{[?]lin
She cares no whit for either but hath blest
Another with her love

3 Opposite this line on the otherwise blank facing verso is the numeral 50 in blue pencil.
10 The caret and "now" are in pencil; "for" is cancelled in pencil.
15 There may be an errant apostrophe between the "e" and "s" of "cares".

disguised
Enter Naschina ~~dressed~~ as a shepherd
Colin
Whom art thou speak
As the sea's furrows on a sea tost shell
{e
Sad histori{ss are lettered on thy cheak
Antonio
It is the shepherd Guarimond who loveth well
In the deep centers of the secret woods
Old miser hoards of grief to tell and tell
Young Guarimond he tells them o'er and o'er
To see them drowned by those vast solitudes
With their unhuman sorrows
Naschina
Cease no more
Of this thou hast ~~an~~ a nimble tongue
{C
{colin —
Thy grief
What is it friend
Antonio
He lost the favouret chief

he loved
and only sheep^of all his flock
Colin
Than thy grief shepherd greater is the stock
Of mine—I like you and I know not why
~~So~~ will you judge must Thernot yon and I
(Fight) for this thing, we love one maid
Naschina
Her name
Colin
Naschina 'Tis
Naschina
I know her well a lame
Dull witted thing with face red
squirrel brown
Antonio
A long brown grasshopper of maids
Naschina
peace sir
Thernot
'Tis clear that you have seen her not

---

5 "So" is cancelled in pencil.

1 The crown
Of beams
^a footing o'er yon lonly fir
2 ~~Of flickering sunlight round yon lonely~~ fir
3 Is not more fair or joyous than she is
4 Naschina
5 There is no way but that ye fight I wis
6 If _her_ ye love
7 Thernot
8 Aye Colin we must fight
9 Colin
10 Aye we must fight
11 Antonio and Naschina turning to go
12 Naschina
13 Tell me Antonio might
14 They get them swords and both or either fall?
15 Antonio
16 No no when that shall be then men may call
17 Unto their feet the stars that sit alone
18 each one at gaze upon his whirling throne
19 ~~Exit Colin and~~ T
20 Exit Antonio and Naschina

---

1 The caret and part of "Of beams" are in the left margin.

2 Opposite this line on the facing verso SB 23.3.42 Yeats wrote: "Nor fairies in the hony heart _of june a stir_".

18 Opposite this line on the facing verso Yeats wrote in blue pencil:
107—counting
stage directions &c

ACT 2⌋
Scene 2
A remote part of the forest
Through knotted and wisted trees
The lake is seen shining under
the red evening
Enter Naschina and Antonio
Antonio
Behold how like a swarm of fiery bees
The light is dancing o'er the knotted trees
In busy flakes reshining from the lake
Though this night vested place the red beams brake
Naschina
From the deep earth unto the lurid sky
All things are quiet in the eves wide eye
Antonio
The air is stil above and still each leaf
As some clenched soul in fixed and tearless grief
Naschina
And boy saw you when through the forest we
Two came, his name and mine on many a tree

carved, here beyond the lakes slow muffled tred
In sand our names are also to be read
Antonio
Yonders the sacred isle for which we came
The white waves wrap it in sheet of flame
And yon a huddling blackness draweth nigh
'Tis that strange boat against the [?~~blazi~~] blinding sky
Naschina
Antonio boy; If I return no more
Then bid them raise my statue on the shore
Here where the round waves come, here let hem build
It facing to the sea and no name ~~build~~ guild
A ~~wite~~ white ~~th~~ ~~lon~~ dumb thing of tears here let it stand
Between the lonly forest and the sand
Antonio
The boat is almost here. You heed me not
Naschina
And when the summer's deep then to this spot
The Arcadians bring and let the stone be raised
As I am standing now as though I gazed

13 Yeats may have first written an "s" at the end of "thing" and then extended the end of the "g" to cover it.
19 The "r" of "raised" may be written over another letter.

One hand brow shading—far into the night
And one arm pointing thus, in marble white—
And once a year let the Arcadians cume
~~And once a year~~ l
and neath it sit and of the woven sum
Of human sorrow let them moralize
And let them tell sad histories till their eyes
Are dim with tears
Antonio
The fairy boat's at hand *800*
You must be gone the rolling grains of sand
Are neath its prow and crushing shells
Naschina (going)
And let the tale be dolerous each one tells
(exit)
Antonio (alone)
In mist of evening boat and maiden sink
lake
Down through the flickering ~~wave~~ the cold stars blink
In companies of ~~gr~~ gold and green and blue
{ s
Pearcing the quivering water{ [?] through and through

1 There may be a dash at line level before "One".

10 The numeral 800 in blue pencil at the right margin is marked to follow l. 10 on the facing recto; Yeats may have written "80" instead.

The sentinels of night who keep their watch
beams
On grief—The world drinks sorrow from the ~~beems~~
~~Of their cold eyes~~ and persecusion of their eyes
(starting)
where the
~~Where yonder lylac~~ blotch
Of lylac oer the the wan [?sea] is
~~Above the edge and~~ pulsing water gleams
Once more those shepherds come
mirth
May hap some∧
I'll have—O absent one 'tis not for dirth
Of grief—And If they say "Antonio laughed"
Say then "A popinjay before griefs shaft
pierced through, chatting from habit in the sun
last
'Till ~~all~~ his wretchedness was oer and done"
A voice from without
Antonio—
Enter Colin and Thernot
Thernot
We have resolved to fight
Antonio
O wonderful

---

8 Yeats may have dropped this half line down because he saw that it would not fit in the remaining space of l. 7.
10 A mark in blue pencil between ll. 10 and 11 leads to the numeral 800 on the facing verso.

Thernot
And we have swords
Antonio
O night
Of wonders eve of prodigies
Colin
Draw draw—~~Draw draw~~
Antonio
He'll snap his sword
~~Colin~~ Thernot
raised is the lyons paw
Colin and Thernot fight
Antonio
Cease Thernots wounded cease, they will not heed
Fearce thrust—a tardy blossom had the seed
But heavy fruit, How swift the argument
Of those steel tongues—crash swords—
—Well thrust—Well bent
Aside
goblin
(a distant burst of∧music)

7 The cancelled "Draw draw" is written in black and purple ink, as though first in purple and then in black; it is cancelled in black.

20 The caret and new word "goblin" are in pencil.

This music told Almintor s end
And of Naschina's now it tells_rend rend
O heart—her dirge—with rushing arms the waves
Cast on the sound on on—This night of graves
—The spining stars—The toiling sea—whirl round
My sinking brain—cease cease—heard ye yon sound
The dirge of her ye love—cease cease
(a far off echo of the music)
again
The echos fling upon my weary brain
The labour and the cadence of their pain
(Exit)
—The scene closes on Colin and Thernot
still fighting—

80 with
stage directions

Lines 15–16 and the diagonal mark above them are in blue pencil.

~~Scene~~ 3.

The island of flowers
Far into the distance reach shadowy
ways burdened with ~~the~~ fairy flowers
Bearded figures of stone are seen
among them — There also is the
statue ~~that~~ once was Almintor —
Over all in the distance a citron
tinctured sky where falter a few stars

Enter Naschina desguised as a shepherd
and the enchantress the beautiful familiar
of the isle

Enchantress,

O youth by this mine ivory staff I swear
I pity thee — turn thou again for fair
and very young thou art and wherefore I
Who'er pitied none so pity thee I know not why
Save that your young and by this staff I swear
My staff with ivory bound that you are fair

~~Scene 3~~ —
The island of flowers
Far into the distance reach shadowy
ways burdened with the fairy flowers
Bearded figures of stone are seen
among them—There also is the
statue that once was Almintor—
Over all in the distance a citron
tinctured sky where falter a few stars

Enter Naschina disguised as a shepherd
And the enchantress the beautiful familiar
of the isle
Enchantress
O youth by this my vine hung staff I sware
{t
I pity thee—{durn thou again for fair
{g
and very youn{y thou art and wherefore I
Who've pitied none so pity thee I know not why
Save that your young and by this staff I sware
My staff with ivy bound that you are fair

Naschina
Where is the flower lady
Enchantress
If I tell
I die by old decre nay seek it not
Sit here—The shade is graceous in this spot
And I will tell thee old world faery tales
About the sorrows of the nighting gales
There sing within the portal of this shell
Naschina
The phantoms of dead waves
Enchantress
And I will tell
There pent up secresies and why they toil
But if I show where is the faery flower
And it be pulled Then by the sacred coil
Of the slow sea snake upon the self same hour
I die
Naschina
Then wake the sleepers from their sleep

SB 23.3.51^{r} and the following ten pages of the scene are cancelled in black ink by various combinations of diagonal lines, on this page by nine mostly diagonal lines from upper left to lower right. There is a pencil sketch, perhaps of a statue, at the upper right.

Of stone
Enchantress
No no I cannot for they keep
Seeled hearts until some mortal touch their lips
With that strange flower [?though] light as some bee sips
They'll wake and some will murmour of old loves
And some of comrades now for ages dust
{O
Seek you {o youth within these shining groves
Some comrade dear and sad whom find you must
Or die—What's love? for breathing faery breath
I know love not at all—I have heard say
It is the clinging friend of change and death
And with these twain full often whispereth
O youth give oer thy hopeless quest—yet stay
Upon this isle—Forget thy hopes and fears
Forget the world and its embattled years
Here all sweet odours by the winds are brought
These gentle as the moth like wings of thought
And here the writhing waves are stilled and calm
[?As]
~~In~~ sleep each burdened oer with poppy balm

4 The "l" of "until" is written over either "ll" or "le".

And hope and memory grow still as these
scarce stir or trouble by these shuddering seas
Naschina
By chance I chose the flower

Enchantress
Stay
But ~~rears~~
Not there—~~But~~ yon^a pillar tall and grey
~~A broken shaft and hanging from~~ its head
a broken shaft
~~There~~ ~~rears high~~ rears high and from its head
^
There hangs a flower like a ruby red
And lapping flame. See shepherd I have told
Yet pull it not though all the wide world gold
Be not it's worth—Your silent and quite still
Be not so silent—Woe is me you will
Take it, and when the busy wings are furled
Of Faeries they are dead indeed—Their life
Tis a happy dream within a dreamless world
Of sleep—'Tis pleasent here the waves have strife

13 The apostrophe of "it's" may be cancelled.

and toil about us—shepherd sit thou here
To thee Ill give mine ivy staff the fear
Of goblins all and I will bring the fruits
Far nurishéd about the huddling ruits
{o
Of the dead wo{wd and many a wide eyed band
Of the pied tiger kittens from thy hand
Will I make feed—But ay you touch the crown
Of the pillar—Thus upon my knees low down
I kneel to thee—O let me live on still
I know not what death is, for I've seen fill
The years whole rounds and seen the summers fling
{ir
The{re scents four thousand years an evil thing
I only know it is—your eyes are wet
spare
Ah you will∧to me my poor life yet
A moment stay
Naschina
Blood from the snapt stem drips
Enchantress
If fade (dies)

Naschina
close seeld
Blue pallor on her ~~perfect~~ lips
And on her forhead dwells and as this hair
I lift or as this cheek nothing so fair
[?citied] earth
The ~~bragard world~~ can show
a voice sings
{I
One on the {island dies
And soon where the white waves call
On the sands away, neath the poplar's grey
Two with the sword blade fall
Naschina (to Almintor)
O
‸Wake wake wake for light as some bee sips
The sacred flower lies upon thy lips
Almintor
I slept—'twas sultry and scarce circling shook
The falling hawhorn bloom
Naschina
knowest thou me—look—
Almintor
Nascina
Naschina
hence
The ~~attendant~~ faeries of the dead enchantress
While
Sing—‸Naschina and Almintor whisper apart

The exchange between Almintor and Naschina comprising ll. 19–22 is written in black ink over the stage direction of ll. 23–24, which is in purple. The black line through "attendant" appears intended to separate ll. 19–20 from 20–21 and not to cancel that word.

4 Yeats may have written "cheak" for "cheek".

5 Yeats apparently forgot to cross the "t" of the word transcribed as "[?citied]".

12 The "O" and caret are in the left margin.

21 Some letters are missing toward the end of "Naschina".

A man has a hoped for heaven
faery
But soulless a ~~spirit~~ dies
As a leaf that is old, and withered and cold
When the wintery vapours rise

Soon shall our wings be stilled
And our laughter over and done
So let us dance~~,~~ where the flaming lance
Of the barley [~~?stoots~~] shoots in the sun

So let us dance on the fringéd waves
And shout at the wisest owls
In their downy caps, and startle the naps
Of the dreaming water fowls

And fight for the black sloe berries
For soulless a faery dies
As a leaf that is old, and withered and cold
{t
When {ahe wintery vapours rise

This leaf in the notebook is loose. The lines on its recto should precede SB 23.3.56v and those on its verso (SB 23.3.58v) should follow that page. The present arrangement follows the Stony Brook numbering sequentially.

Naschina
wake
~~Sea farer wake~~ ~~for~~ light as some bee sips
The sacred flower lies upon thy lips
first sleeper (awaking)
Have I slept long
Naschina
long years
Sleeper
With hungry heart
with [?all]
Doth still the wanderer rove ~~within~~ his ships
I saw him from sad Dido's shore depart
Enamoured of the waves impetuous lips
Naschina
These twain are dust
—Wake light as some bee sips
The sacred flower lies upon thy lips
sea farer
~~Wake~~ ~~sleeper~~ wake
2 Sleeper
Was my sleep long
Naschina

4 There may be an "e" between the "k" and "i" of "awaking".

long years
Sleeper
A rover I who come from where mens ears
flair
love storm and stained with mist the new moons∧
Doth still the man whom each stern rover fears
{A
The austere {arthur rule from uther's chair
Naschina
{W
He is long dust—{wake light as some bee sips
The sacred flower lies upon thy lips
3 Sleeper
Was my sleep long O youth
Naschina
long long and deep
Sleeper
Youth as I came I saw god Pan he played
An ~~otten~~ otten pipe unto a listening fawn
would weep
Who oft with eyes ~~to grief unused~~ to grief unused∧
Doth he still dwell within the forest shade
And rule the shadows of the eve and dawn
Naschina

long dust he is—wake light as some bee sips
[?brood]
The sacred flower ~~lies~~ upon thy lips
{ A
Sleeper { [?]wake
4 Sleeper waking
How long my sleep
Naschina
Unnumbered
goblin
Are the years of ~~faery~~ sleep
Sleeper
While I slumbered
How in Troyea passed the years away
Doth it still hold the Achean host at bay
Where rise those walls magestical avove
The windy plains a fair haired maid I love
~~Naschina~~ [?alas]
She is long ages dead
Sleeper
Ah woe is me
1 Sleeper
Youth here we will abide and be
chief
Be ~~thou our king O youth and~~ be thou king

---

15 ''Naschina'' is in purple ink; the cancellation line and ''[?alas]'' are in black ink.

Of this lake nurtured isle—

Naschina

Let thy king be

Yon archer he who hath the halcyon's wing
High fixed like a glad thought on his crest

The awakened sleepers shout

Clear browed Arcadian thou shalt be our king

Naschina

O my Almintor worthy was thy quest
For this was worthy and most noble it hath been

Sleepers

Clear browed Arcadian thou shalt be our king

Almintor (to Naschina)

and thou the queen

END

Of this lake nurtured isle—
Naschina
Let thy king be
Yon archer he who hath the halcyon's wing
High fixéd like a glad thought on his crest
The awakened sleepers shout
{C
{slear browed Arcadian thou shall't be our king
Naschina
{A
O my {almintor worthy was thy quest
[?] yay worthy and most noble it hath been
Sleepers
{A
Clear browed {arcadian thou shall't be our king
Almintor (to Naschina)
And thou the queen

E N D
And til we d
And til we die with the charmed ring
[?our]
of this star shuddering sky you are the queen

This page is written on the inside back cover of the notebook.

10 This line is crowded between ll. 9 and 11; it was probably added later.

13 This line is crowded between ll. 12 and 14; it was probably added later.

16–18 These lines, which became the final ones of the play, are written nearly diagonally and apparently later. There may be one or more letters missing from "queen" in l. 18. Two pencil sketches of insects appear at the bottom right of the page.

Fourth Version: Scenes 2 and 3 of Act 2

The manuscripts in this section represent stages of parts of act 2 intermediate between the third draft (transcribed in the previous section) and the King's School version (transcribed in the following one). Their dates must thus fall between completion of the previous version in August 1884 and publication in the *Dublin University Review* beginning in April 1885. The first two pages comprise a single loose leaf (NLI 30,457), 18 cm by 22.4 cm, folded to make a bifolium, with a blank bifolium folded into it; chain lines in the paper run vertically at intervals of 2.7 cm. The text on 1^r (SB 22.3.44) reworks the first half of Antonio's speech at Naschina's departure for the island in scene 2 (VP 2,2:37–46) and the text on 4^v (SB 22.3.45) presents the earliest surviving version of his subsequent lines at the reentrance of Colin and Thernot (VP 2,2:56–60). Found in separate notebooks (NLI 30,328), each of the other two manuscripts pertains to scene 3. The earlier comes from a notebook containing this scene, ten pages of prose on Eastern psychology, two pages of *The Seeker,* and three pages of an unpublished early play; the second comes from a notebook labelled "Island of Statues / Part 2 / and / The Seeker". None of the other material is transcribed here.

The final scene of the verse drama gave Yeats the most trouble. Even by the end of the third version of the entire work the dialogue between Naschina and the Enchantress (interspersed with occasional spirit voices) which comprises the first two-thirds of the scene remained wholly different from the eventual version, and the remaining third (in which Naschina wakes the sleepers) contained smaller differences and still lacked the crucial concluding stage direction about Naschina's shadow. SB 23.3.68–80 provided for the first time a draft of the opening lyric and a recognizable outline of the encounter between Naschina and the Enchantress as far as the eventual line 188 of the VP numbering, when it breaks off abruptly. Yeats then integrated a revision of the new opening, a draft of additional lines through the Enchantress's death, and a revision of the old conclusion to create in SB 23.3.115–146 an approximation of the final form of the scene.

All these manuscripts are in black ink, with the last containing occasional pencil revision as well. The unlined loose leaf is folded in half to make pages that measure 11.3 cm by 17.8 cm. The lined notebooks are similar to those used for *Mosada* and for earlier versions of *The Island of Statues.* Inside the front cover they bear the oval device of "W. CARSON BOOKSELLER & STATIONER". Because the Stony Brook numbering assigns a different number to each page, I have added a superscript r or v to indicate whether a given page is a recto or verso. In general, Yeats used the rectos of the notebooks for composing and transcribing, reserving the facing versos for insertions or corrections. A special feature of the most advanced draft is the appearance, upside down in pencil on two successive versos, of an apparent brief review in Yeats's hand of the work under composition, which may be a wishful fantasy by Yeats himself or else possibly his transcription at a later date of an as yet unidentified early notice. These prose pages are transcribed at the end of the manuscript.

1 I would have gone with her
But far away
2 The faery thing flew with
her oer the grey
and
3 Slow waters ~~where~~ the boat
and maiden sink
4 Away from me where mists
of evening drink
5 To ease there world old
that along the brink
waves
6 Of sword blue ~~deeps~~ of calm[?ness]
oe head blink
7 The mobs of [?stars] in gold and green
and blue
8 Piercing the quivering water through and thr
9 [?] ageless [?] ~~who keep~~
who watch
10 Oer grief

This is the first of two pages on a loose bifolium (NLI 30,457) containing drafts of part of two speeches by Antonio in act 2, scene 2. Yeats reached the margin of the narrow leaf before completing most of the lines, which he finished immediately below.

1 To yonder Ile from ~~which~~ whence
wh[?] never sail w[?]
theres no return
2 [?] from whos green banks no living thing
can rove
3 Naschinas gone drawn there
by thirst of love

4 or see again the dear arcadian light
5 and that was strange but [?this] is
many a world
6 more wonderful

Act 2—
Scene 3—
The island
Flowers of many colours every where
In a citron coloured sky falter
a few stars
A voice
so fair and bright
What do you weave ~~with wool so white~~
2 voice
The cloak I weave of sorrow
O lovely to see in all mens sight
shall be the cloak of sorrow
In all mens sight
3 voice
What do you make with sails for flight
{4
{3 voice
A boat I build for sorrow
O ~~lovely~~ swift on the seas all day and night
Saileth the rover sorrow
all day and night

This page begins a section of a notebook in which Yeats reworked scene 3 of act 2 as far as l. 188 of the VP numbering. The opening lyric was titled "Voices" for its separate publication in the *Dublin University Review* (March 1885); it was included in later collections as "The Cloak, the Boat, and the Shoes."

5 voice
What do you weave with wool so white
6 voice
The sandals these of sorrow
~~O lovely to see in all~~
Soundless shall be the foot fall light
In each mans ears of sorrow
Sudden and light
Enter Naschina with the
Enchantress of the Isle—
Naschina
What are the voices that in flowery ways
Have cloathed their tonges with song of songless days
Enchantress
They are the flowers guardian sprights
With streaming hair as wandering lights
They passed a tiptoes ever where
And never heard of greaf or care
Until this morn—as adders back
The sky was banded oer with wrack
They were sitting round ~~the~~ a pool

---

10 One or more letters may be missing near the end of ''Enchantress'' here and in l. 14.

At their feet the waves in rings
gently shook their mothy wings
For their came an air breath cool
From the ever moving pinions
Of the happy flower minions
But a sudden melencholy
Filled them as they sat to geather
{ N
{ [?]ow their songs are mournful holy
As they go with drooping feather
Naschina
{ it
O lady thou whos vest{ urure of green
Is rolled as verdend smoke
O thou who's face
Is worn as thou with fire O goblin queen
thee
lead me I prey to the statued place
Enchantress
wandering
O youth allong a ~~folded~~ ~~path~~ way
~~Were fruit~~
I led the here and as a wheel
around place
We turned ~~about~~ the ~~isle~~ alway

---

8 There may be a second ''l'' at the end of ''mournful''.

10 At this point in the manuscript the ink changes from deep black to a more faded, nearly brown ink, used also for the final two letters in l.7, above.

1 lest on thine heart the stony seel
2 As on these others hearts were laide
3 Behold the brazen gatéd glade.
4 (casts open the brazen gates
5 throu which the statues are seen
6 some bent as though to pull a flower
7 others holding flowers in their hands)
8 Naschana
9 Let me pas in The spells from of his heart
10 At Touch of the enchanted flower depepat
11 Let me pass in
12 Enchantes (holding the gate [?with]
[?hand]
13 That flower none
14 ~~Who seek may find save only~~ one
years
15 A ~~shepherdess for long for~~ told
16 ~~And even she will never hold~~
17 ~~That blossom save some things be found~~
18 ~~To die for her in air or ground~~
[?there]
19 None such their are if such were
20 Een then before her shepherd hair

---

12 "holding" is missing one or more letters at the end.

1 had felt the Island breeze my lore
Will drive her forth for ever more
2 ~~Will drive her by the bubbling~~ shore
to wander by the bubbling shore
3 lafter lipped but for her brain
4 A guerdon of deep rooted pain
5 and for her eyes a lightles stare
for from { o
6 if ~~once~~ severed ~~were~~ the r{ [?]ot
7 That enchated blossom were
8 From my wizard iland fair
9 I die as music that grows mute
10 on a girls forgotton lute
11 Naschina
12 Your eyes are all a flash she is not here
shepherd
13 I am a youth
14 Enchantress
{N { r
15 {nay do not fea{ rt
16 With you I am all gentles in truth
17 There is but little Id refuse thee youth
18 Naschana
19 I have ~~I have~~ a whim let some attendet sprite
land water
20 ~~cry~~ of thine cry over ~~thine~~ and white

---

2 Yeats cancelled this line and expanded it into two, one above and one below the original line.
6 "for" is written in the left margin.
8 The "i" of "iland" was either first capitalized and then written over in lowercase or vice-versa.

That one must die unless one die for her
Tis but to see if any thing would stir
a
For such ~~ere~~ call [?een] let the words be cried
As though she whom you fear had crossed the tide
Though she has not
Enchantress ~~It shall be as you~~ wish
A litle thing that is
{n done
A{sd shall be ~~as you ask~~
If you will dane to kiss
fair youth my lips
{n
Nascha{sa
It shall be as you ask
Enchantress
you
Forth Forth O spirits ~~thou~~ have head yor task
voices we are gone
Enchantress—(sitting down)
good yoth as we two hither came
the [?in] | [?Iland]
I begd∧this∧to remain
And banish ever more the flower quest
But thou rufussed for then thou [?wiret] unblest

1 And stony hearted now thou hast grown kind
2 And thou wilt stay, ~~soon~~ ~~all th~~
All thouts of what the find
{ll
3 Within the world wi{th vanish from thy mind
4 And you'l rember only how the sea
5 Has fenced us twain around eternally
6 But why are you so silent did you hear
7 I laughed
8 Naschina
9 And why is that a thing so dear
10 ~~From of thy lips I caught it~~
~~I caught~~
From thy lips I caugh it en
11 ~~From thee I learnt~~ ~~een~~ the fay that that trips
at
12 ~~And~~ morn and with her feet each cobweb rends
It ~~O~~ alone
13 laughs not, for ~~laughter~~ dwells on mortal lips
14 ~~Alone~~
{ing
15 Youl teach me laugh{ter and I'll teach the peace
{ing
16 For peace and laugh{ter have been seldem friends
a boy
17 But for how long your hair has grown
18 Long cirton coils that hang around you blown

---

17 There may be a dash at the end of the line.

a voices—
~~Harken harken~~ ~~let thy voice seas~~
[?] {c
Hear [?] let sealed voices {sease
~~O youth and~~ ~~thou hot hearted~~ one
hot e
O thou h arted one and thou
wave
o mortal things by ~~sea~~ and waste
Where cypris is and ousy pine
{I
{a did
did I on suddering pinion hast
you bid me cry
I cried the thing ~~to bird and steer~~
[?~~not~~] an owl who in an alder tree
Had had hoed hooted for an hundred years
raised (up) his voice and hooted me
{en
{Th thou his wings were plumles stump
And all his veins had near run drys
From out the ashen alder trunk
He hooted as as I wandered by
And so with bore and bird and stear
And wone of all alone would ~~hart~~ hark
A man who by a dead man stood

---

2 This line is cancelled by various horizontal marks difficult to distinguish from each other.

6 The "th" of "things" is written over "one".

9–10 The following two lines on the otherwise blank facing page SB 23.3.75v are marked for insertion between lines 9 and 10:

And all was quiet round me spred
As quiet as quiet as the key cold dead

[SB 23.3.77^{r}] [VP 2,3:125–144]

A star lit rapier half blood dark
{ d
Was broken in his quivering han{ ds
where the of
As blossom ~~in a~~ wind ~~of~~ ~~marsh~~ March
Hold festival acros the land
He shrank before my voce and stood
low dumb
~~Stil~~ bowed and ~~mute~~ upon the sand
A foolish quest thou gavest me
{th
For each within himself ha{ [?] all
The world within his folded heart
{his temple
{[?] ~~castles~~ and his banquet hall
And who will throw his mansion down
{ B
{[?]ut for anothers buggle call—
Enchantress—
but why this whim of thine—A strange unrest
Is on thy face thy lips are closely prest
And why so silent for I'd hear thee speak
Soon wilt thou smile for hear the winds are weak
As moths with broken wings and as we sit
The heavens all strar throbing are a lit
Naschan
But art thou happy

4 This line is squeezed into the same ruled space of the notebook as l. 5.

Enchanter.

Let me gaze on thee

at arm, [illegible] thou [illegible] [illegible],

I could ever gaze upon thine eyeballs ~~blue~~ grey

~~Gaze on until the final trumpet~~

~~or until~~ the lily crumble, time itself decay

~~gaze on until the earth had passed away~~

~~En~~

If you were weeping here should sorrow cease

Naschina

But art thou happy

Enchanter

Youth I am at peace

[illegible] Naschina

But ~~are you happy~~ happy, not

Enchanter

Have ~~you never seen~~ thou

These eyes so grey of thine

Have they never seen the eyes of beast or kine

Or aught remote or have you never heard

1 Enchantress
2 Let me gaze on thee
3 At arms lenth thus unto entenity
grey
4 I could en gaze upon thine eyeballs ~~blue~~
5 ~~gaze on until the final trumpet~~
~~un until the~~ till crumbling time itself decay
6 gaze on ~~until the earth had passed away~~
7 ~~En~~
8 Ay you are weaping here should sorrow cease
9 Naschana
10 But art thou happae
11 Enchantress
12 Youth I am at peace
13 [~~?~~] Naschina
happyness
14 But ~~are you happy~~
15 Enchantress
~~thou~~
16 ~~Have you never~~ ~~seen~~
17 These eyes so grey of thine
18 Have they neer seen the eyes of beast or kine
19 Or aught remote or have you never heard

8 The "A" in "Ay" appears to be written over the start of another letter.
15 One or more letters are missing near the end of "Enchantress".

Naschana ~~But you must seak~~
For [?joy]
Nay ~~for~~ we
joy
Must seek for ~~faith~~ Nor yet forget to seek
for faith from [?Mary/?Murcy] and the psalery
and holy wells

he
and called alone for her I die →

In the notebook this page contains insertions for the facing page SB 23.3.80^{r}. Lines 1–6 are marked for insertion after l. 8 there, and l. 7 to go after l. 19 there. Neither insertion found its way into the final version of the scene. In the present volume the facing page 348 is blank so that the facsimiles on pages 346 and 350 can face their transcriptions.

7 This line is in a darker black ink than the rest of the page, as is the arrow indicating its location.

Nevin

moss clotted leaves the voice of song except bird
who passed the forest through with flower wreath
Or have you never seen with the visage meek
hoary old hunter lean upon his staff
alone as you passed by and did he cough
all then they are at peace.

A voice that is eared

cease - cease - cease
I did from this foot short upward dart
Till the fretful wanderers under my feet
and the lake that hid song in its golden heart
Bright a rippling Lakes' thing on the surface moved
as the canker worm on a milk white rose
and down I came as a falcon swoops
When his sinewy wings he doth up close

and I lit by the thing twas a cowering maiden
The same who had stood at the bloody oak bank
and I cried the words that you bid me cry
and at the rais'd her armour gurgling sank
and thither I came when I saw her die

1 ~~Never~~
2 Mong clotted leaves the voice of song wrapt bird
3 who passed the forestt through with fluting week
with
4 Or have you never seen ~~the~~ visage meek
{ Some hoary
5 { [?] ~~mute old~~ hunter lean upon his staff
{ y laugh
6 Alone as { [?]ou passed by and did he ~~lague~~
7 ~~all~~ these ~~they~~ are at peace.
8 that is enough
9 A voice
10 ~~peace~~ cease—cease—cease
stool
11 I did from thy foots upward dart
12 Till the fretful [?birds] were under my feet
13 And the lake that has song in its folded heart
But rigling
14 ~~And~~ a ~~dusky~~ thing on its surface moved
{ c
15 As the { [?]anker worm on a milk white rose
falkan
16 And down I came as a ~~phantom~~ swwops
17 When his sinewy wings he doth upclose
18 And I lit by the thing twas a swimming [?man] [~~?I~~]
19 The same who had stood on the blood dark bank
20 And I cried the ~~th[?]~~ words ~~that~~ you bid me cry
arm and
21 And ~~it~~ he raised his^gurgling sank
22 And thither I came when I saw him die

Passages for insertion from the facing page SB 23.3.79v are marked to follow ll. 8 and 19, respectively.

8 "that is enough" is squeezed into the same ruled space of the notebook as l. 9.

14 "rigling" and the cancellation mark through "dusky" are in darker ink.

19 Written in darker ink, this line is squeezed into the same ruled space of the notebook as the following one.

ACT 2—
scene 3—
The Island—
Flowers of many colours fill the scene
a across the stage a brazen gate
above which in a citron coloured
sky falter a few stars—
[?] 1 voice
{ir
What do you weave so fa{re and bright
2 voice
~~f~~ of
The cloak I weave ~~of~~ sorrow
O lovely to see in all mens sight
Shall be the cloak of sorrow
In all mens sight
3 voice
What do yo build with sails for flight
4 voice
A boat I build for sorrow
O swift on the seas all day and night
Saileth the rover sorrow

Yeats wrote this version of the final scene in a notebook labelled "Island of Statues / Part 2 / and / The Seeker". Inside the front cover is the following column of addition:

193
290
483
100
583
77
660
760
80
840

all day and night
5 voice
What do you weave with wool so white
6 voice
The sandals these of sorrow
Sound less shall be the footfall light
In each mans ears of sorrow
Sudden and light
Enter Naschina with the enchantress
of the Island
Naschina
What are the voices that in flowery ways
Have clothed their tongues with song of songless days
Enchantress
They are the flowers guardian sprights
With streeming hair as wandering lights
They passed a tiptoe every where
And never heard of grief or ~~eor~~ care
~~And~~ Until this morn—as addars back
The sky was banded o'er with wrack

6 There is an unclear mark between ''Sound'' and ''less'' which may be intended to eliminate the space between them.

17 There may be a hyphen between ''tip'' and ''toe''.

whose
They were sitting round a pool
At their feet the waves in rings
Gently shook their moth like wings
For their came an air breath cool
From [?thee] ever moving pinions
Of the happy flower minions
But a sudden mencholy
Filled them as they sat togeather
~~mo~~ Now their songs are mournful holy
As they go with drooping feather
Naschina
O lady thou who's vestiture of green
Is rolled as verdent smoke
O thou who's face
Is worn as though with fire, O goblin queen
Leed me I prey thee to the statued place
Enchantress
Fair youth along a wandering way
I led the here and as a wheel
We turned around the place alway

---

1 "whose" is written in a lighter ink than the rest of the page as a trial spelling rather than a revision.

14 Presumably, Yeats saw that he could not finish the line before reaching the margin and completed it immediately below.

stony
1 Lest on thine heart the ~~silent~~ seel
2 As on these other hearts, were laid—
3 Behold the brazen gated glade
partialy
4 she ~~easts~~ opens the brazen gates
5 The statues are seen within some
6 are bending with their hands among
7 the flowers Others are holding
8 Withered flowers ~~in their hands~~
9 ~~Naschina (resting with an arm~~
10 ~~over each gate)~~
11 Naschina
~~the~~
~~his~~ the
12 O let me pass, the spells from off ~~his~~ heart
13 ~~Of my sad hunter lover shall de~~
14 ~~At touch of the enchanted flower depart~~
15 O Let me pass ~~in~~
16 Enchantress (resting with an
17 arm over each gate)
18 That flower none
19 Who seek may find save only one

---

4 The "s" probably was added later to "open".

12 Apparently, Yeats first cancelled the original "his" and substituted "the", then cancelled "the" and wrote a new "his", and finally cancelled that "his" and wrote a new "the".

13 This line is squeezed between ll. 12 and 14. Two lines on the facing page SB 23.3.118^v are marked for insertion here:

> Of my sad hunter friend shall all depart
>
> If on his lips the enchan{t / ded} flower be laid

That verso also has the numeral 580 in pencil opposite l. 18 of the present page. Upside down in pencil are the last three lines of the prose review on SB 23.3.120^v, which are transcribed with that page at the end of the draft.

A shepherdess long years foretold
And even she shall never hold
The flower save some thing be found
to air
~~Who'll~~ ~~will~~ die for her in ~~wave~~ or ground
And none their are, If such their were—
En then before her spepherd hair
{f
Had {selt the island breeze my lore
Would drive her forth for ever more
To wander by the ~~bubbling~~ pulsing shore
Laugher lipped but for her brain
A guerdon of deep rooted pain
in
And ~~for~~ her eyes a lightless ~~stair~~ stare—
^
For if severed from the root
~~The~~ The enchanted flower were
wizard
From my ~~winged~~ Island lair
And the happy wingéd day
I, as music that grows mute
On a girls forgotton lute,
pass away—

4 Yeats appears to have written first "Who will", then changed that to "Who'll", and finally settled on "to".
15 "winged" is cancelled by multiple lines and followed by an uncertain mark which may be a caret.

~~En~~ <u>Naschina</u>
Your eyes are all a flash—She is not here
~~I am a spepherd youth~~
<u>Enchantress</u>
kill
I would ~~slay~~ her if she were—Nay do not fear
With you I am all gentleness in truth

There's little I'd refuse to the—o youth
~~h~~
~~There is but little I'd refuse thee~~ ~~yout~~{ ~~[?]~~
<u>Naschina</u>
I have a whim let some attendent sprite
Of thine cry over [?] wold and water white
That one shall die unless one die for her—
I ~~fain would see if any thing would stir~~
Tis but to see if any thing would stir
For such a call e'n let the word be cried
As though she whom you fear had crossed the tide
Though she has not
<u>Enchantress</u>
A little thing that is
And shall be done if you will dain to kiss
Fair youth my lips

Naschina
It shall be as you ask
Enchantress
            { O
Forth, Forth { [?] spirits you have heard your task
voices
We are gone
Enchantress (sitting down by Naschina)
Good youth as we two hither came
                                                    { e
I besaught thee in this island to r{ amain
                                                    { e
Where dream fed passion is and peace { uncloses
Where revel of foxglove is and revel of roses
And banish ever more thine hopeless quest
wouldst not
But thou refused, for then thou wert unblest
And stony hearted now thou hast grown kind
And thou wilt stay—All thaught of what they find
Within the world will vanish from thy mind
And you'll remember only how the sea
Has fenced us round for all eternity
But ~~why are you so silent did you~~ hear
~~I laughed~~

The cancellation marks in ll. 19–20 are in pencil.

In shaddowy dimness to be fair as thee
Id give ~~mine~~ my faery fleetness thoug I be
Far fleeter than the million footed sea
And all the quiet of my faery brow

to be restored

100

[?202]

Lines 1–4 are marked for insertion at the end of the Enchantress's speech on the facing page SB 23.3.125^{r}.
6 The numeral is in pencil.
7 The numeral is in blue pencil.

Naschina
and [?] why is that a thing so dear
Enchantress
From thy lips I caught it en the fay that trips
At morn and with her feet each cob web rends
Laughs not—It dwells alone on mortal lips—
You'll teach me laughing and I'll teach thee peace
For peace and laughing have been seldom friends—
thine
But for a boy how long ~~your~~ hair has grown
thee
Long citron coils that hang around ~~you~~ blown
a voice
~~O thou hot~~
{a
He{er—and let thy whispiring cease
O thou hot hearted one and thou
O mortal thing by wave and waste
Where cypris is and ousy pine
Did I on shuddering pinnions haste
And all was quiet round me spred
clay
As quiet as the ~~key~~ cold dead

Lines 1–10 are cancelled in pencil by a combination of pencil strokes and are overwritten by three linked letters which look like "esp". The lines on the facing verso SB 23.3.124v are marked for insertion at the end of the Enchantress's speech, and the direction "to be restored" there probably refers to the entire speech.

{a
I ~~e[?]~~ cried the thing you b{ide me cry
An owl who in an alder tree
Had hooted for an hundred years
Up raised his voice and hooted me
En though his wings were plumeless stumps
And all his vains had near run dry
From forth the hollow alder trunk
He hooted as I wandered by
And so with wolf and boar and steer
And one alone of all would hark
~~And~~ A man who by a dead man stood
A starlit rapier half blood dark
Was broken in his quivering hand
As blossoms when the winds of March
festival
Hold ~~revelry~~ across the land
He shrank before my voice and stood
Low bowed and dumb upon the sand
A foolish word thou gavest me
For each within himself hath all
The world within his folded heart

3 The otherwise blank facing page SB 23.3.126v contains an alternate reading in light black ink: "Was hooting for his hundreth year".

5 The "gh" at the end of "though" appears to be added later.

His temple and his banquet hall
And who will throw his mansion down
thus at
~~But for~~ anothers buggle call
Enchantress
But why this whim of thine—a strange unrest
As a ∫ k
Alien as ∧ coc{[?]o in a robins nest
Is in thy face and lips togeather prest
And why so silent—I would hear thee speak
Soon wilt thou smile, for hear the winds are weak
As moths with broken wings and as we sit
The heavens all star throbbing are a-lit
Naschina
But ar't thou happy
Enchantress
Let me gaze on ~~me~~ thee—
At arms length thus for all eternity
~~I could en gaze for all eternity~~
I could en gaze upon thine eyeballs grey
gaze on till (knavish) time himself decay—

Opposite ll. 10–13 on the facing page SB 23.3.128v the phrase "To be extended" is written in pencil.
6 The "A" of "As" is in the left margin.
19 The circle around "knavish" and the line extending from it are in pencil. The line runs to the facing page of the notebook, where a substitute word—probably "ragged"—is written and circled in pencil.

bubbling

an hoary hunter leening on his bow
To watch the pass. Yet deeper than men know
These are at peace

180

---

1 "bubbling" is a substitution for "clotted" in l. 12 of the facing page on the right, SB 23.3.131^{r}.
2–4 These lines rework ll. 15–17 of the facing page.
5 The numeral 180 is aligned with the last line of the facing page.

all grief
Ay you are ~~we~~ weeping, here should sorrow cease
Naschina
But ar't thou happy
Enchantress
Youth I am at peace
Naschina
But happiness
Enchantress
These eyes so grey of thine
Have they nee'r seen the eyes of lynx or ~~ky~~ kine
has't thou
Or aught remote or ~~have you~~ never heard
mong clotted leaves a wandering song wrapt bird
going the forest through with fluttings weak
{h
Or {sas't thou never seen with visage meek
An hoary hunter lean upon his staff
Alone as thou passed by and did he laugh
These are [~~?ar~~] at peace
a voice
~~O love sick~~ ~~Cease cease cease cease~~
{a
Sad [~~?a~~] Lady ce{[?]se

12 The line around the bottom of "clotted" is in pencil; the substitution "bubbling" is given in pencil on the facing page to the left, SB 23.3.130v.

15–17 The large "X" at the right, and the indeterminate mark which it covers, are both in pencil. An alternate wording for these lines is given in pencil on the facing verso.

20 This line may be in a slightly different color of ink.

I rose I rose
From the dim woods foundation
I rose I rose
Where in white exultation
~~The lilies einclose~~
The long ~~lilly~~ lily blows
And the wan wave that lingers
{o
From flo{ud time encloses
{n
With infanti{[?]e fingerrs
roots
The [~~?forests~~] of the roses
{n
From the{[?]ce I came winging
I there had been keeping
A mouse from his sleeping
With shouting and singing
Enchantress
How sped thy quest, this prelude we'll not hear it
was't
In truth thou ever ~~were't~~ a wordy spirit
voice —
A rigling thing on the white lake moved
As the canker worm on a milk white rose

4 Yeats misspelled "exultation" as either "exulation" or "exutation".

and down I came as a falchon swoops
When his sinewy wings he doth up close
and I lit by the thing 'twas a shepherd young boy
who swimming sawed stern to reach the island bank lone
with in his clenched teeth a sword
I heard the deathful monotone
The water serpent sings his heart
Before a death — Over wave and bank
I cried the thing word you bade me cry
The shepherd raised his arms and sank
His rueful spirit fluttered by

Naschina (aside)
I must bestir myself both dead for me
~~Both dead. No time to think I must bestir~~
both dead no time to think
~~myself. Both dead for me~~

(aloud) I am she

The long foretold ~~wanderer~~ arises and bring to me
In silence that famed flower of wizardry
For I am mightier now by far than thee
~~That Thou dead with foul Phantoms and black art~~
For faded now is all thy far wondrous art

1 And down I came as a falchon swoops
togather
2 When his sinewy wings he doth up close
~~boy~~
3 And I lit by the thing 'twas a spepherd ~~young~~ boy
swimming saught
4 who ~~strove~~ ~~to reach~~ the island ~~bank~~ lone
5 with in his clenchéd teath a sword
6 I heard the deathful monatone
7 The water serpent sings ~~him~~ his heart
8 Before a death—Oer wave and bank
words
9 I cried the ~~thing~~ you bade me cry
^
10 The spepherd raised his arms and sank
11 His rueful spirit fluttered by
12 Naschina (aside)
I must bestir myself both dead for me
13 ~~Both dead—no time to think I must bestir~~
both dead no time to think
14 ~~myself. Both dead for me~~
she
15 (aloud) I am ~~her~~
that shepherdess
16 ~~The long foretold~~ ~~I am her~~ arise and bring to me
17 In silence that famed flower of wizerdry
18 For I am mightier now by far than thee
19 ~~T[?] Thou dealer with foul Phantoms and black art~~
20 For faded now is all thy ~~fa~~ wondrous art

13–14 The revised wording also appears in pencil on the otherwise blank facing page SB 23.3.133v of the notebook.

1 The Enchantress points to a cleft in
2 the rock
3 Naschina
4 I see within a cloven rock dispart
5 ~~A starry bloom~~
dying faery
6 A scarlet bloom O ~~wizard~~ one
famous
7 Why dwells the ~~scarlet~~ minion of the sun
8 In shadow thus—What mean the lights that rise
9 As light of triumph in thy goblin eyes
10 In thy wan face
11 Enchantress
12 Hear thou o daughter of days
ways
13 Behold the loving loveless flower of lone ~~days~~ [~~?de~~]
~~sign~~ token of {O
14 The ~~star~~ of ~~thy~~ lone life {o daughter of days
15 Well nigh imortal in this charmed clime
16 thou shalt out live thine amerous happy time
17 And dead as are the lovers of old rime
18 ~~The~~ shall be the hunter lover of thy youth
Yet {y
19 ~~Yeth~~ ever more through all th{e days of ruth
20 Shall grow thy beauty and thy dream less truth

14 On the otherwise blank facing verso of the notebook are the number 200 in pencil and an indecipherable squiggle in blue pencil.
15 There may be a stress on the ''ed'' of ''charmed''.

ceasless
~~Thy soul~~, as an hurt ~~pe~~ leperd fills with∧moan
And aimless wanderings the woodland lone
pityless and bright
Thy soul ~~so~~ shall ~~it~~ be, Though ~~laughter~~ ~~bright~~
It is, yet shall it fail thee day and night
Beneath the burden of the infinite,
far
In Those [~~?fare~~] years—O daugher of the days
Yet when thou hast these things for many ages felt
a
The red squirel shall rear her young where thou h{[?]s't dwelt
Naschina
know
I ~~no~~∧not of the things you speak [~~?~~] but what
Of him on yonder brazen gated spot
By thee spell bound
Enchantress (going)
Thou shall't ~~ne~~ know more
When thou shall't meet two ravens by the shore
[?hence] mortal
~~Long hence~~ (goes)
~~*out*~~
Naschina (following her)
Will he have happiness
(exit)

---

1 "Thy soul" is cancelled in pencil.
6 "In" was added to the start of the line in the left margin.

                voices sing
A man has an hoped for heaven
  But soulless a faery dies
As a leaf that is old, and withered and cold
  When the wintery vapours rise

Soon shall our wings be stilled
  {A
  {and our laughter over and done
So let us dance where the yellow lance
  Of the barley shoots in the sun

So let us dance on the fringéd waves
  And shout at the wisest owls
In their downy caps, and startle the naps
  Of the dreaming water fowls

and fight for the black sloe berries
  for soulless a faery dies
as a leaf that is old, and withered and cold
  When the wintery vapours rise

9 The number 200 (or 280), amended to 250, is written in pencil opposite this line on the otherwise blank facing verso of the notebook.

Enter Naschina
Naschina
I plucked her backward by her dress of green
To question her. Oh no I did not fear
Because St Francis' image hangeth hear
Upon my necklace. But the goblin queen
Faded and vanished nothing now is seen
saving a green frog dead upon the grass—
As figures moving mirrered in a glass
The singing spepherds to have passed away
~~would be [?felt]~~
~~Ah me~~ ~~I knew some~~ ~~evil~~ ^ ~~on this day~~
~~'En since the solitary magpie crost~~
~~My road,~~ ah now Ill whake these sleepers lost
and woe begone, For them no evil day
(~~Opens~~ throws open the brazen
gates)
Naschina (to Almintor)
O wake wake wake for soft as a bee sips
The faery flower lies upon thy lips

---

4 The punctuation mark may be either a comma or a period and is written in pencil.
8 The punctuation mark in pencil at the end may be either a dash or a period.
11–13 Opposite these lines on the otherwise blank facing page SB 23.3.138^{v} of the notebook Yeats wrote:

O arcady, {O / of Arcady} this day
A deal of evil and of change has crost
Thy peace—

Almintor
I slept. T'was sultry and scarce circling shook
The falling hawthorn bloom, by mere and brook
The otters dreamed—You ~~here~~ in the spell bound isle
Naschina
Ay gaze but gaze in silence yet a while
(to the second sleeper)
Old warrior wake for soft as a bee sips
The faery ~~flower~~ blossom lies upon thy lips
——→ ————————————————→
2 Sleeper
With hungry heart
ships
Doth still the wanderer rove, With all his ~~sp~~
I saw him from sad Dido's shore depart
Enamoured of the waves impetuous lips
Naschina
These twain are dust.
for
Wake wake∧light as a bee sips
The faery blossom lies upon thy lips
Sea farer wake

3 sleeper
was my sleep long
Naschina
long years
Sleeper
A rover I who come from where men's ears
Love storm and stained with mist the new moons flair
Doth still the man whom each stern rover fears
The austere Arthur rule from [?] Uther's chair
Naschina
He is long dead
Wake shepherd soft as a bee sips
lieth on
The goblin flower ~~lies upon~~ thy lips
4 Sleeper
Was my sleep long o youth
Naschina
long long and deep
~~Youth as I came~~
Sleeper
Here
~~Youth~~ as∧I came I saw god {P / pan played

---

9 The arrows on SB 23.3.141[r] indicate insertion of the following passage from the otherwise blank facing page SB 23.3.140[v]:

1 Sleeper
Have I slept long
Naschina
long years

1 An oten pipe unto a listening fawn
2 Who oft with eyes to grief unused would weep
3 Doth he still dwell with the woody shade
~~weeping~~
4 And rule the shadows of the eve and ~~trembling~~ dawn
5 *and rule the shade's of evening and of dawn*
6 Naschina
gone
7 ~~O he~~ Yea he is ~~gone~~ ~~wak~~
8 wake wake for as a bee sips
9 The feary blossom broods upon thy lips
10 Sleeper awake
{5
11 {4 Sleeper
12 How long my sleep
13 Naschina
14 unnumbered
15 are the years of goblin sleep
16 Sleeper
17 While I slumbered
in
18 How have the years ~~of~~ Troyea flown away
are still the Achaian's tented chiefs
19 ~~Do they still hold the Achean host~~ at bay
^ ^ ^
20 Where rise the wall majestical above
21 The plain, a little fair haired maid I love

4 The cancellation mark through "weeping" is in pencil. On the otherwise blank facing page of the notebook is the number 300.
19 The words transcribed as "Do they" may be "Doth it".

All

~~Nas~~ Naschina
She is long ages ~~dust~~ dead
Shepherd (showing his breast)
Ah woe is me
—
—
—
1 sleeper
Youth here we will abide and be thou King
Of this lake nurtured isle
Naschina
Let thy King be
Yon archer, he who hath the halcyons wing
~~High fixed like a glad thought on his crest~~
~~St~~ All the sleepers cry
Clear browed Arcadian thou shalt be our King
~~O thy Almintor worthy was thy quest~~
~~Yea~~ Naschina ~~noble~~
O my Almintor ~~worthy~~ noble was ~~was thy~~ thy quest
Yea ~~no~~ noble and most kingly it hath been

all
~~Ma~~ ~~Naschina~~
She is long ages ~~dust~~ dead
h
Shepherd (showing ais broach)
Ah woe is me
~~Behold in this a ringlet of her hair is curled~~
—~~All~~—
~~as a~~
~~Truely the grey hound, sorrow coarses through the world~~
1 sleeper
Youth here we will abide and be thou King
O*f* this lake nurtured isle
Naschina
Let thy King be
Yon archer he who hath the halcyons wing
~~High fixéd like a glad thought on his crest~~
~~Sl~~ All the sleepers cry
Clear browed Arcadian thou shall't be our King
~~O my almintor worthy was thy quest~~
~~Yea [?]~~ Naschina
~~noble~~
~~knightl~~ noble was
O my Almintor ~~worthy was the~~ thy quest
Yea ~~mo~~ noble and most knightly it (hath) been

5–7 These lines are cancelled by various marks in pencil.
14 An arrow on the facing page SB 23.3.144v indicates the following line as substitute:

flaming minstril
Like a ~~minstrels flaming~~ word upon his crest ——————→

20 On the facing page opposite this line are the number 317 written and cancelled in pencil and an indecipherable word in blue pencil cancelled in ordinary pencil.

Sleepers
Clear browed arcadian thou shallt be our
King
Almintor
Until we die within the charmed ring
Of these star shuddered skies you ar the queen

E N D

(*320* <

---

7 This line is in pencil.

a new poet has appeared among us
in the person of Mr W B Yeats
a yong student of Trinity College
Dublin The Island of Statues
An Arcadean Fairy tale compled
in the June [?numer] of the
University review is a
sufficient proof of powers
distinctly out of the common
Mr Yeats has only to be careful
that his evident facily shall
not tempt him to [?over] production
and if we judge from the
promise of his published
verse ~~will~~ his performance
should yet justify the most
flattering predictions
Nor is Mr. Yeats to be judged alone
by a single poem Voices in
another number of the review is even
more remarkable as the
production of ~~so~~ a very
[?yongh] writer

This prose review (or perhaps pseudo-review by Yeats himself) is written upside down in pencil on two successive versos of the notebook. The first twenty lines appear on SB 23.3.120^{v} and the last three on SB 23.3.118^{v}.

18 The mark that appears to be a period after "Mr" may be the dot of the "i" of "single" in the next line.

Fifth Version: Printer's Copy of "The Island of Statues"

The exceptionally full manuscript record of the evolution of *The Island of Statues* culminates in the printer's copy transcribed below. Yeats probably prepared the manuscript in early 1885, in time for the first installment of the verse drama to appear in the *Dublin University Review* for April of that year. He signed the manuscript in four places, corresponding to the four installments of it in the magazine, and included directions for sending proof at the end of the first one. Yet the manuscript is by no means a fair copy. It contains heavy revision and even so differs in numerous particulars from the published version. Yeats must have executed the final changes in now-lost proofs.

A special problem of the manuscript is the presence of a hand other than Yeats's. At the end of the first installment (KS 7) Yeats included a note directing proofs to be sent to himself at 10 Ashfield Terrace and to T. W. Lyster at 89 Marlborough Road. Under the direction is a two-line pencilled note in a different hand. Line 1 reads: "Corrections made by", with an arrow pointing to "Lyster". The second line reads "W. Frazer". Thus, the note appears to assign the corrections to Lyster, on the authority of Frazer; it is possible, however, that the arrow applies to the entire two lines, which would then assign the corrections for the first installment to Frazer. But the presence of the arrow, the similarity of the corrections to Lyster's handwriting, and Yeats's later recollection (discussed in the Introduction to the present volume) all make Lyster the more probable candidate, even though both the ambiguity of the pencilled notation and the brevity of many changes (sometimes amounting only to punctuation) make it imprudent to rule out Frazer's possible participation. The changes do represent an additional stage of composition and must have been approved by Yeats.

In view of such complexities, the following transcriptions employ one additional type style (***boldface italic***) for any correction definitely in a hand other than Yeats's. In addition, line notes indicate when emendations are probably the work of another hand. But it has proved impossible to ascribe every change with certainty. Because facsimiles are included for so few pages, I have followed a conservative policy of indicating the presence of another hand only when the evidence appears reasonably clear. Brief corrections whose origin appears ambiguous have been transcribed as though by Yeats. The manuscripts are written basically in black ink, often faded to brown, with Lyster (and perhaps Frazer) apparently using a slightly darker black than Yeats and with occasional pencil corrections. As elsewhere in this volume, Yeats's pencil corrections are rendered in italics. But for the special cases of a pencil correction overwritten in darker black ink by another hand, I have opted for the boldface italic type used elsewhere to indicate those contributions, and have described in a note to the appropriate line the presence of both instruments. Similarly, I have recorded all overwritings that change actual spellings but have passed over the numerous instances where Lyster (or Yeats himself) merely reinforced Yeats's own letters.

The manuscript is in the Hugh Walpole Collection, King's School, Canterbury. It consists of forty-nine leaves, written on rectos only and bound in green morocco gilt, with Walpole's bookplate inside the front cover. On the manuscript the leaves are numbered in four groups, corresponding to the four magazine installments, as follows: folios 1–7; 1–13 (folios 5 and 6 of this group are missing); 1–12 (folios 7 and 12 of this group lack numbers); and folios 1–20 (this group lacks a page with the number 19, but there is no gap in the text). Their dimensions vary: the first group is on long sheets measuring from 26.7 cm to 27.3 cm by 20.2 cm; the remaining groups are on shorter sheets with dimensions varying from 22.2 cm to 19.8 cm high by 18.7 cm to 15.9 cm wide. The pagination on the first group of leaves (1 through 7) does not appear to be in Yeats's hand. For simplicity of reference in the transcriptions, I have recorded the given pagination where it occurs but have also assigned consecutive numbers to each page of the manuscript in a bracket at the top left, from 1 to 49. Thus [KS 19] indicates the nineteenth leaf of the King's School manuscript.

The black rectangles extending from the right margin on KS 29, 36, 39, and 40 direct that those lines be moved to the right by the printer. The manuscript also contains a loose envelope of the National Library of Ireland, Science and Art Department, addressed to "W. Frazer Esq M. D. 20 Harcourt Street" and inscribed "From T. W. Lyster MSS of W. B. Yeats' Poem 'Island of Statues' ".

The Island of Statues
An Arcadian faery tale in Two Acts —
Dramatis Personae

Naschina — Shepherdess — Almintor a hunter
Colin — Shepherd — Antonio — His page
Thernot — Shepherd — Enchantress of the Island
And a company of the sleepers of the isle

Act I.
Scene I.

(Before the cottage of Naschina, it is morning and away in the depth of the heaven the moon is fading.
Enter Thernot with a lute

Thernot: Maiden come forth, the woods keep watch for thee,
Within the drowsy blossom hangs the bee.
'Tis morn, thy sheep are wandering down the vale,
'Tis morn, like old men's eyes the stars are pale,
And thro the odorous air love-dreams are winging,
'Tis morn, and from the dew-drenched wood I sped
To welcome thee, Naschina, with sweet singing —
(sitting on a tree-stem he begins to tune his lute)
(Enter Colin Abstractedly)
Colin. Come forth, the morn is fair; as from the pyre
Of sad Queen Dido shone the lapping fire
Unto the wanderers' ships, or as day fills
The brazen sky, so blaze the daffodils;
As Argive Clytemnestra saw out-burn
The flagrant signal of her Lord's return,
Afar clear-shining on the herald hills
In vale and dell so blaze the daffodils;
As when upon her cloud o'er-muffled steep,
Oenone saw the fires of Troia leap,
And laughed, so, so along the bubbling rills
In lemon-tinted lines, so blaze the daffodils.
Come forth, come forth, my music pours for thee,
A quenchless grieving of love melody (raises his lute)
Thernot (sings) Now her sheep all browsing meet
By the singing water's edge
Tread and tread their down feet
On the ruddy river-sedge,

1

([~~?1~~] [~~?sheet~~])

The Island of Statues

Two

An Arcadian faery-tale—in ~~2~~ Acts—

Dramatis Personae

~~These are the people thereof~~

Naschina—Shepherdess—Almintor—a hunter

Colin —Shepherd —Antonio —His page

Enchantress of the Island

Thernot —Shepherd —And a company of the sleepers of the isle

Act I.

Scene I.

~~Act 1. Scene 1.~~ (Before the cottage of Naschina; it is morning

and ~~afar~~ away in the depth of the heaven the moon is fading.

Enter Thernot with a lute

keep watch for thee,

Thernot. Maiden come forth, the woods [~~?are ?waiting ?thee~~]

Within the drowsy blossom hangs the bee,

down

'Tis morn, thy sheep are wandering ~~in~~ the vale,

'Tis morn, like old men's eyes the stars are pale,

thro ***o***

And ~~in~~ the od{erous air love-dreams are winging,

'Tis morn, and from the dew-drenched wood I sped

N

To welcome thee, {naschina, with sweet singing—

(sitting on a tree-stem he begins to tune his lute)

C ***A***

(Enter {colin {abstractedly)

O{A

Colin. Come forth, the morn is fair; {as from the pyre

Q D

Of sad {queen {dido shone the lapping fire

Unto the wanderers' ships, or as day fills

The brazen sky, so blaze the daffodils; ///

A ***C***

As {argive {clytemnestra saw out-burn

The flagrant signal of her lord's return /,

herald hills

Afar clear-shining on the [~~?herald ?hills~~], ///

In vale and dell so blaze the ~~dafo~~ daffodils;

upon

As when ~~from [?on]~~ her cloud o'er-muffled steep,

Troia a

OEnone saw the fires of ~~Troyea~~ le{ep;

And laughed, so, so along the bubbling rills

t

In lemon-tin{ded lines, so blaze the daffodils.

Come forth, come forth, my music pours for thee,

A

{a quenchless grieving of love melody (raises his lute)

her

Thernot (sings) Now ~~thy~~ sheep all browsing meet

By the singing water's' edge

a ***a*** ***~~little~~*** cloven

Tred and tred their ~~cloven~~ feet

On the ruddy river-sedge,

4–5 “Naschina” and “Colin” are double-underlined lightly in pencil.

6 The underlining here, as in ll. 9–10 and 19–20, is in darker black ink and possibly by another hand. The phrase “Enchantress of the Island” was squeezed into the space between ll. 5 and 6.

10 Yeats may have omitted the “t” in “depth”.

16–17 The hyphens are probably by another hand.

21 The caret, inserted “O”, and capital “A” were written in ink (possibly by another hand) and then imperfectly erased.

24 The dash after “daffodils” was cancelled and the original comma or colon changed to a semicolon.

25 The hyphen in “out-burn” is probably by another hand.

26 The apostrophe in “lord's” is probably by another hand.

27 The hyphen, caret, and the phrase “herald hills” are in purple ink or pencil and probably by another hand.

30 “Troia” is in blue pencil overwritten in black ink and probably by another hand. At the end of the line, the dot of the original semicolon was cancelled to result in a comma.

31 The second comma, like the one in l. 32, is cancelled in blue pencil.

35 A loop in blue pencil has been added to the “N” of “Now”. “her” here and “cloven” in l.37 may be by another hand.

All hyphens on this page seem to be in darker ink and may be by another hand.

3 The cancelled question mark in the right margin may represent a query to Yeats about the new wording.

6 The first comma is in blue pencil overwritten with darker ink, probably by another hand.

8 The new wording is in another hand, and the question mark in the right margin may represent a query to Yeats about the new wording.

9 The final “e” and question mark are probably by another hand.

12 “s” was presumably added to “light” at the same time that “is” was changed to “are”; the question mark at the right may represent a query to Yeats about the new wording.

13 “to” is in blue pencil overwritten with black ink.

21 Yeats first wrote “troup” in black ink; then “op” was written over “up” in blue pencil, and “troop” was written above; and finally, “oop” was written in darker black ink over the original “oup”. Lyster probably had a hand in the revision.

22 The dot of the semicolon is cancelled in darker black ink.

24 The hyphen and comma are in blue pencil overwritten in darker black ink.

25 The cancelled illegible word is a misspelling of “young”.

32 In the main body of the line, the loop on the “n” of “neck” is in blue pencil. At the end of that word, “ 's” has been added in darker ink, and the caret and cancel mark are in blue pencil. The letter through which the cancel mark passes looks like an “e” but may be an “s”. The “neck's” in the left margin is in black ink over blue pencil and is probably by another hand.

33 The “ies” of “beauties” is in blue pencil overwritten in black ink; the caret is in blue pencil.

([~~?2~~] [~~?sheet~~]) 2

For the dawn the foliage fingereth,
And the waves are leaping white,
She my
~~Thou~~ alone, ~~o~~ lady, lingereth [?]
While the world is rolled in light.
~~Colin. [?Shepherd ?to ?morning ?hast ?thou ?come]~~
Colin. Shepherd, to mar the morning hast thou come,
Hear me, and shepherd hearing me grow dumb.
Where is the owl that lately flew
(sings) ~~The owl has gone from where she flew~~ [?]
Flickering under the white moon-shine?
She sleeps with owlets two and two,
Sleepily close her round bright eyne;
are
O'er her nest the light*s* ~~is~~∧blending: ?
to
Come thou, come, and [~~?two~~] this string,
Though my love-sick heart is rending,
Not a sad note will I sing.
~~Thernot (sings)~~
Thernot I am not dumb, I'd sooner silent wait
Within the fold to hear the creaking gate.
the
(sings) The wood~~land~~ and∧valley and sea
Awaken, awaken to new-born lustre,
troop
A new day's tro{op / up} of wasp and bee
Hang on the side of the round grape-cluster;
on
Blenching∧high the dull stars sicken
Morn-bewildered, and the cup
young
Of the tarn where [—?—] waves quicken
Hurls their swooning lustre up.
Colin. I'll silence this dull singer—
gleaming
(sings) Oh more dark thy ~~lustrous~~∧hair is,
pansy's
Than the peeping ~~pansies'~~ face,
[~~?ae~~]{y
And thine eyes more bright than faer {ie's
Dancing in some moony place,
neck's And thy neck∧{' / ~~e~~s} a poiséd lily
beauties
See, I tell thy [~~?beautys~~]∧~~o're~~ o'er,
As within a cellar chilly
Some old miser tells his store,

The underlining in ll. 6, 15, 24, 25, 30, and 33 is in darker ink and probably by another hand.

1 The caret and separate "y" are in blue pencil.

3 "Till" is in blue pencil overwritten in black ink, probably by another hand.

14 The correction of "a" to "e" in "persistance" is in blue pencil overwritten in black ink, probably by another hand.

18 The "is" above the line is written in blue pencil and cancelled in ink; and "marks" is cancelled in blue pencil and ink. The corrections of "burden" and "persistance" are probably by another hand.

23 Another hand probably supplied the period.

24 The caret, line, and loop are in ordinary pencil.

([?3] [~~?sheet~~]) 3

memory *y*
And thy ~~memory~~ ^ I keep
Till all else is empty chaff,
Till {e
~~And~~ I laugh when others we{ap,
Weeping when all others laugh ⊙ ⊙
Thernot I'll quench his singing with loud song
{C
(sings wildly) {come forth, for in a thousand bowers
[~~?Blossoms ?ope ?their ?dewy ?lips~~]
Blossoms open dewy lips,
O'er the lake the water-flowers,/
Drift and float
~~Floating are~~ ^ like silver ships,
Hundred throated dawn
~~All the dawning day~~ ^ is singing
{e
Joy and love are one exist{ance,
{E
{ever ringing, ringing, ringing,
{e
With unfaltering persist{ance.
Lone and wanting
Colin (sings) ~~Alone and waiting~~ ^ thee, I weep;
Love and sorrow, one existence,
Sadness, soul of joy most deep,
~~*is*~~ {***th*** {***e***
Is [~~?Marks~~] the bur{den and persist{ance
Of the songs that never sleep.—
Love from heaven came of yore
As a token and a sign,
o'er,
Singing ~~oer'~~ and o'er, and o'er,
Of his death and change malign ⊙
yon
Thernot. With fiery song I'll drown ~~yon~~ ^ puny voice
(sings, (leaping to his feet))
~~[?] with her sickle of light~~ ^
~~The moon has gone with sickle bright,~~
Passeth the moon with her sickle of light,
Slowly, slowly fadeth she,
Weary of reaping the barren night,
And the desolate shuddering sea ⊙
crieth
Colin (sings) ~~standing~~ Loud for thee, the morning [~~?cryeth~~]
~~dieth~~
And my soul in ~~darkness~~ waiting ~~dyeth~~
dieth
{E ***dieth, dieth, dieth.***
{ever ~~dyeth~~ ^ ~~ever dyeth~~ ^
Thernot (sings) Far the morning vapours shatter,
As the leaves in autumn scatter.

5 The capitalization of ''Lift'', along with ''Stricken'' in l. 6 and ''Music'' in l. 7, is probably by another hand.
10 The closing parenthesis after ''Naschina'' appears to be written over a dash.
11 Another hand probably supplied the capital ''O''.
17 Another hand probably supplied the extended dash here and the capital ''C'' in the next line.
21 The hyphen is in blue pencil.
23 ''named'' is in blue pencil overwritten in black ink, probably by another hand.
24 Another hand supplied the capital ''A'' and probably the underlining.
25 Another hand supplied the capital ''A'' and probably the exclamation point.
26 There are illegible corrections in blue pencil under the cancellation marks through ''subtle'' and ''subtile''.
33 Another hand probably supplied the capital ''A'' of both ''Almintor'' and ''Antonio''. The ''a'' of ''togather'' was cancelled in blue pencil and overwritten in black ink, also probably by another hand.

([~~?4~~] [~~?sheet~~]) 4

w
Colin (sings) In the heart of the da{[?]n the rivers are singing ~~//~~
Over them crimson vapours winging—
Thernot (sings) All the world is ringing, ringing,
All the world is singing, singing.
L
Colin (sings) {lift my soul from rayless night—
S
Thernot (sings) {stricken all the night is past— —
M
Colin (sings) {music of [~~?his~~] my soul and light—
Thernot (sings) Back the shadows creep aghast—
(They approach one another while singing with angry
E
gestures.—{enter Naschina~~)—~~
O
Naschina. {oh, cease your singing! wild, and shrill, and loud,
On my poor brain your busy tumults crowd.
Colin. I fain had been the first of singing things
To welcome thee, when o'er the owlet's wings
And troubled eyes, came morning's first-born glow,
But yonder thing, yon idle noise, yon crow
Yon shepherd——
~~The~~ ***C***
Thernot {came your spirit to beguile
With singing sweet as e'r round lake-lulled isle
S
{sing summer waves—But yonder shepherd vile,
All clamour-clothed
Colin Was't clamour when I sung,
named
Whom men have ^ ~~called~~ Arcadia's sweetest tongue
A
({a horn sounds)
A
Colin {a horn! some troop of robbers winding goes
~~Along the wood~~ subtle
[—? ?—] ~~subtile [?tread] and bended bows~~
Along the wood with subtle tread and bended bows.
F
(An arrow passes) {fly!
Above
F
Thernot—{fly!
(Colin~~in~~ and Thernot go)
S both
Naschina [~~?Col~~] {so these brave shepherds ~~both~~ are gone ^
Courageous miracles—
A ***A*** ***e***
(Enter {almintor and {antonio, talking tog{~~a~~ther)

2 ''thro'', the caret, and the question mark in the right margin are probably by another hand.

11 ''Their'' is written in black ink over ''eir'' in blue pencil.

17 Another hand may have supplied ''woolly''.

18 The first comma and dash are in blue pencil overwritten in black ink, probably by another hand.

20 The hyphen is in darker ink and probably by another hand.

21 The ''e'' of ''lonely'' and the cancelled punctuation after ''moon'' are in blue pencil overwritten in black ink, probably by another hand.

25 The caret under ''ash-trees' '' and the cancellation mark through the apostrophe before ''mong'' are in blue pencil; the ''trees'' of ''ash-trees' '' is in blue pencil overwritten in black ink, probably by another hand.

26 The hyphen is in blue pencil and black ink.

33 Both ''e''s of ''ere'' and the second ''z'' of ''whizzed'' are in blue pencil overwritten in black ink; the caret is in blue pencil.

([~~?5~~] [~~?sheet~~]) 5

Almintor. The sunlight shone
thro
Upon his wings, ~~in~~^yonder green abyss ?
I sent an arrow
Antonio And I saw you miss,
And far away the heron ~~soars~~ sails I wis.
~~Nay~~
I missed him not
Almintor. Nay, Nay, ~~I did not miss~~, his days
Of flight are done.
(seeing Naschina and bowing low)
Most fair of all who graze
Their
~~There~~^sheep in Arcady, Naschina, hail!
Naschina, hail!—
Antonio (mimicking him) ~~and bowi~~
Most fair of all who graze
{ir {A
The{re sheep in {arcady, Naschina, hail!
Naschina, hail!
woolly
Almintor I'll drive thy ~~wooly~~ sheep,
If so I may,—along a dewy vale,—
Where all night long the heavens weep and weep
Dreaming in their soft odour-laden sleep,
Where all night long the lonely moon~~, //~~the white
Sad Lady of the deep, pours down her light,
[~~——?——?——?——?——~~]
[~~——?——~~]
[~~——?——?——?——?——~~]
ash-trees'
And 'mong the stunted ~~ashes~~^drooping rings,
All flame-like gushing from the hollow stones,
All day and night a lonely fountain sings,
And there to its own heart for ever moans.
Naschina I'd be alone
Almintor We two by that pale fount,
Unmindful of its woes, will twine a wreath
As fair as any that on Ida's mount
whizzed
Long [~~?~~] ere an arrow ~~whized~~, or sword left sheath,
The shepherd Paris for Oenone made,
Singing of arms and battles some old stave,

2 Another hand probably supplied the hyphen in "live-long".

7 Another hand probably supplied the semicolon.

8–9 The "m" is partially erased.

11 Another hand probably supplied the question mark, which is in darker black ink written over an original comma.

The "u" of "furred" is written in darker ink over an illegible letter.

15 Part of the substitute wording is written over blue pencil; the period and the cancellation line through the "s" of "needs" are probably by another hand.

16 "Lynx's" may not be in Yeats's hand.

19 The phrase below line level is cancelled in blue pencil.

22 "the" is written in darker ink over blue pencil, probably by another hand.

23 The capital "F" of "Fear" here and in l. 24 is written in black ink over blue pencil, probably by another hand.

28 There may be a hyphen between "shining" and "scaled".

29 The corrections may be by another hand.

33 Alternate readings for "will" were entered below l. 34.

([~~?6~~] [~~?sheet~~]) 6

{A
                                    murmurous
{as sleeps dark water in a^ ~~murmerous~~ glade,
Dreaming the live-long summer in the shade,
            flashing flight
Dreaming of [~~?speed~~]^and of the plumed wave.
Antonio.   Naschina, wherefore are your eyes so bright
{W
{with tears? [~~?~~]
                                    ~~[?no] [?one]~~
~~Naschina.   [?I ?weary] of ye there is none~~
Naschina   [~~?~~] I weary of ye; there is none
Of all on whom Arcadian suns have shone
                    m
[~~?~~] sustains his soul in courage or in might:
Poor race of leafy Arcady—Your love
To prove what can ye do? What things above
Sheep-guiding, or the bringing some strange bird,
Or some small beast most wonderfully furred,
                                    {***es***
Or sad sea-shells where little echo{s sit
      quests as these I trow
Such ~~questing~~ ~~methinks~~ needs little wit⊙
      [~~?And on/?Anton~~]
            {A   [?] (Lynx's)
Antonio.   {and the great grey^[?lynxes] skin!
            Naschina.   In sooth methinks
~~Naschina~~   ***That I myself could shoot a great grey Lynx*** [~~? ?~~ ///]
            with bow and arrow
~~[? ? ?] great grey Lynx~~
~~With bow and arrow~~ (~~turns to go~~) [~~?~~] (~~turns to go~~)
                        ~~[?] going~~
(Naschina ~~makes no reply but~~ turns to go)
Almintor   Stay, Naschina, stay!
                                    the
Naschina   Here, where men know^gracious woodland joys
            Fear,
Joy's brother, ~~fear~~, dwells ever in each breast,
            Fear, lurks [?] in each
Joys brother, ~~fear, [? ?] each~~ leafy way;
      I
[~~?I'm~~]^weary of your songs and hunter's toys. ~~//~~
To prove his love a knight with lance in rest
Will circle round the world upon a quest
            {***appears***
      afar {[?] the gleam of dragon-scales
Until ~~hes found a dragon, shining sealed,~~
            battling   {s
From morn the^twain until the evening pale{d [?]
Make havoc   he'll   [?]
~~[?With] war~~; or ~~else~~ ~~he'd~~ seek enchanter old
      sits
Who [~~?sat~~] in lonely splendour mailed in gold
      will   'mid   wondrous
And they^ ~~would~~ war ~~'mong~~ ~~wonderous~~ elfin-sights—
      may
Such ~~will~~ I love; the shuddering forest lights
Of green\Arcadia do not hide, I trow,
      ~~[?may ?can]~~

7

Such men, such hearts. But, uncouth hunter, thou
Know'st naught of this. (she goes)
Antonio And uncouth hunter now—
Alminton ay, boy!
Antonio Let's see if that same heron's dead

(Antonio
(the boy runs out followed slowly by Alminton)
(End of Scene 1.)
W B Yeats—

Please send proof to W. B Yeats
10 Ashfield Terrace
Rathgar
and to:— T. W. Lyster
189 Marlborough Road
Donnybrook
Corrections made by
H. Frazer

7

{S
{such men, such hearts. But, uncouth hunter, thou
Know'st naught of this. (she goes)
Antonio And uncouth hunter now—
Almintor Ay, boy!
Antonio Let's see if that same heron's dead
({~~A~~
({~~antonio~~
(the boy runs out followed slowly by Almintor)
(End of scene 1.)
W B Yeats—

Please send proofs to W. B Yeats
10 Ashfield Terrace
Rathgar
and to:—T. W. Lyster
Corrections made by→89 Marlborough Road
W. Frazer Donnybrook

---

12 "Rathgar", like "Donnybrook" in l. 15, is probably not in Yeats's hand.

14–15 The phrase "Corrections made by W. Frazer" and the accompanying arrow are in ordinary pencil, presumably in Frazer's hand.

(1)
~~ACT. 1~~—Island of Statues
Act 1. Scene 2.
sundown a remote forest valley
~~An~~
Enter Almintor followed by
Antonio
~~Anton~~
uncouth
Antonio. And whither ~~uncooth~~ hunter
Why so fast?—
'mid the willow-glade
So! ~~'mong these moss grown trees~~ you pause at last.
~~Almintor~~
Almintor. Here is the place, the cliff-encircled wood;
Here grow that shy retiring sisterhood,
anemones⊙ {W ***sought***
The pale [~~?enemonies~~] {we've ~~searched~~^all day
And found. ~~///~~
Antonio. 'Tis well! another mile of way
{[{]
I could not go {(they sit down{)
Almintor. Let's talk and let's be sad
Here in the shade.
Antonio Why? Why?
Almintor For what is glad?
For look you, sad's the murm~~o~~ur of the bees,
Yon wind goes sadly, and the grass and trees

---

13 The first two corrections in this line may be by another hand, as may the period in the next line.

(2)

{R
1 {reply like moaning of imprisoned elf
~~[?all] things are~~ [~~—?—?—~~]
2 The whole world's sadly talking to itself.
3 ~~In yo~~ The waves [~~—?—~~] in yonder lake where
points my hand
{B
4 ~~The waves~~ {beat out their lives lamenting o'er the sand
sad
5 The birds that nestle in the leaves are ~~sand~~
rhapsodists.
6 —Poor sad wood-~~wrapsodists~~
{y 're
7 Antonio Not so: the{ir∧glad
8 ~~All wrapsody hath sorrow for it's soul.~~
rhapsody
9 Almintor All∧~~wrapsody~~ hath sorrow for its soul.
10 Antonio Yon eager lark that fills with song
the whole
{*s*
11 Of this wide vale, [~~?E~~] embo{~~s~~somed in the air,
12 Is sorrow in his song, or any car~~e~~!
13 Doth not yon bird, yon quivering bird, rejoice?
14 Almintor. ~~All wrapsody hath~~
15 I hear the whole [~~?skiy's~~] sky's sorrow in one voice
{*N* {*N* Almintor song
16 Antonio {nay ~~nay~~ {nay∧yonder∧~~bird~~ is glad.
17 Almintor [~~?I't~~] 'Tis beautiful and therefore it is sad
{H sooth
18 Antonio {have done this phrasing, and say why in ~~sooth~~
hast grown
19 Almintor thou∧[~~—?—?—~~] so full of ruth,
20 And wherefore have we come?
{A
21 Almintor {a song to hear
But
22 Antonio [~~?from~~]∧whence, and when?

---

16 The capital "N"'s are in pencil.
18 The capital "H" is in darker ink and the rest of the line overwritten, probably by another hand.

(3)—

sere
Almintor. Over the willows ~~seer~~
Out of the air.
Antonio And when?
Almintor When the sun goes down
Over the crown of the willows brown.
Oh boy, I'm bound on a most fearful quest
so
For∧she willed—you heard? Upon the breast
green
Of yonder lake from ~~off~~ who'se∧banks alway
The poplars gaze across the water's grey,
And nod to one another, lies a green
{S
{small island, where the full soft sheen
Of evening and glad silence dwelleth aye,
For there
[~~ ? ~~] [~~?where~~] the great enchantress lives
Antonio And there
{G of joy,
{groweth the goblin flower∧~~all~~ her care
sought forest
By many [~~?saught~~]∧and 'tis a [~~?fireside~~]∧tale
How all who seek are∧doomed to (ever) fail;
{tou
{reach
Some say that all who∧~~seek~~ the island lone
Are changed forever into moonwhite stone

1 The correction may be in another hand.
8 The "e" of "whose" appears to have been added later, probably at the same time that the apostrophe was cancelled.
16 The corrections may be in another hand. There is a penciled "o" above the incorrect "a" of "saught".

(4)

Almintor—
^That flower I seek
(You)
Antonio ~~And~~^ never will return
Almintor Ill bring that flower to her and ⌐so may ~~ear~~ earn
Her love {: , ~~//~~ to her who wears that bloom ⌐comes truth
elvish
And ^ ~~elfin~~ wisdom, and long years of youth
Beyond a mortal {'s s {years time. I wait the song
That calls
evil
Antonio O ~~veil~~ starred
Almintor It comes along
The wind at evening when the sun goes down
~~the~~
Over the ~~co~~ crown of ^ willows brown—
See yonder sinks the sun, yonder a shade
Goes flickering in reverberated light
There! There! {D
~~Yon, yon,~~ do you not see?
Antonio I see the night
~~Slow-footing down the~~
~~In [?dewy] [?sandals] coming down the glade~~
Deep-eyed slow-footing down the empty glade
~~a voice~~ A Voice [sings]
~~For~~ From the ~~shade-vested~~ {shadowy hollow
Arise thou and follow!

6 The revision may be in another hand.
15 The revisions may be in another hand.
17 The final wording may be in another hand.
19 "shadowy" may be in another hand.
The next two pages, which would be numbered 5 and 6 at the top and would contain the remainder of the scene, are missing from the King's School manuscript.

(7)

Scene 3 –

– The Birth of Night The Island

Far into the distance reach shadowy
ways burdened with the faery
flowers: knee-deep amongst them
stand the immoveable figures of those
who have failed in their questing

First voice

See, oh see the dew drowned bunches
Of the monke-hood how they shake,
Nodding by the flickering lake,
There where yonder squirrel crunches
Acorns green with eyes awake.

Second Voice

I followed him from my green lair
But wide awake his two eyes were

First voice

Oh learned is each monkshood's mind,
And full of wisdom is each bloom,
As, clothed in ceremonial gloom,
They hear the story of the wind,
That dieth slow with sick doom

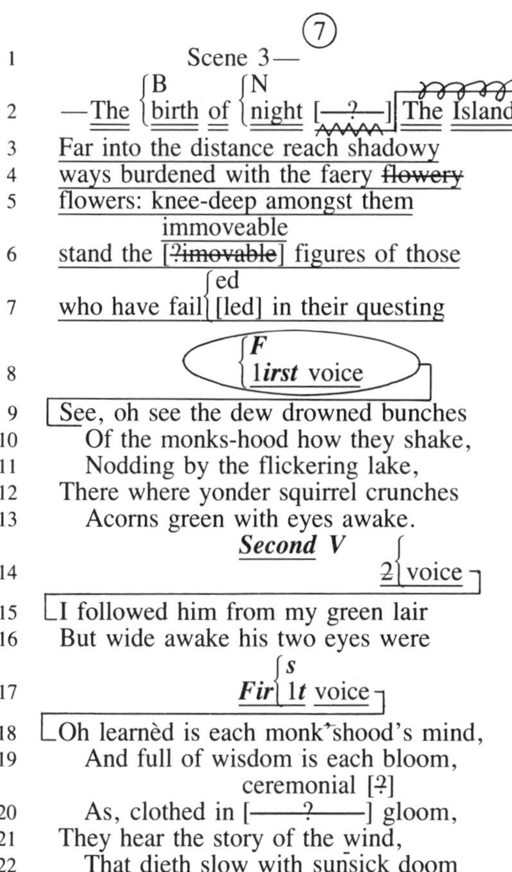

(7)
Scene 3—
—The {B birth of {N night [—?—] The Island
Far into the distance reach shadowy
ways burdened with the faery ~~flowery~~
flowers: knee-deep amongst them
immoveable
stand the [?~~imovable~~] figures of those
who have fail{ed [led] in their questing
{F 1irst voice
See, oh see the dew drowned bunches
Of the monks-hood how they shake,
Nodding by the flickering lake,
There where yonder squirrel crunches
Acorns green with eyes awake.
Second V
~~2~~{ voice
I followed him from my green lair
But wide awake his two eyes were
Fir{s 1t voice
Oh learnèd is each monk'shood's mind,
And full of wisdom is each bloom,
ceremonial [?]
As, clothed in [——?——] gloom,
They hear the story of the wind,
That dieth slow with sunsick doom

5 There may be a cancelled punctuation mark after the colon.
6 The revision may be in another hand.
20 The revision may be in another hand.

(8)

Second Voice

The south breeze now in dying fears
Tells all his sinning in their ears.

First Voice

He says 'twas he and 'twas no other
Blew my crimson cups away
O'er the lake this very day —
Hark! he's dead — my drowsy brother
And has not heard Absolvo te

[A pause]

First Voice

Peace peace the earth's aquake, I hear
Some barbarous un-faery thing draw near

Enter Alminitor

Alminitor The evening gleams are green and gold and red
Along the lake — The crane has home-ward fled
Each flower 'mid clustering thousands near and far

(8)

Second Voice
1 ~~2 voice~~
{e
2 ^The south bre{aze now in dying fears
3 Tells all his sinning in their ears.
4 ***First Voice*** ~~1 voice~~
5 He says 'twas he and 'twas no other
{B
{blew my crimson cap away
6 ~~[?Blew] my cap of crimson blew away~~
7 O'er the lake this very day—
8 Hark! he's dead—my drowsy brother
{A
9 And has not heard {absolvo te=
10 ~~2 voice~~ [A pause]
11 ~~Now I hear the grains of sand [?A]~~
12 ~~[?agrating]~~ ^~~***Second Voice***~~
13 ^~~The [?] has to sing to his soul asleep~~
~~two~~
14 ~~and we^[?alone] our watching keep~~
15 ~~1 voice~~
First Voice
aquake
16 ^Peace peac the earth's ~~a shake~~, I hear
{a
17 Some barb{erous un-faery thing draw near
18 Enter Almintor
19 ~~Alminto~~
and red
20 Almintor The evening gleams are green and gold^
~~and red~~
~~red~~
21 Along the lake. The crane has home-ward fled
22 ~~And flowers around in clustering [?thousands] are~~
Each flower 'mid clustering thousands near and far

---

16 Yeats first substituted "quake" for "shake" and then added and overwrote letters to substitute "aquake" for "a shake".

17 The second "a" in "barbarous" is in darker ink and may be by another hand.

9)
Shines clear as ever shone unbaffled star
~~Shines radiant each~~ (9)
~~Each shining clear as some unbaffled star~~
The skies more dim, though burning like a shield,
Above these men whose mouths were sealed
Long years ago
~~Full long ago~~∧and unto stone congealed
And oh! the wonder of the thing! each came
When low the sun sank down in clotted flame
wave
Beyond the lake whose smallest ~~wave~~ was burdened
With rolling fire, beyond the high trees turbaned
wanderer came
With clinging mist, each star faught∧
{ose
As I to cho{se beneath day's dying flame—
And they are all now stone
~~Each one around is stone~~ as I shall be
me
Unless some pitying god shall succour∧[?~~me~~]
In this my choice
{[{]
{(stoops over a flower, then pauses{)
Some god might help If so
I throw
May hap [—?—] 'twere better that aside ~~I [—?—]~~
[—?—] All choice and give to chance for guiding
chance
Some cast of die, or let some arrow glance
For guiding of the gods. The sacred bloom

1 The revisions may be in another hand. Yeats presumably rejected the changes in proofs, for the printed text follows the original wording. Because the corrections obscured the original ''(9)'' at the top of the page, an additional ''9)'' was added in the left margin above the corrections.

9 Yeats nearly reached the margin with ''faught'' and used a caret to gain space to complete the line.

10 The correction may be in another hand.

16 The corrections at the end of the line may be in another hand.

17 There is a dot like a period after ''chance'' which is probably a stray mark.

(10)

seek
To ~~find~~ not hopeless have I crossed the gloom
With that song leading where harmonic woods
Nourish the panthers in dim solitudes,
{R
Vast greenness where eternal {rumour dwells
her
And hath [?his] home, by many folded dells
I passed, by many caves of dripping stone~~s~~
each) (echo) (her)
And heard ~~the~~^ unseen^ ~~echos~~ on ~~their~~^ throne~~s~~
Lone regent~~s~~ of the woods, deep muttering
murmurs
And then new ~~murmours~~ came new uttering
In song from goblin waters swaying white
Mocking with patient laughter all the night
vast
Of those ~~va~~ woods; and then I saw the boat
Living, wide wingéd, on the waters float;
Strange draperies did all the sides adorn
And the waves bowed before it like mown corn.
all ***Faery Land***
The wingéd wonder of [?]^ ~~faery land~~
It bore me softly where the shallow sand
Binds as within a girdle or a ring
{s
The lake embo{ssomed isle—Nay this my quest

4 The capital "R" of "Rumour" may be in another hand.
5 "her" may be in another hand.
7 The corrections may be in another hand; and the "d" of "heard" appears to have been added later.
9 "murmurs" may be in another hand.

(11)

Shall not so hopeless prove: some god may rest
Upon the wind and guide mine arrow's~~'~~ course
From yonder pinacle above the lake
I'll send mine arrow now, my one resource,
blossom
The nighest ~~flower~~ ^ where it falls I'll take
{~~Exit~~ ***Goes out***
{(~~goes out~~ fitting an arrow to his bow{]
{)
{A {V
{a {voice
Fickle the guiding his arrow shall find!
{a
Some goblin my serv{ent on wings that are fleet,
That nestles alone in the whistling wind
Go pilot the course of his arrow's deceit—
re-enter
[—?—]
~~A~~ [The arrow falls—[~~?enter~~] ^ Almintor]
Almintor 'Tis here the arrow fell, the breezes laughed
Around the feathery tip; unto the shaft
most {Oh
This blossom is [~~?nigh~~] near—Statue! {o thou
Whose beard a moonlight river is, whose brow
Is stone, old sleeper, this same afternoon
O'er much I've talked, I shall be silent soon
wrong
If ~~rong~~ ^ my choice, as silent as thou art

5 The revisions may be in another hand.
8 There is additional cancelled and illegible punctuation at the end of the line.
12 The revision may be in another hand.
15 "Most" is written in black ink over pencil.
19 "wrong" is written in black ink over pencil.

(12)

i an a
1 O grac{eous ***P***{pan, take now thy serv{ents part

a
2 He was our ancient god, if I spe{ek low

new
3 And not too clear how will the [~~?~~] god know
4 But that I called on him

{[
5 {(Pulls the flower and becomes stone~~)~~
6 from among the flowers a sound as of a multitudes of horns]
7 ~~[?]~~ ~~[?voice]~~

A Voice
8 Sleeping lord of archery

shalt
9 No more a-roving [~~?shall't~~]^thou see,
10 The panther with her yellow hide

~~dreamy and~~
11 Of the forests all the pride,
12 Or her ever burning eyes
13 When she in a cavern lies

Watching
14 ~~guarding~~ o'er her awful young

sinewy
15 Where their [~~?sinewy~~] [~~?sinewey~~]^might is strung
16 In the never lifting dark

(standest)
17 No thou^~~standeth~~^still and stark

of old wert moving ever
18 That ~~wert [?wont] to move for ever~~—
19 But a mother panther never
20 Oer her young so eagerly
21 ~~Did her~~

---

3 The second "o" of "too" appears to have been added later.
6 This line is crowded into the same ruled space of the page as l. 7 and was apparently added later.
14–15 The revisions may be in another hand.
17 The revision may be in another hand.

(13)

Did her lonely watching take
{A my watching
{as I ~~in guarding~~ lest you wake
{S
{sleeping lord of archery
End of ~~Sc~~ Act 1—
W B Yeats

W. B. Yeats

---

5 The signature here is nearly illegible, and is repeated more clearly in the next line in a mixture of cursive and printed letters, possibly by another hand.

1—

Island of Statues
ACT 2
Scene 1.–
The wood in the early evening
Enter Antonio and Naschina
Naschina I as a shepherd dressed will seek and seek
Untill I find him. What a weary week
My pretty child since he has gone 't 'as been
Tell oer again how unto you was seen
His passage oer the lake
Antonio When we two came
From the wood's ways then like a silver flame
{o he
We saw the dol{erous lake; and ~~then~~ thy name
Carvéd on trees, and with a sun dry weed
He wrote it on the sands (The owls may read
And ponder it if they will); then near at hand
The boats prow grated on the shallow sand
{A
{and loudly twice it's living wings flapt ~~wide~~
wide
And leaping to their feet far echos cried
Each other answering—and between each wing

2—

He sat and then I heard the white lake sing
Curving beneath the prow; as some wild drake
Half lit—so flapt the wings across the lake
Alas!
~~But see~~, I make you sadder shepherdess
<u>Naschina</u>. Nay, grief in feeding <u>on old grief</u>
grows less.
<u>Antonio</u>. Grief needs much feeding then—
ear
of him I~~'ll~~ sw are
We've talked and talked not
~~A deal we've said~~∧ and∧a whit more rare
Become
~~Do come~~ your weeping fits
strait
<u>Naschina</u> Look you, so∧[~~?straight~~]
barred
[~~?shy~~] [?]
The [~~?small~~]∧woodpecker's mansion is and deep
No other bird may enter there
<u>Antonio</u> ~~Look you so straight~~
~~Well~~ Well?
<u>Naschina</u> Late—
Aye
[~~?aye~~]∧Very lately, sorrow came to weep
within mine heart, and naught but sorrow now
Can enter there—
<u>Antonio</u> Above yon brow
<u>Of hill</u> two shepherds come
<u>Naschina</u> Fare well. I'll don~~e~~

There is a diagonal mark between ll. 11 and 13, a vertical one between ll. 13 and 14, and another vertical one between ll. 17 and 18; the purpose of all three lines is probably to align the wording.

20 The "e" of "done" is cancelled in a darker ink like that of the revisions in another hand on this page.

3—

My shepherd raiment and return anon
(goes)
{o
Enter Colin and Thern{et
Thernot Two ~~men~~ who ~~love one~~ maid have ample⌐
⌜cause
strife
Of war. Of yore two shepherds, where we pause
{o
F{aught once for self same reason on the hem
Of the wide woods.
Colin And the deep earth gathered them.
Thernet We must get swords
Colin Is't the only way? Oh see
Yon is the hunter***'s***, Sir Almintor's, page
Let him between us judge for he can guage
[~~— ? ? —~~] ~~[?fingers ?deftest]~~ ~~[?]~~
~~And [?measure] out the ways of chivalry~~
With deftest measures things of chivalry
Thernot Sir page, Almintor s friend and therefore l[?]
⌜learned
all
{a
In∧such ~~like~~ things—pr{ey let thine ears ⌐
⌜be turned
{***And***
{Prey hear, and judge!
Antonio My popinjay what now?
~~two~~ two
Colin ~~M~~ This thing we ask—must we∧fight—Judge ⌐
⌜thou
Each came one morn, with welcoming of song
~~Beside~~ ~~break~~
~~Before~~ her door, for this where nod the long
Unto
we ***have*** {o
And shore-ward waves∧nigh∧~~had we~~ f{aught⌐;
⌜waves bring
The brown weed burden, so the sword brings fear
To us

4—

[?] a
Thernot Oh wise art thou in such ~~like~~ thing
^
Being Almintor's page—Now judge you hear
We love Naschina both
Antonio Whom loves she best
Colin She cares no whit for either but has blest
Almintor
~~Another~~ with her love—
^
[Enter Naschina disguised as a shepherd
boy—]
a
Colin Whom art thou? spe{ek
—As the sea's furrows on a sea tost shell
cheek
Sad histories are lettered on thy ~~cheak~~
G
Antonio It is the shepherd {[?]uarimond
who loveth well
res t
In the deep cent{ers of the secre{d woods
Old miser hoards of grief to tell and tell
Young
~~Y[?]g~~ Guarimond he tells them oer and oer
To see them drowned by those vast solitudes
With their unhuman sorrows
Naschina Cease! No more!
T an over-
~~Of this~~ {thou hast ~~a~~^nimble tongue
Colin Thy grief
What is it friend?
Antonio He lost i'the woods the chief

12 The overwriting may be in another hand.
18 The capital "T" of "Thou" may be in another hand.

5

the troop
And only sheep he loved of all ~~his flock~~
More great is mine. No man shall ever stoop
Colin ~~Than thy grief shepherd greater is the [?st]~~
~~stock~~
~~of mine. I like you and I know not why~~
Beneath the weight of greater grief than
~~So will you judge must [?] Thernet~~
~~yon and I~~
I like ~~thee~~ you though in sooth I know not why
Now judge must shepherd Thernot there and I,
For this thing fight, we love one maid.
Naschina Her name***?***
Colin Naschina. [~~?'Tis~~]
{O
Naschina {Ah I know her well a lame
Dull witted thing, with face red squirrel brown
Antonio. A long brown grasshopper of maids!
{s
Naschina Peace, {Sir!
~~Colin~~
'Tis clear that you have seen her not. ~~The~~
(Colin) The crown,
Is not more fair and joyous than she is—
a-flicker {n e
Of beams ~~a-footing~~ o{r yon lonly fir
^
honey
~~Or~~ Nor fairies in the ~~hony~~ heart of June a-stir
~~I sware by bosky June and by her [?] and her~~
[~~?mir~~]
{ear
By bosky June I sw{are, and by the bee her minister
Naschina There is no way but that ye fight I wis
If her ye love
Thernot Aye Colin we must fight
fight
Colin Aye^we must ~~fight~~

The insertion of l. 5 by another hand in the manuscript separates the cancelled phrase "yon and I" from l. 4, which it completes; in the transcription, I have moved that phrase above l. 5 to facilitate comprehension.

8 The question mark is probably in another hand.

12 The second "s" of "grasshopper" may have been added later.

16 The caret and inserted "e" of "lonely", like "honey" and the hyphen in "a-stir" of the next line, may be in another hand.

6⌋

h

Antonio and Nascina turn to go
^

{A
[~~?Na~~] Naschina Tell me {antonio, might
They get them ~~s[?]~~ swords and both or either fall?
Antonio No, No, when that shall be then men ⌐
⌈may call

{D
{down to
~~Unto~~ their feet the stars that sit alone
upon
Each one at gaze ~~[?from] on~~ his whirling throne
[They go

The line around the ''6'' at the top of the page extends through the left margin.

6 The correction may be in another hand.

Scene 2
A remote part of the forest
Through black and twisted trees the
lake is seen shining under
the red ~~e[—?—]~~ evening
Enter Naschina ~~and~~ as a shepherd
boy, and Antonio—
~~Antonio~~
Antonio Behold how like a swarm of fiery bees
The light is dancing oer the knotted trees
{i
In busy flakes reshin{gng from the lake
red *break.*
Through this night-vested place the ~~red~~ beams^ ~~brake~~
=
Naschina The air is still above, and still each leaf
And loud the grashopper that lies beneath
~~As some clenched soul in fixed and tearless grief~~
Antonio From the deep earth unto the lurid sky
All things are quiet in the eve's wide eye.
Naschina And boy saw you when through the forest we
Two came, his name and mine on many a tree
Carved; here beyon***d*** the lake's slow-muffled tread
[—?—] ***I've***
In sand his name and mine^ ~~are~~ also ~~to be~~ read

A mark that is probably the bottom of a "7" is visible at the closely cropped top of the page.
6 The double underlining of "Naschina", and of "Antonio" in the next line, is in a slightly different black ink and may be by another hand.
14 The pencilled revision may be in another hand.
19 The "d" of "beyond" is in another hand.

8

isle in sea[?]
the ~~island seeking which~~ we came
<u>Antonio</u>. Yonder's ~~the sacred isle for which came~~
The white waves wrap it in a sheet of flame
yonder
And [—?—]∧huddling blackness draweth nigh—
Tis that strange boat against the blinding sky
<u>Naschina</u>. Antonio, boy, if I return no more
Then bid them raise my statue on the shore,
Here where the round waves come, here let them build
gild;
It facing to the sea, and no name∧~~guild~~—
A white dumb thing of tears here let it stand
Between the lonely forest and the sand.
draws near and near
<u>Antonio</u> The boat∧~~is almost here~~, You heed me not
~~When summers~~
<u>Naschina</u> And when the summer's deep, then to this spot
The {A / arcadians} bring, and bid the stone be raised,
As I am standing now, as though I gazed,
One hand brow shading—far ~~in~~ acros the night.
And one arm pointing thus, in marble white
And once a year let the Arcadians come
And 'neath it sit, and of the woven sum
Of human sorrow let them moralize
And let them tell sad histories till their eyes

---

1 The page is cropped in the middle of a diagonally slanting word whose first three letters are "sea" and which is probably "search".
5 The comma after "Antonio" is in darker ink and probably by another hand.
10 The "e" of "lonely" appears to have been added later, perhaps in another hand.
12 The apostrophe of "summer's" is in darker ink and probably by another hand.

9—
Are dim with tears
{a
Antonio The fairy boat's {ut hand
You must be gone, the rolling grains of sand
Are 'neath its prow, and crushing shells
turning *sorrowful*
Naschina (~~going~~ ^ to go) And let the tale be ^ ~~dolerous~~
each ~~one~~ tells
~~(goes)~~
(Antonio and Naschina go o)ut
~~Antonio [alone]~~
Re-enter
~~Reenter~~ Antonio
also,
Antonio I would have gone ~~with her~~ ^ but far away
flew
The faery thing [~~?~~] ^ with her oer the grey
Slow waters, and the boat and maiden sink
Away from me where mists of evening drink
To ease their world-old [~~?thrist~~] thirst along the brink
; while
Of sword-blue waves of calm~~ness~~ O'er head blink
The mobs of stars in gold and green and blue
{ie
P{earcing the quivering waters through and through,
The ageless sentinels who hold their watch
Oer grief. The world drinks sorrow from ~~the bea~~
the beams
And penetration of their eyes
[starting ~~up~~ forward

---

2 The apostrophe is in darker ink and probably by another hand.
9 "also," is in darker ink and probably by another hand.
11 The comma is in darker ink and probably by another hand.
13 The hyphen between "world" and "old" is in darker ink and probably in another hand.

(10)

Where yonder blotch
lilac ***pulsing waters*** l
Of ~~lylac~~ ^ o'er the ~~waves slow pulsing~~ g{reams
Once more those shepherds come. Mayhap some
mirth
Oh, ***dearth***
I'll have. ~~O~~ ^ absent one 'tis not for ^ [?~~dirth~~]
A
Of grief. And If they say, "{antonio laughed"
Say then, "a popinjay before grief's shaft
Pierced through, chatting from habit in the ~~su~~
sun
Till his last wretchedness was o'er and done."
~~the~~
~~A voice from without~~
~~A voice~~
among
A voice from ^ the trees: Antonio!
Enter Colin and Thernot
Thernot We have resolved to fight
furled
Antonio. To yonder isle where never sail was ~~furld~~
whose ~~roam~~
From ~~who's~~ ^ green banks no living thing may ~~rome~~
rove
And see again the happy woodland light,
[?] a
Naschina's gone, drawn ~~their~~ by thirst of love
And that was strange, but this is many a world
More wonderful!
Thernot And we have swords

12 The double underlining of "Colin" and "Thernot" is in darker ink and probably by another hand.
17 The " 's" of "Naschina's" was added later.
18–19 The punctuation is in darker ink and probably by another hand.

(11)

1 Antonio O night
2 Of wonders! eve of prodigies!
3 Colin Draw! Draw!
(aside)
4 Antonio He'll snap his sword
5 Thernot |Raised is the lion's paw
6 (Colin and Thernot fight
{T {'s
7 Antonio Cease! {thernot{s wounded, cease!
they will not heed—
{ie
8 F{earce thrust—A tardy blossom had the seed
{a
9 But heavy fruit,—How swift the {[?]rgument
10 Of those steel tongues—crash swords—
—well thrust—well bent
11 Aside—
12 [a far-off multitudinous sound of horns)
13 The wild horns told Almintor s end
14 And of Naschina's now they tell—rend, rend,
15 O*h* heart!—Her dirge!—With rushing arms the waves
16 Cast on the sound, on, on—This night of graves—
17 —The spinning stars—The toiling sea—whirl round
18 My sinking brain!—Cease! Cease! heard ye
yon sound?
19 The dirge of her ye love—cease! cease!
in a cliff
20 [An echo^~~away [?in] [?the] fore~~-in the heart of the
mournfully
21 forest sends^back the blast of the horns]

The punctuation in ll. 2–3, 14, 16, and 18–19, together with the exclamation points and dash in l. 7 and the exclamation points in l. 15, are in darker ink and probably by another hand. So, too, in ll. 5 and 13 are the rectangles that extend from the right margin.

5 The vertical mark before "Raised" is probably intended to align it with the end of "He'll" in the preceding line.

7 The correction's are in darker ink and probably by another hand.

8 The correction "ie" is in darker ink and probably by another hand.

15 The "h" of "Oh" is in darker ink and probably by another hand.

20–21 These lines and the phrase "yon sound" in l. 18 are substantially overwritten by another hand to reinforce the letters. The square brackets may be written over original parentheses.

Antonio
The Echos fling upon my weary brain
The labour and the cadence of their pain
[rushes away the scene
closes on Colin and Thernot
still fighting

W B Yeats

Now facing KS 30, the verso of the previous page KS 29 contains the following, heavily cancelled distinction:
statue—an image
statute—a law.

(1)
The Island of Statues
Act 2
Scene 3—
~~The Island.~~ {F
flowers of ^[~~?many~~] ~~manyfold~~ manifold
colour are knee-deep before a gate
of brass, above which in a citron-
tinctured sky falter a few stars
at intervals come mournful blasts from the horns among
the flowers
1 Voice
What do you weave so fair and bright
2 Voice
The cloak I weave of sorrow
Oh lovely to see in all men's sight
Shall be the cloak of sorrow
In all men's sight
{3
1 Voice
What do you build with sails for flight
4 Voice A boat I build for sorrow,
O swift on the seas all day and night
Saileth the rover sorrow,
All day and night

---

4 The capital "F" of "Flowers" and the cancelled circle and arrow relocating "The Island" are in darker ink and probably by another hand.

8 This line is crowded between those above and below it and may have been added later.

21 There is a smudge after "night" that may have been intended as a period.

(2)

~~5~~
5th Voice What do you weave with wool so white?
6th Voice The sandals these of sorrow,
Soundless shall be the footfall light
In each mans ears of sorrow,
Sudden and light
a
~~Naschina~~
Naschina disguised as a shepherd boy enters
E
with the enchantress the beautiful familiar
of the Isle ~~at intervals come~~
~~mournful blas~~
Naschina What are the voices that in flowery ways
Have clothed their tongues with song of songless
days
Enchantress They are the flowers' guardian sprights;
With streaming hair as wandering lights
They passed a ~~p~~ tip-toe everywhere,
And never heard of grief or care
Until this morn; as adder's back
The sky was banded o'er with wrack;

15 Yeats wrote "every where" as separate words that were later joined.

17–18 The semicolons are in darker ink and may be by another hand; a dash before "as" in l. 17 has been cancelled by a solid black spot.

(3)

They were sitting round a pool,
At their feet the waves in rings
Gently shook their mothlike wings,
{re
For the{ir came an air-breath cool
From the ever moving pinions
{O
{of the happy flower minions,
But a sudden melancholy
together
Filled them as they ~~sh~~ sat^[?~~togeth~~]
wholly
Now their songs are mournful^~~holy~~
As they go with drooping feather
Naschina O Lady, thou who'se vestiture of green
{a
Is rolled as verd{ent smoke!, O thou, whose ~~flace~~
face
~~I wo~~ Is worn as though with fire! !
Oh goblin queen
{a
Lead me, I pr{ey thee, to the statued place! ^
Enchantress Fair youth, along a wandering way
  I'*ve* led thee here, and as a wheel
  We turned around the place alway,
{a
  Lest on thine heart the stony se{el
  As on these other hearts were laid;
  Behold the brazen-gated glade

---

11 The "e" of "whose" appears to have been added later, probably at the same time that the apostrophe was cancelled.

12 Yeats nearly reached the margin with "whose", wrote a barely legible "face" after it, then cancelled that word and wrote it more legibly below. The exclamation marks here and at the end of the next two lines are in darker ink and possibly by another hand.

13 Yeats did not have room to finish the line after "fire", and he completed it immediately below.

17 The comma at the end, like the semicolon in l. 19 and hyphen in l. 20, is in darker ink and may be by another hand.

(4)

She partially opens the brazen gates, the
statues are seen within, some are
bending with their hands among
the flowers, others are holding
withered flowers
Naschina. O let me pass, the spells from off the heart
will
Of my ~~sh~~ sad hunter-friend ~~shall~~^all depart
If on his lips the enchanted flower be laid,
O let me pass!
[Leaning
Enchantress ~~[resting~~ with an arm upon
each gate] That flower ~~mo~~ none
{W
~~May find~~ {who seek may find save only one
{A
{a shepherdess long [~~?yeas~~] years foretold
{A
{and even she shall never hold
The flower, save some thing be found
To die for her in air or ground
And none there is, If such there were
E'en
~~E'n~~^then, before her shepherd hair
Had felt the ~~ila~~ island breeze, my lore
Would drive her forth for ever more,
To wander by the bubbling shore,

The commas in ll. 1, 4, 15, 20, and 21, together with the period in l. 6 and hyphen in l. 7, are in darker ink and possibly by another hand.

10–11 The square brackets before "~~resting~~" and after "gate" may be written over earlier parentheses. The capital "L" of "Leaning" may be written over a small "l", and the entire word has been reinforced.

(5)

Laughter lipped, but for her brain
A guerdon of deep rooted pain,
And in her eyes a lightless stare,
For if severed from the ~~foo~~ root
The enchanted flower were,
From my wizard island lair
And the happy wingéd day
growing ~~m~~
I, as music ~~that grows~~ mute
On a girl's forgotton lute,
Pass away—
Naschina Your eyes are all a-flash, she is not here
I'd
Enchantress ~~I would~~^kill her if she were. Nay do not fear!
With you I am all gentleness; in ~~th~~ truth
There's little Id refuse thee, dearest youth.
{a
Naschina I have a whim: bid some attend{ent sprite
wold
Of thine cry over^~~wold~~ and water white
That one shall die unless one die for her
Tis but to see if anything will stir
For such a call, let the wild word be cried
As though she whom you fear had crossed the tide,
{h
Though she {sas not—

8 The revision is in darker ink and probably by another hand.
12 The exclamation point is in darker ink and possibly by another hand.
21 The dash is in darker ink and possibly by another hand.

(6)

Enchantress A little thing that is
And shall be done if you will ~~[illegible]~~ deign to kiss,
Fair youth, my lips
Naschina It shall be as you ask
Enchantress Forth! forth! O spirits ye have heard your task!
Voices We are gone
Enchantress [sitting down by Naschina
~~[illegible]~~
~~[illegible]~~
Fair shepherd as we wandered hither
My words were all: "here no loves fade and wither,
Where dream-fed passion is and peace encloses
Every revel of foxglove is, and revel of roses, ~~[illegible]~~
~~[illegible]~~ My words were all "O whither, whither, whither
Wilt ~~[illegible]~~ roam away from this rich island rest
O stay I bid thee, ~~[illegible]~~ renouncing thy mad quest unblest
But thou wouldst not, for then thou wert ~~[illegible]~~
And stony-hearted; now thou hast grown kind
And thou wilt stay — All thought of what they find
In the far world, will vanish from thy mind
Till thou remember, only how the sea

(6)
Enchantress A little thing that is
And shall be done if you will ~~dain~~ ***deign*** to kiss,
Fair youth, my lips
Naschina It shall be as you ask
Enchantress Forth! forth! {O / o} spirits ye have heard your task!
Voices We are gone
Enchantress {[/ (}sitting down by Naschina
~~Fair shepherd as we hither came~~
~~I besaught thee in this island to remain~~
Fair shepherd as we wandered hither
My words were all: ~~he~~ "here no loves ^fade and^ withir,
Where dream-fed passion is and peace {e / incloses}
Where revel of foxglove is, and revel of roses," Transpose
~~Roses [?]~~
[~~?May~~] my words were all "O whither, whither, ***whither***
Wilt ~~thou~~ roam away from this rich ^***island***^ rest
~~O stay stay~~ I bid thee ^stay ~~and~~ ***renouncing***^ ~~banish~~ thy mad quest."
But thou wouldst not, for then thou ~~[?wert] unkind~~ wert unblest
And stony-hearted; now thou hast grown kind
And thou ~~willt~~ ***wilt*** stay—All thought of what ~~is found~~ they find
In the far world, wil{l / t} [?] vanish from thy mind
Till ~~you~~ ^***thou***^ remember***est*** only how the sea

The rectangles extending from the right margin in ll. 1, 4, and 10 are in darker ink and possibly by another hand.
5 The exclamation points and capital "O" are in darker ink and possibly by another hand.
7 The square bracket and underlining are in darker ink and possibly by another hand.
12 The dot of the "i" of the original "incloses" has been cancelled; the new "e" for that word is in darker ink and probably by another hand.
13 The final comma is in darker ink and possibly by another hand.

(7)
Has fenced us round for all eternity
art thou ***didst thou***
But why ~~are you~~^so silent ~~did you~~^hear ~~I laughed~~
I laughed
Naschina And why is that a thing so dear
From thee I snatched ***it e'en***
Enchantress ~~From thy mouth~~ ~~I caught~~ ~~it e'n~~ the fay
^ that trips
At morn and with her feet each cobweb rends
Laughs not. It dwells alone on mortal lips
Thou'lt
~~You'll~~ teach me laughing and I'll teach thee peace
Here where laburnum hangs her golden fleece
For peace and laughing have been ~~s[?]~~ friends—
seldom
But for a boy how long thine hair has grown
Long citron coils that hang around thee blown
In shadowy dimness. To be fair as thee
fleetness
I'd give my faery [~~?fleetness~~]^though[?] I be
Far fleeter than the million-footed sea.
~~I'd give~~
~~And [?all] the quiet of my faery brow~~.
~~And all the quiet of my faery brow.~~
{A {V
{a {voice By wood antique, by wave and waste
{ess ~~ousy~~ ~~pine~~
Where cypr{is is and ~~willows bow~~ oozy pine
quivering
Did [?] I on^~~shuddering~~ pinions haste
{ead
And all was quiet round me spr{ed
As quiet as the clay cold dead.

---

8 The second "e" of "thee" is in darker ink and appears to have been added later, perhaps by another hand.
9 This line is crowded between ll. 8 and 10; it may have been added later.
21 The correction may be in another hand.

(8)

I cried the thing you bid me cry,
An owl, who in an alder tree
Had hooted for an hundred years,
Up raised his voice and hooted me
E’*e*n though his wings were plumeless stumps,
And all his veins had near run dry,
From forth the hollow alder trunk
He hooted as I wandered by,
And so with wolf, and boar, and steer,
And one alone of all would hark,
A man who by a dead man stood,
{ l
A star lit rapier half b{ [?]ood dark
Was broken in his quivering hand—
As blossoms, when the winds of March
Hold festival across the land,
He shrank before my voice, and stood
Low bowed, and dumb upon the sand,
A foolish word thou gavest me,
For each within himself hath all
The world, within his folded heart.
His temple and his banquet hall
throw
And who will ~~through~~ his mansion down
bugle
Thus for another’s ~~bugle buggle~~ call

Most of the commas on this page are in a darker black ink and were probably added later by another hand, particularly those in ll. 1, 3, 5–6, 8–11, 14–15, 17–18, and 20.

5 The “ ’e” of “E’en” is in darker ink and was probably added by another hand at the same time that the original apostrophe between “e” and “n” was cancelled.

(9)

1 Enchantress But why this whim of thine—
{A
—{a strange unrest
2 As alien as a cuckoo in a swallow's nest
together pressed
3 Is in thy face, and lips ~~togeather prest~~
4 And why so silent?—I would hear thee speak
here
5 Soon wil't thou smile, for ~~hear~~ ^ the winds are weak
6 As moths with broken wings, and as we sit
7 The heavens all star-throbbing are a-lit
8 Naschina. But art thou happy?
9 Enchantress Let me gaze on thee
10 At arm's length thus till ~~dim~~ dumb eternity
away
11 Has rolled ^ the stars ~~away~~ and dried the sea
12 I could gaze, gaze upon thine eye-balls grey
13 Gaze on till ragged time himself decay.
here
14 Ah! you are weeping, ~~hear~~ should all grief cease.
15 Naschina But art thou happy
16 Enchantress Youth I am at peace
17 Naschina But happiness
18 Enchantress Those eyes so grey of thine
19 Have they ne'er seen the eyes of lynx, or kine,

The rectangles extending from the right margin in ll. 9, 16, and 18, like the question marks in ll. 4 and 8, are in darker ink and possibly by another hand.

11 There may be a period after "sea".

14 The exclamation point and commas appear to be in the same dark ink as the cancellation and new word "here", and hence are probably in another hand.

(10)

[~~?~~] or aught remote, or hast thou never heard
'Mid
~~Mong~~ bubbling leaves a wandering song-wrapt bird
flutings
Going the forest through with [~~?fflutting~~]^weak
Or hast thou never seen with visage meek
{A
{An hoary hunter leaning on his bow
To watch thee pass—yet deeper than men know
These are at peace ~~A Voice~~
A voice Sad lady cease!
~~m~~

I rose, I rose,
From the dim woods foundation
I rose, I rose,
Where in white exultation
The long lily blows,
And the wan wave that lingers
From flood-time, encloses
With infantine fingers
The roots of the roses,
{***T***
~~From~~ {thence I came winging,
I there had been keeping
~~an~~ A mouse from his sleeping
With shouting and singing⊙

The punctuation of the voice's song is in darker ink and appears to have been added later, probably by another hand. So, too, does the rectangle extending from the right margin of l. 8.

2 There may be a cancelled "a" above "Mong" and before "'Mid".

5 The "A" appears to have been added later in darker ink, probably by another hand.

6 The second "e" of "thee" appears to have been added later in darker ink, probably by another hand.

18 The cancel mark and capital "T" are in darker ink and in another hand.

(11)

Enchantress How sped thy quest? this prelude we'll
not hear it

wordy
In truth thou ever was't a ~~w[?]d~~ spirit
{V
The {voice ***A wriggling***
~~A[?]~~ ~~A wriggling~~ thing on the white lake moved
As the canker worm on a milk-white rose,
falcon
And down I came as a ~~falchon~~ ~~f[?]~~^swoops
together
When his sinewy wings ~~togeather~~^close
I lit by the thing, [?] t'was a ~~sp~~ shepherd boy
sought
Who swimming ~~saught~~ the island lone
{e
Within his clenchéd te{ath a sword
I heard the deathful monatone
The water serpent sings his heart
Before a death. O'er wave and bank
I cried the words you bid me cry
The shepherd raised his arms and sank
His rueful spirit fluttered by
Naschina [aside] I must bestir myself! both dead for me
Both dead no time to think
(aloud) I am she
That shepherdess, arise and bring to me
In silence that famed flower of wizerdry
For I am mightier now by far than thee
For faded now is all thy wondrous art

---

1 The question mark is in darker ink and possibly by another hand.

2 The cancellation mark through the apostrophe is in darker ink and possibly by another hand.

12 There is a cancellation above the apostrophe through what may be another apostrophe.

15 The mark transcribed as a period after "by" may be intended instead as the top of an exclamation point after "myself" in the next line.

17 Presumably, Yeats realized that he did not have space to complete the line, and well before reaching the margin he completed it below.

(12)

[The enchantress points to a cleft in a
rock]
Naschina I see within a cloven rock dispart
A scarlet bloom. O dying faery one
Why dwells the famous minion of the sun
In shadow thus—what mean the lights that rise
As light of triumph in thy goblin eyes—
In thy wan face?
{O
Enchantress Hear thou {o daughter of the days
Behold the loving loveless flower of lone ways
immortal
Well nigh ~~imortal~~^in this charméd clime
amorous
Thou shal't out live thine^~~amerous~~ happy time,
And dead as are the lovers of old rime
Shall be the hunter lover of thy youth,
Yet ever more through all thy days of ruth
Shall grow thy beauty, and thy dreamless truth
As an hurt ***leopard***
~~And [? ?]~~ ~~leperd~~ fills with ceaseless moan
And aimless wanderings the wood-lands lone
pitiless
Thy soul shall be, though ~~pityless~~ and bright
It is, yet shall it fail thee day and night
Beneath the burden of the infinite
In those far years, O daughter of the days—
{e
And when thou hast thes{s things for many ages felt
red {rel
The [~~?red~~] squir{all shall rear her young where thou hast [~~?~~]
dwelt

---

8 The question mark is in darker ink and possibly by another hand.
9 The capital "O" is in darker ink and possibly by another hand.
24 The "rel" of "squirrel" is written in darker ink over "all", probably by another hand.

(13)

{A
And—{ah me! I go from ~~an~~ sun and shade
streams
And the joy of the [?~~strems~~] where long limbed herons wade
And never any more the wide eyed bands
Of the pied panther kittens from my hands
Shall feed. I shall not in the evenings hear
{o
Again the wo{ddland laughter and the clear
Wild cries grown sweet with lulls and lingerings long.
I fade and shall not see the mornings wake
{ace
A fluttering the painted popul{ous of lake
And sedgy stream, and in each babbling brake
And hollow lulling the young winds with song
—I dream—I cannot die—No! No! ~~No! [?]!~~
I hurl away these all unfaery fears.
Have I not seen a thousand ~~seas~~ seasons ebb and flow
{H
The tide of stars? {have I not seen a thousand years
The summers fling their scents? Ah subtile and slow
The warmth of life is chilling, and the shadows grow
More dark beneath the poplars, where yon owl
{ie {e
Lies torn and rotting; the ~~f[?]~~ f{earce kestr{il birds
sibyl
Slew thee—poor ~~sybil~~, comrades thou and I
For ah our lives were but two starry words
Shouted a moment ~~it~~ 'tween the earth and sky
Oh death is horrible and ~~foul~~ foul foul foul
Naschina I [?~~know~~] know not of the things you speak
but what
brazen
Of him on yonder^gated spot
By thee spell bound

---

9 The "ace" of "populace" is written over "ous" in darker ink, probably by another hand.

19 The "ie" of "fierce" and second "e" of "kestrel" are written over "ea" and "i" respectively in darker ink, probably by another hand.

(14)

~~thou shal't~~

know
<u>Enchantress</u> Thou shal't ~~no~~ more
^
Meeting long hence the phantom herdsman, king
along their russet floor
Of the dread woods, ~~on their unruffled~~ ~~frloor~~
{ e
His sl{ oeuth-hounds follow every faery thing
[<u>turns to go. Naschina [?~~try~~] trys to prevent her</u>
Before I am too weak fearce mortal let me fly
<u>And crouch</u>| ~~in some far stillness~~
in ~~stilness by the talking lake~~
↓ ~~And~~ some far [?~~leafy~~] stilness of the isle and die
[goes
<u>Naschina</u> <u>[following]</u> ~~Will he~~
Will he have [?] happiness—great sobs her being
shake
~~V~~
<u>Voices</u> [sing]—A man has an hoped for heaven
But soulless a faery dies
As a leaf that is old, and withered and cold
{ 'r
When the wint{ ery vapours rise
[—Soon shall our wings be stilled
And our revelry over and done
[[?] So let us dance, where the yellow lance
Of the barley shoots in the sun
So let us dance on the fringéd waves
And shout at the wisest owls
In their downy caps, and ~~stratle~~ the naps
startle
Of the dreaming water fowls

4 "floor" is in darker ink and possibly by another hand.
7 The final "o" of "too" was added later in pencil.

(15)

And fight for the black sloe berries
  For soulles a faery dies
As a leaf that is old, and withered and cold
  When the wintery vapours rise
                                          re
~~Enter Naschina~~ Enenter Naschina
Naschina   I plucked her backwards by her dress of green
To question her oh no I did not fear
Because St Joseph s image hangeth here
Upon my necklace. But the goblin queen
Faded and vanished nothing now is seen
Saving a green frog dead upon the grass.
As figures moving mirrored in a glass
The singing shepherds too have passed away
O arcady O arcady this day
A deel of evil and of change has crossed
T
thy peace. Ah now I'll wake these sleepers lost
And ~~w~~ woe begone. For them no evil day
[Throws open the brazen gates

---

5 The "re" of "reenter" is written in pencil over "En", perhaps by another hand.

16 The "'ll" of "I'll" has been reinforced in pencil. The periods here and in l. 17 could also be read as commas.

(16)

1 ~~Naschina~~
2 [To Almintor—O wake wake wake for soft
as a bee sips
3 The faery flower lies upon thy lips
4 Almintor I slept 'Twas sultry and scarce circling shook
5 The falling hawthorn bloom. by mere and brook
6 The otters dreaming lay. The faeries' isle ~~//~~
7 ~~—[?You/?Yon]~~ lay dre—[?you/?yon]
8 Naschina gaze but be thou dumb a while
9 [to the second sleeper]
10 Old warrior wake for sof*t* as a bee sips
11 The faery blossom lies upon thy lips
12 (1(sleeper) Have I slept long
13 Naschina Long years
14 The sleeper With hungry heart
15 Doth still the wanderer rove; with all his ships
16 I saw him from sad Dido's shore depart
17 Enamoured of the waves impetuous lips
These
18 Naschina ~~The~~ twain are dust—Wake, Wake for light
(*~~to the Sleeper~~*) (*~~To third sleeper~~*) as a bee sips
19 The faery blossom lies upon thy lips
20 Seafarer wake

---

2 There may be a comma after the second "wake".
6 The apostrophe is in pencil.
10 The "t" of "soft" is in pencil.
18 The pencil corrections may be in another hand.

(17)

Third sleeper   Was my sleep long
Naschina   ~~Was my sleep long~~
{ l
{ [?]ong years——————————]
the sleeper   A rover I who come from where men's ears
new
Love ~~st~~ storm and stained with mist the ~~me~~
moons flare
Doth still the man whom each stern rover fears
{ U
The austere Arthur rule from { uther s chair
Naschina   He is long dead
Wake shepherd soft as a bee sips
The goblin flower lieth on thy lips
sleeper
fourth ~~shepherd~~.   Was my sleep long oh youth
Naschina   long long and deep
{ P
the sleeper   As here I came I saw god { pan he played
An Oaten pipe unto a listening fawn
Who oft with eyes to grief unused would weep
woody
Doth he still dwell within the wood~~s~~y shade
And rule the shadows of the eve and dawn
Naschina   Yea he is gone. Wake wake as a bee ~~sp~~
sips

The pencilled corrections in ll. 11 and 16 may be by another hand.
5 There may be an apostrophe between the "n" and "s" of "moons"; "flare" is heavily reinforced in pencil.

(18)

The faery blossom broods upon thy lips
Sleeper awake
Fith Sleeper How long my sleep
n
Naschina Unumbered
^
goblin
Are the years of ~~faery~~ sleep
^
the Sleeper While I slumbered
How have the years in Troia flown away
Achaans
Are still the [~~?Achains~~] tented chiefs at bay.
Where rise the walls majestical above
The plain a little fair haired maid I love
the sleepers *all together*
~~All.~~ ^ She is long ages dead
The Sleeper Ah woe is me
{*re*
First Sleeper Youth he{ar we will abide and be thou ~~King~~
King
Of this lake-nurtured isle
Naschina Let thy King be
Yon archer, he who hath the halcyon's wing
{il
Like a flaming minstr{el word upon his crest
All the sleepers Clear browed Arcadian thou shalt be our King
Naschina. O my Almintor noble was thy quest

The pencilled corrections in ll. 4, 11, 13, 16, and 17 may be in another hand.
4 The caret and inserted "n" are in pencil.
11 "all together" is written in pencil by another hand.
13 The corrected "re" of "here" is in pencil. Yeats squeezed a barely legible "King" into the space remaining as he approached the right margin, then cancelled it and wrote the word more legibly below.
16 The apostrophe of "halcyon's" is in pencil.

(20)

Yea noble and most knightly hath it been
All the sleepers
Clear browed Arcadian thou shal't be our king
Almintor Until we die within the charmed ring
Of these star shuddered skies you are the queen
~~End~~
End

W B Yeats

send proofs to me
and to Lister

There is a pencil sketch of a man's head on the bottom half of the page.

Appendix One: Additional Materials

To complete the record of surviving manuscript materials, this appendix records changes by hand in four sources—galley proofs, two annotated copies of *The Wanderings of Oisin and Other Poems* (1889), and a typescript prepared by Mrs. Yeats in connection with the Cuala Press 1943 edition of *Mosada.*[1] None pertains to *The Island of Statues;* the first and last pertain exclusively to *Mosada.* From the two annotated copies, I have indicated here only changes to *Mosada* and will present the changes to other work from those volumes together with the relevant transcriptions in volume two of the early poetic works.

Because each source represents a distinct occasion on which Yeats revised his texts, I have noted all the changes in any one source before proceeding to the next. The reader who prefers a synoptic arrangement by line number of *Mosada* will find such a presentation for all the materials except galley proof in Finneran, *Editing Yeats's Poems,* together with discussion of some of the problems involved.[2] Because the changes are so small, and because two sets of them are not actually in Yeats's hand (though made from his directions), the tabular form followed below serves the purposes of clarity better than would the elaborate principles followed in transcription of actual manuscripts. Changes are keyed to scene and line number according to *The Variorum Edition of the Poems of W. B. Yeats.* The left-hand column represents the original material and the right-hand one gives the new reading incorporating the emendation.

Galley Proof of *Mosada*

A set of galley proof for the 1886 version of *Mosada* is included with other *Mosada* materials in the library of Trinity College Dublin (MS 3502/4). The phrase "2 Revises" in ordinary pencil and circled numeral 2 in blue pencil at the start indicates that these are a second revise. The galleys are very clean and contain only minor corrections in black ink in four places, all pertaining to punctuation. (In a fifth case, a pencilled correction raises the "r" of "matter" in line 3 of scene 2 to line level.)

[1]Two additional sources that I have been unable to locate include Yeats's own annotated copy of *The Wanderings of Oisin and Other Poems,* which Mrs. Yeats presented to Thomas Mark in April 1949, and his annotated copy of the *Dublin University Review* numbers containing *The Island of Statues.* For information on the first of these see Richard J. Finneran, *Editing Yeats's Poems* (New York: St. Martin's Press, 1983), pp. 101–102; and for information on the second see the catalogue compiled by R. O. Dougan, *W. B. Yeats: Manuscripts and Printed Books* (Dublin: Friends of the Library of Trinity College, 1956), p. 5.

[2]Finneran, pp. 101–105.

[VP 1,72]	you let	you, let
[VP 3,90]	thee	thee—
[VP 3,92]	foot worn:way is long	foot-worn way is long,
[VP 3,118]	world.	world!

The Reading Copy of *The Wanderings of Oisin*

The Ellis Collection of the University of Reading library holds a copy of *The Wanderings of Oisin and Other Poems* (1889) that contains pencilled corrections and the following pencilled inscription on the "Contents" page: "corrections in this book made / at my dictation / May 7. 1889 / W B Yeats". This copy belonged to Edwin Ellis, Yeats's collaborator on the Blake edition.

[VP 2,42]	wages	wage
[VP 3,5]	long-lost footstep	lost footstep
[VP 3,6]	will pass	now pass
[VP 3,7]	Quite soon the	Along the
[VP 3,10]	Will be	Will move
[VP 3,13]	And Hassan will be with them—	Hassan is with them too—
	(The left margin opposite l. 13 contains the additional phrase "should be there".)	
[VP 3,58]	the flags	the stones
[VP 3,79]	Afar along	Far, far along

The Princeton Copy of *The Wanderings of Oisin*

The Robert H. Taylor Collection at the Firestone Library, Princeton University, contains a copy of *The Wanderings of Oisin and Other Poems* (1889) inscribed "Edward Garnett / from W B Yeats / Sept 26 / 1890". Like the inscription, the five changes to *Mosada* are in black ink. Yeats's friend Garnett was a reader for the firm of Fisher Unwin.

[VP 2,42]	wages	wage
[VP 3,10]	Will be	Will move
[VP 3,13]	be with them—he	be one—he
[VP 3,41]	". . . Yonder a leaf" is cancelled	
[VP 3,42]	Of apple-blossom	An apple-blossom

Mrs. Yeats's Corrections to a Typescript of *Mosada*

A typescript from the collection of Michael B. Yeats, now in the National Library of Ireland (NLI 30,193), contains pencilled corrections by Mrs. Yeats which follow the emendations in Yeats's own copy of *The Wanderings of Oisin,* the copy she later presented to Thomas Mark. The confusion emanating from Mrs. Yeats's assumption that the typescript itself derived from the *Wanderings of Oisin* (1889) version rather than the *Dublin University*

Review (1886) one is described by Finneran in *Editing Yeats's Poems.*[3] Mrs. Yeats indicated that the epigraph was to be deleted.

[VP 1,38]	and comes	and rises
[VP 1,97]	ha ha! they come, they come!	They come, they come, they come!
[VP 2,23]	By the	Beside the
[VP 2,24]	And he shouted	The stranger shouted
[VP 2,42]	wages . . . No use.	wage . . . No use. No use.
[VP 3,5]	a long dead	a dead
[VP 3,6]	brothers will be	brothers now be
[VP 3,7]	Quite soon the	Along the
[VP 3,10]	Will be	Will move
[VP 3,12]	is scarcely dawning	is dawning
[VP 3,13]	And Cola will be with them	Cola is with them too
[VP 3,41]	". . . Yonder a leaf" is cancelled	
[VP 3,42]	Of apple blossom	An apple blossom
[VP 3,58]	the flags	the stones
	(A question mark after "stones" indicates Mrs. Yeats's uncertainty about the reading "stones" in l. 58.)	

[3]Ibid.

Appendix Two: Conversion Table for Manuscript Designations

For the convenience of readers in North America who might wish to consult the manuscripts, the identification numbers for the archive at the State University of New York at Stony Brook (SB) have been provided, while for the convenience of readers in the United Kingdom and Ireland the following table of equivalents for holdings of the National Library of Ireland (NLI) has been included. The manuscripts at Trinity College Dublin and at King's School, Canterbury, were not filmed for the Stony Brook archive and hence are not included in the table.

SB	*NLI*	*Title*
22.3.44–45	30,457	*Island of Statues*
22.7.14–15	30,430	*Mosada*
23.2.199–200	30,328, 1st loose leaf	*Island of Statues*
23.2.201–202	30,328, 2d loose leaf	*Island of Statues*
23.2.203–204	30,328, 3d loose leaf	*Island of Statues*
23.2.205–275	30,328, 1st notebook	*Island of Statues*
23.2.276	30,328, 4th loose leaf	*Island of Statues*
23.3.1	30,328, 5th loose leaf	*Island of Statues*
23.3.3–61	30,328, 2d notebook	*Island of Statues*
23.3.68–80	30,328, 3d notebook	*Island of Statues*
23.3.115–146	30,328, 4th notebook	*Island of Statues*